T0247946

NAMASTE, NEW RECRUITS

L O

S-T

BACK TO THE ISLAND

The Complete Critical Companion
to the Classic TV Series

EMILY ST. JAMES &
NOEL MURRAY

Abrams Press | New York

Library of Congress Control Number: 2024936203

ISBN: 978-1-4197-5050-2
eISBN: 978-1-64700-112-4

Printed and bound in the United States
10 9 8 7 6 5 4 3 2 1

Abrams books are available at special discounts when purchased in quantity for premiums and promotions as well as fundraising or educational use. Special editions can also be created to specification. For details, contact specialsales@abramsbooks.com or the address below.

Abrams Press® is a registered trademark of Harry N. Abrams, Inc.

ABRAMS The Art of Books
195 Broadway, New York, NY 10007
abramsbooks.com

To every *Lost* fan who jumped into the comment section to theorize, analyze, and add to the conversation.

CONTENTS

125 **SEASON THREE**
THE END OF THE BEGINNING

FOREWORD

PREVIOUSLY ON . . .

When it debuted in September 2004 on ABC, *Lost* landed like a meteor right in the middle of the television lineup. Soon, even if you didn't watch the show, it was hard to escape its cultural impact. Whether you wanted to or not, you were living on the Island.

Though the show drew upon a vast web of influences, including everything from the short-lived cult TV series *Twin Peaks* to the collected works of Stephen King, the series felt wildly, wholly original. With its blend of sweeping sci-fi elements, compelling mystery box conundrums, and intimate personal drama, the show followed in the footsteps of so many breakthrough TV hits—just familiar enough to be approachable, just wildly original enough to become an obsession.

For six seasons, *Lost* remained one of the signature TV series of its era—even as it aired alongside shows now considered to be all-time classics like *The Sopranos*, *The Wire*, *Mad Men*, and *Breaking Bad*. When it ended in 2010, with a finale that proved divisive, to say the least, the show's influence and impact were never in question. It changed TV in ways both big (its enormous, diverse ensemble cast became the norm for TV dramas) and small (ABC's agreement to set an end date for the series three seasons in advance set a new benchmark for how to end a serialized TV series). What no one might have anticipated is just how thoroughly *Lost*'s long tail continues to sprawl through the modern TV landscape—and not just in the form of the many, many shows indebted to it.

In 2024, the year of this book's initial publication, the year of *Lost*'s twentieth anniversary, the legacy of the series is more complicated than ever before.

To be sure, plenty of people still love the show with an abiding fervor, and its overall impact on the TV medium has been enormously positive. Even some of the elements that weren't fully beloved at the time have become better appreciated in the intervening years. As an obvious example, the finale's choice to prioritize the characters over answering big questions created huge blowback at the time, but after over a decade of limp finales that *did* try to answer everything, *Lost*'s approach looks a little more dead-on with every passing year.

Yet into the middle of this narrative has come a growing knowledge that not everybody had the best time making *Lost*. Yes, some of the people who had issues behind the scenes were airing their concerns back when the show was airing. Actor Harold Perrineau, who played Michael Dawson, gave interviews during the show's run about how badly he felt the series had let down his character's storyline—and the show's opportunity to tell a unique, much-needed story about a nuanced but ultimately loving Black father in a TV landscape too often dominated by bad Black dads.★

Since the show ended, even more people have told their own difficult stories of working on it. Writers have detailed how many of the show's famed mysteries didn't have solutions when they were first dreamt up, and even more actors have criticized how the show handled their characters, especially Evangeline Lilly, who played Kate Austen. For the most part, these people are proud of the work they did on *Lost*—but they also think that the show's status as a titan of television requires understanding that making *Lost* too often left people who weren't white men behind in the dust.

In 2023, journalist and critic Maureen Ryan published *Burn It Down: Power, Complicity, and a Call for Change in Hollywood*, which featured an entire chapter that dug the deepest anybody had into *Lost*'s workplace environment. In particular, Ryan chronicled a writers room filled with

★ "Walt just winds up being another fatherless child," Perrineau told *TV Guide* in 2008, shortly after his character was killed off. "It plays into a really big, weird stereotype and, being a Black person myself, that wasn't so interesting."

jokes that ranged from badly off-color to outright racist and sexist. Ryan used *Lost* as a synecdoche for larger, systemic issues throughout the TV industry. If this was happening on a TV show *everybody* was paying attention to, Ryan argued, then the industry had no incentive to shut down or punish bad behavior. Ryan's larger systemic points are well-taken, yet if you're a *Lost* fan, you might have focused more on feeling a deep sadness that so many people had such an awful time making a show you loved. (For whatever it's worth, *Lost* co-creator and co-showrunner Damon Lindelof later issued an apology for the behavior outlined in Ryan's book, while co-showrunner Carlton Cuse denied having been part of any bad behavior.)

In 2020, when we sold this book, we planned to write about the show episode by episode, yes, but also to delve into the ways in which it fell short, especially considering criticisms from Perrineau and Lilly. (This is a *critical* companion, of course.) Yes, *Lost* was hugely innovative and diverse for its era, but to look back on it now is to see many places where it might have gone further—and where the series it inspired have both pushed past *Lost* and stumbled in many of the same ways.

As an obvious example, Netflix's *Orange Is the New Black* took many lessons from *Lost* in how to tell stories, and then created an even more diverse cast, full of women that TV wouldn't normally tell stories about. Yet that series, too, encountered sustained criticism for how its mostly white writing staff told stories about its mostly Black cast of characters.

The thing about loving any work of art—especially one that is receding in your rearview mirror—is that all works of art are created under imperfect circumstances. We live in a world that is deeply broken and filled with systemic problems that filter their way up into the art we create. We should not use this truth to excuse bad behavior—people who treat other people monstrously in the course of making something as trivial as a TV show need to make restitution for their behavior—but we should use it to examine our own relationships to the art we love. If the world we live in is broken, then the art created in that world can't help but reflect it.

As a working critic for fifteen years, I have come to understand criticism not as an act of hate but as an expression of love. I will only get this particular about the things I really care about, and when it comes to *Lost*, well, I can get very particular indeed. To love *Lost*—and I really, *really* love *Lost*—has always been to love something that is imperfect by design. No TV show that lasts more than 120 episodes can hit a home run every time, and fans of the series have always known that. Yet in 2024, to love *Lost* also means learning to dig deeper into how those imperfections might reflect the darker qualities of the world.

So, then, let's venture forth, back into the deep and abiding mysteries of the Island. —*Emily St. James, September 2024*

INTRODUCTION

ORIENTATION

What is the legacy of *Lost*?

For most of *Lost*'s six-season run on ABC, this sprawling saga about plane crash survivors stranded on an uncharted, mystical island was one of the most popular series on television, around the world. Fans were heavily invested in the characters—an eclectic, multiethnic group of strangers who gradually came to realize that their lives were more connected than they knew—and fascinated by the secrets of their strange new home, where polar bears came roaring out of the jungle, a monster made of smoke could strike at any time, and there were remnants everywhere of a decades-old clash between a utopian humanitarian organization and a band of violent reactionaries. *Lost* was thrilling, thought-provoking, and—by the time it ended—divisive. It's perhaps remembered as much for the arguments over its conclusion as it is for its dominant status in pop culture of the mid-2000s.

Between the show's first episode in September 2004 and the finale in May 2010, the authors of this book wrote easily over one hundred thousand words about *Lost*: reviewing episodes, writing essays about its themes, and swapping theories with fans about where the story was going. There's a good chance that many of you who have picked up this book did so because you read (and we hope enjoyed) what we wrote about the show as it was airing.

I, Noel Murray, covered *Lost* for The A.V. Club from Season Four to the finale. Emily wrote about Season Six for the *Los Angeles Times*. During that time, we also conversed with readers in comment sections and on social media; and we formed bonds with many of our colleagues (including each other) by reading what everyone wrote and chatting about it online. A lot of the ideas in these pages originated in what we wrote at that time, but also in our back-and-forths with esteemed TV critics like Alan Sepinwall, Maureen Ryan, Myles McNutt, James Poniewozik, Emily Nussbaum, Ryan McGee, Joanna Robinson, and the most high profile of the *Lost* theorizers in the entertainment media, *Entertainment Weekly*'s Jeff "Doc" Jensen. Give credit to them all for a virtual assist to what you read herein.

Since "The End" aired, Emily and I have written thousands more words, often defending the series from people who have insisted that its final season—and in particular its finale—went so disastrously off the rails that it ruined everything amazing about the show. So now, twenty years after *Lost*'s premiere, we wanted to look again, with eyes as clear as possible, and consider what this show's primary creative team of Damon Lindelof and Carlton Cuse accomplished over their six-year run on ABC. We still believe that *Lost* mattered. Its phenomenal success—and even the backlash that came later—both changed and defined the way people talk about television with each other, and even the way television is made. And yet it's possible that today both TV fans and TV producers take the wrong lessons from what *Lost* was and what it became.

This book consists of new essays and conversations, covering all 121 *Lost* episodes, with special attention paid to the forty we consider pivotal. These essays are aimed at those who've watched the show. (Warning: There will sometimes be spoilers, though we've tried to keep them to a minimum so that newcomers can read along as they watch for the first time.) For fans who need a refresher on what actually happened on *Lost*, the shorter episodic write-ups begin with brief summaries; each section of the book starts with an overview of each season's general plot and primary characters, as well as some reminders of what was happening behind the scenes and in the fandom at the time. (Warning: These intros *definitely* contain spoilers and are more for people who've seen the whole series.) Each section ends with a longer essay about *Lost*'s larger themes and concerns.

We should make this clear at the outset: The forty episodes we've chosen for deeper study are not meant to be our picks for the forty *best* episodes. Sure, some of them absolutely are top tier. (There was no way we weren't going to dig deep on "The Constant" or "The Man Behind the Curtain.") But mainly we tried to find a variety of episodes from across all six seasons that would allow us to discuss some of the show's motifs and main characters . . . and sometimes to talk about *Lost*'s failures, too.

Make no mistake: Even now, we are approaching this show as fans. But we can't and *shouldn't* ignore Lindelof and Cuse's creative missteps— nor should we breeze too quickly past the reports that have emerged in recent years about some cast members and writers feeling neglected, disrespected, and even abused because of their gender and/or ethnicity.

So, no, we can't talk about what worked on *Lost* without talking about what flopped—especially given that a lot of what made this series special sprang from Lindelof, Cuse, and their collaborators doing the hard work of making a weekly TV drama, which required a lot of scrambling and adjustments when things went awry. We don't speak for those creators, nor do we offer any excuses for any of the choices they may wish now they could correct. Instead, we accept that they're part of *Lost*'s larger legacy.

Besides, every believer knows that doubt is an essential component of faith. And every *Lost* fan knows that half of the fun of watching the show is arguing about it afterward.

So, for people of faith and people of science alike, let's have those discussions again. It's been too long, and there's a lot still to say. We have to go back. —*Noel Murray*

SEASON ONE

EYE-OPENING

In 2004, network television was in trouble. Between the boom of new cable channels, surging DVD sales, and the improved quality of streaming via the internet, the "Big Four"—ABC, CBS, NBC, and Fox—had begun a slow process of bleeding audience share that would soon accelerate. Even worse, it seemed increasingly that the nets had nothing unique to offer. Sophisticated, award-winning dramas? HBO already had that covered; and with *The Shield*, FX had shown that basic cable could compete, too. Clever comedy? The average episode of *South Park* was funnier and more cutting-edge than most network sitcoms.

In Bill Carter's book *Desperate Networks*, he writes about this time of transition, when the executives making programming decisions at the Big Four were scrambling. They overpaid to keep still-popular but creatively sputtering shows like *Friends* on the air for an extra season or two, and compensated for the high price tag by programming relatively inexpensive reality shows and game shows like *Fear Factor, Joe Millionaire*, and *Extreme Makeover: Home Edition*, hoping that one or two would become breakout sensations.

Then, in the fall of '04, ABC—regularly trounced in the ratings by Fox's gimmicky reality experiments, CBS's senior-friendly crime shows, and NBC's leftover '90s hits—took a gamble on originality. Throughout the '90s, as NBC became a juggernaut, ABC had played the role of the scrappy innovator, buying and airing distinctive dramas that critics loved but that rarely appealed to large audiences: *Murder One, Cupid*, and the like. They went back to that well in '04, banking on two shows unlike anything else on TV at the time: *Desperate Housewives* and *Lost*.

Lost almost didn't make it to air. The germ of the idea for the series came from the chairman of the ABC Entertainment Group, Lloyd Braun, who thought a scripted TV series inspired by the reality show *Survivor*[*] and the movie *Cast Away*[†] could offer a lot of human drama and visual pizzazz. When the first few scripts he commissioned didn't deliver what he'd envisioned, Braun and some of his closest allies at ABC turned to J. J. Abrams, the wunderkind writer-director-producer they had worked with on *Alias*. Abrams realized right away that the premise needed something extra, so he proposed that the characters be stranded on a magical island, with mysteries to explore. In need of a writing partner, ABC paired him with the simpatico young writer Damon Lindelof, who was well-versed in Abrams's nerdier inspirations. Some of Braun's bosses at ABC remained skeptical, but since they had already committed millions of dollars to an ambitious two-hour pilot, they tried to figure out what to do with what they'd bought.

This movie-length pilot introduced the passengers of Oceanic Airlines Flight 815 from Sydney to Los Angeles, who would crash-land on an uncharted island and begin experiencing some inexplicable, possibly supernatural phenomena. There were concerns that too much mystical woo-woo might eventually turn off the audience. And there was talk about making the series into a miniseries—or even reconfiguring the pilot as a movie.

Instead, ABC took a chance on breaking the two-hour pilot into two separate episodes, airing on consecutive Wednesday nights at eight P.M., to kick off the prime-time schedule each night. The first part ended with a cliffhanger: the sound of a monster roaring in the jungle and shaking the trees, just past the beach where a big chunk of the plane had landed, followed by the question that would define the first season. "Guys," Charlie asked. "Where are we?"

Charlie is **CHARLIE PACE** (Dominic Monaghan), the drummer for the one-hit-wonder Britpop band Drive Shaft—and a heroin addict. Although around seventy people (and one dog) survived the 815 crash, the early *Lost* episodes really focused only on fourteen. The others are

---

[*] A Top 10 show in the Nielsen ratings when it debuted in the summer of 2000 and still in the Top 10 in its ninth season, which began one week before *Lost*'s premiere.

[†] The third-highest-grossing film in the US in 2000.

JACK SHEPHARD (Matthew Fox), a brilliant surgeon and control freak, still reeling from a recent divorce and the death of his father.

JOHN LOCKE (Terry O'Quinn), a lifelong sad sack and spiritual seeker who was a paraplegic when he got on the flight but can walk again on the Island.

JAMES "SAWYER" FORD (Josh Holloway), a selfish con man who turned to crime when another con man ruined his childhood.

KATE AUSTEN (Evangeline Lilly), a free spirit pushed into a life of crime after a childhood marred by an abusive and dysfunctional family.

SAYID JARRAH (Naveen Andrews), an Iraqi who reluctantly served in the Republican Guard under Saddam Hussein, and specialized in torture.

HUGO "HURLEY" REYES (Jorge Garcia), an amiable guy who had suffered a run of catastrophic luck ever since he won millions of dollars in the lottery.

SUN-HWA KWON (Yunjin Kim), the daughter of a wealthy Korean crime boss, and **JIN-SOO KWON** (Daniel Dae Kim), her husband, who is also one of her father's hired guns.

MICHAEL DAWSON (Harold Perrineau), a divorcé trying to be a better dad to his son **WALT LLOYD** (Malcolm David Kelley), a bookish kid who may have psychic powers.

SHANNON RUTHERFORD (Maggie Grace), a self-absorbed socialite who was cut off from a lot of her wealth when her father died and had been relying for help from her stepbrother **BOONE CARLYLE** (Ian Somerhalder), who is hopelessly in love with her.

CLAIRE LITTLETON (Emilie de Ravin), a heavily pregnant young woman.

The two-part pilot—called "Pilot"—offered a brief introduction to these characters, and also introduced the narrative structure that *Lost* would, with some significant variations, hold on to for six seasons. Every so often, the action on the Island would lead to a "whoosh" on the soundtrack, cutting to flashback, showing what the characters were doing in the days, weeks, months, years, or even centuries before the plane crash. Throughout the first season, *Lost* filled in details about these fourteen characters' lives that were often startling and revelatory, changing our understanding about the choices they were making on the Island.

The TV audiences of 2004 and '05 ate it up. "Pilot (Part 1)" debuted after an extensive and clever marketing campaign that made the show look like a must-see—without ever really explaining what it was about.* The ratings for the premiere out-performed expectations, drawing over 18 million total viewers. Of those, an impressive 17 million came back the next week for "Pilot (Part 2)." The viewership hovered around that level all season, never dropping below 16 million viewers and sometimes drawing over 20.

But what did they come back for? The flashbacks? Or the "Where are we?" mystery? That remained an unsettled question all the way to the series finale, in 2010. One thing was certain early on (even if some ABC execs couldn't quite believe it): The mystical woo-woo did not scare people off. If anything, the viewers who fell deeply in love with the show by the end of episode one were clamoring for all the science-fiction/fantasy/horror craziness *Lost* had to offer.

Still, compared to the furiously mind-bending show *Lost* would later become, Season One today looks surprisingly simple and sedate. The episodes are slower-paced and quieter, with only one or two "wow" moments per hour. There are fewer sets and locations. The piles of money spent on the pilot (much of it shipping huge pieces of an airplane to a Hawaii beach) left less for the rest of the season, so the production value is a bit lower than what would come later. Though the pilot suggested flashy drama, the season's focus was largely on establishing who the characters were and are, pre- and post-crash—and in suggesting, without expressly stating, that everyone who ended up on this Island was there for some cosmic reason. The secrets of the Island itself? Those were lower priority.

What we did learn was enticing. The two-part "Pilot" introduced "the monster" but also threw in a mysterious message in French that had been transmitted on repeat for sixteen years. By the end of the season, we would meet that Frenchwoman—**DANIELLE ROUSSEAU** (Mira Furlan)—and would learn that during her decade-plus on the Island she

---

* The crashed plane was the dominant motif in both the print and TV ads, along with some common desert island imagery (beaches, trees, etc.). The show's potential audience knew it was about castaways and had a few hints that there was something mysterious and dangerous afoot, but that's about it.

had been in conflict with an unwelcoming group of residents she called "the Others." There were other signs of the Island's long, strange history, too: skeletons in a cave entombed with black and white rocks; a small airplane filled with Virgin Mary statuettes (each one filled with heroin), stuck on a cliff; an ancient sailing vessel, nestled way inland; a roving polar bear; and a sealed hatch atop a deeply buried concrete bunker. While some of these "signs" may have initially felt random or far-fetched, it would be revealed over the course of six seasons that each Easter egg served an explicit purpose—all introduced very early on in the show's narrative arc.

Lost's first season also laid the groundwork for the themes and conflicts that would continue to animate the series. Should we approach every difficult situation with the cold logic of Jack or the open-minded wonder of Locke? Is it better to be a builder like Sayid or a taker like Sawyer? Are people wholly good or bad, or can they change? Has anybody ever had a healthy relationship with their parents?

If nothing else, the fact that *Lost* was poking at difficult ideas while also building an increasingly complex mythology was a signal that network TV in the twenty-first century could generate new ideas, and could compete with cable's sophistication, critical acclaim, and fan engagement. Season One was nominated for twelve Emmys and won six, including Outstanding Drama Series (beating HBO's *Deadwood* and *Six Feet Under*, as well as Fox's *24* and NBC's *The West Wing*).

How long could this smash hit run? How long *should* it? Answering those questions in the seasons to come would change the way people thought about and talked about television. —*NM*

WHERE ARE WE?

"PILOT"

—

SEASON 1, EPISODES 1 & 2
ORIGINAL AIRDATES 9/22/04 & 9/29/04

NOEL: It's hard to talk about the beginning of *Lost* without wanting to race ahead to the ending—or even to the middle. Once you've seen the whole series, watching the first episode again raises all kinds of questions I itch to answer. The most immediate may be: How much of the show that *Lost* would become is already evident in its first two hours?

But before we get to that, right here at the top we should take a moment to appreciate just how terrific "Pilot" is. With *Lost*, there's no "it starts slow but give it four or five episodes and then it gets good." This show comes roaring out of the gate at such an incredible clip—with a plane crash on an uncharted island, and the rapid-fire introduction of about a dozen immediately engaging characters—that it easily could have coasted on that "Pilot" momentum for a whole season. (I might even argue that it did, at times.)

When I watch it now, four things stand out:

THE TWO CRASH SCENES. The first is the most memorable, with Jack running around on the beach for roughly the first ten minutes of the episode, trying to steer a bunch of panicked survivors to safety while enlisting the more capable ones to help, as a roaring jet engine and a collapsing fuselage threaten lives. (The engine yanks one man to an unforgettable death.) We don't know who any of these people are yet, but we know right away that when in doubt, we should probably focus our attention on Jack. But I often forget that toward the end of "Pilot," in the flashback to Kate on the plane, we also see the moment when the tail section of Oceanic 815 rips off, sending several passengers flying into the air.

HOW FEW FLASHBACKS THERE ARE. I mistakenly remembered seeing what nearly every key castaway was doing on the plane before it broke apart; but the pre-crash 815 flashbacks in this episode are really limited to Jack, Charlie, and Kate.

HOW WELL THE MAJOR CHARACTERS ARE INTEGRATED INTO THE ISLAND ACTION. Even during the mayhem after the crash, we get at least glimpses of Michael, Hurley, Locke, Claire, Shannon, Boone, Jin, Charlie, and Rose. Not long after the situation stabilizes, we meet Kate, Sayid, and Sawyer (with Sawyer getting a cool bad-boy close-up, smoking a cigarette), and Sun and Walt aren't far behind. That's a lot of people introduced within the first twenty minutes; and it sets up the show with lots of stories to tell in Season One.

HOW QUICKLY SOME OF THE ISLAND MYSTERIES ENTER THE PIC-TURE. There's a polar bear attack. A radio salvaged from the plane picks up Rousseau's sixteen-year-old call for help. And oh yeah, there's some kind of monster howling and shaking the trees—even killing 815's pilot. Again: What a way to hook an audience. Who wouldn't stick around for at least a few more episodes to see where all this is headed?

I'll also add that J. J. Abrams handles the action masterfully, balancing the mad rush when the 815ers are in crisis with quiet, still moments of reflection. (At one point there's a shot of a sunset over the ocean and the wreckage that is lyrical in a way unlike anything I can recall in any of the episodes to come.) The performances too are razor sharp from minute one. I was never all that invested in the Jack/Kate romance; but even I have to admit that the first scene between the two of them, where Jack talks Kate through sewing up his wound, is a charmer.

EMILY: I recently rewatched *Lost*, and I kept sending messages to a friend that amounted to "How has TV fallen so far from this?" Not every element of *Lost* clicks at every single moment. Sometimes, the storytelling is more functional than poetic. Sometimes, the direction can be a bit slapdash. Sometimes, the performances lack nuance or depth. Sometimes, the show feels like it's going to disappear into its own navel and never come out.

And then you'll have a moment like the sunset you called out, Noel, and on come the waterworks, sparked by nostalgia for how good TV was back in the day. While every element may not work well together in every episode, more often than not, at least a couple of things are cooking. And when every element of your show has the potential to be some of the best TV of all time, well, then it's a real treat to just *watch* the show.

I first saw the *Lost* pilot in a stuffy, too-warm apartment in Milwaukee, Wisconsin. It was the summer after I had graduated from college, and a handful of network pilots for the fall had leaked★ onto file-sharing sites online.† One of them was *Lost*. My wife and I crowded together in bed and watched as an instantly compelling cast of characters crashed on a mysterious island and found themselves immediately drawn into a series of improbable mysteries. That fall season was the first I paid attention to with a real critical eye, and *Lost* set the bar horribly high. I just assumed that every fall season would have a pilot as good as *Lost*'s.

Now, twenty years removed, *Lost* is still the answer I give to the question "What's the best pilot ever made?"‡ I think there are probably pilots that are better as artistic works, and I think there are probably pilots that are better simply as episodes of television. (The *Lost* pilot, after all, very much resembles the movie it would have become overseas to defray costs had ABC not picked the show up.) I don't think, however, that there is another pilot that works so well as both an episode of TV and an artistic work simultaneously. The pilot takes a whole bunch of character types and storytelling tropes you know backward and forward from watching TV, then shakes them all up together. *Then* it makes room for moments of quiet mournfulness and strange melancholy. It tells its story as often through images as it does through words. It offers big action but also laser-sharp character writing. It doesn't do everything perfectly, but it does everything well. I've been doing this long enough now to know how impossible doing *anything* well in a pilot is. On those grounds, *Lost*'s pilot is a low-grade miracle.

★   Considering how many of them were from ABC and considering how far behind the other networks ABC was at the time, I've always wondered if some enterprising person in ABC's marketing department looked at how good the *Lost* and *Desperate Housewives* pilots were and thought, "Couldn't hurt!" before putting them online.

†   Yes, I am admitting to an extremely minor crime in the pages of a major publication, but (a) the statute of limitations has surely passed, and (b) I've spent so much money on *Lost* stuff over the years. Don't arrest me, Disney!

‡   Interestingly enough, many of the best drama pilots of the past ten years—*Mr. Robot*, *The Handmaid's Tale*, *Yellowjackets*, Lindelof's own *Watchmen*—take big lessons from *Lost*'s pilot, often by keeping a tight character focus on deeply traumatizing events, then veer in their own directions.

It's tempting to write about the *Lost* pilot as unprecedented. It was (probably) the most expensive pilot to that point, costing around $14 million, it took huge storytelling swings, and it melded together several TV subgenres—the sci-fi drama, the *Twin Peaks*–style mystery show, the *Love Boat*–style "shove a lot of characters into one exotic location" show, the *thirtysomething*-style intimate character drama—into a new TV storytelling type that we still . . . mostly compare to *Lost*. The closest antecedent to it in TV history is probably the *Twin Peaks* pilot,★ but *Lost* is pulpier and more eventful. *Twin Peaks* was all mood and vibes; *Lost* is all blood and guts.

The real precedent for *Lost* can be found in a slightly more disreputable corner of TV history: the light anthology drama. These shows proliferated in the 1970s, seeing the apex of their success with the ABC series *The Love Boat* and *Fantasy Island*. The shows were evolutions of the anthology dramas that had dominated the 1950s but proved harder and harder to produce as networks lost easy access to standing backstage sets on studio lots in an era of Hollywood contraction. A show like *The Love Boat* had a skeleton crew of series regulars, whose stories (such as they were) would continue throughout the series, but the real attraction was the guest stars of the week, who would have their own crises and love stories to celebrate.

The smartest thing about *Lost* was how it took the anthology-style cast of characters and stranded them on the same beach; the showrunners used a full season of television to make every single one of them the focal point in one hour or another. And in the pilot, the sharpness of Abrams and Lindelof's character writing is the hidden spine holding together the wilder mysteries.

Noel, you and I have seen the full series, but try to put that out of your mind for a second. Which characters grab you the most immediately when watching the pilot?

NOEL: It's tempting to say Hurley, just because he's so likable from the get-go, with his honest reactions to dire situations and his willingness to do what's needed of him anyway. Without spoiling too much, I will say that I do think the scene where Jack asks for Hurley's help with

★ See also: pilots that are better as artistic works than the *Lost* pilot.

his impromptu surgery on Kate's marshal perhaps unintentionally fore-shadows where this story is going to wind up.

It's also tempting *not* to say Jack or Kate, given that both characters become more problematic later. (We'll get to that.) But I have to admit that both of them are incredibly charismatic in the pilot. In fact, given the way things play out in the series, it's odd that Jack comes off so charming and my beloved Sawyer is so abrasive. Meanwhile, Locke—who has a powerful scene with Walt, explaining the rules of backgammon—has an air of men-ace about him that forecasts villain. (In a way I guess he is, eventually.)

I'm actually going to pick another character, though, who represents the show's thematic complexity and unapologetic thorniness—and who in retrospect is an odd choice to be one of only three 815ers to get a flashback showcase, alongside Jack and Kate. I don't know if J. J. Abrams and Damon Lindelof decided to center Charlie in "Pilot" because Dominic Monaghan was one of the show's most famous faces—having just been in the *Lord of the Rings* trilogy—but even if so, the way we meet him is incredibly effec-tive. He's so affable from the get-go; but then we find out that the reason he's so eager to join Jack and Kate on their expedition to retrieve the radio from the cockpit is that he stashed some heroin in the lavatory.

That one revelation (coupled with the later reveal that Kate spent Flight 815 in handcuffs) says so much about what this show's going to be. Some characters will perform heroic acts for selfish reasons, and some flashbacks will give us information about the characters that no one else on the Island knows. There are secrets within secrets here.

EMILY: One thing I find interesting about the early seasons of *Lost* is that it's a simpler show. To some degree, that's to be expected. All TV shows become more complicated the deeper they get into their runs—which is not a criticism, necessarily. The storytelling of the pilot is so propulsive and the mysteries so immediately intriguing that the show likely couldn't have sustained a bunch of intricate character portraits, even if it had the real estate for them.

It does mean, however, that the characters mostly function as arche-types you might be more familiar with from other TV shows. There's a Heroic Doctor (Jack) and a Mysterious Older Man (Locke) and a Charm-ing Rogue (Sawyer) and an Addict Rock Star (Charlie) and so on and so on. And in the weeks to come, the show will mostly spend its time inverting those archetypes in relatively predictable ways, complete with more capital letters. Kate's the Beautiful Criminal? Well, would you believe that she's maybe also Misunderstood?

Abrams left the show fairly early in its run,* but this approach to building a TV show had his fingerprints all over it—surround characters you feel like you know already (because you kind of do) with a swooping, swirling curlicue of a plot. You can see a lot of what he would do in *Lost* on the (also terrific) pilot for *Alias*, where he surrounds a star-making performance by Jennifer Garner with some of the goofiest spy movie shenanigans imaginable, as well as a bunch of characters you understand almost from looking at them. This isn't easy; there's a real skill to knowing how to make an audience understand what they're looking at almost *immediately*, and Abrams has it. It's likely why he's so successful.

It extends to other projects. I'd argue that Abrams's gift for complex simplicity was core to *Lost*'s quick ascension. He knows exactly which screws to turn and when, and he knows how to get you on board with a character almost immediately. Yet within this version of the show is little of what it would become, even beyond the sense of "all shows get more complicated as they go along." *Lost* eventually became this pseudo-spiritual series of parables about people who were lost metaphysically before they became lost more literally. While you can sense that idea lapping at the edges of the pilot, it's not nearly as present as the pulpier version of this story about archetypal characters you already know and love from a billion other things getting trapped on an island where nothing is quite as it seems.

Perhaps that's why every time I revisit the pilot, I'm struck anew by how different it is from what the show became. It's recognizably *Lost* on a plot level, but the deeper thematic weight the series would develop as soon as two episodes from now† is mostly hinted at. Again, I don't want to hold that against the pilot, because pilots are inherently cumbersome beasts, and they never possess all the thorny complications of the shows that follow. But I do think the version of *Lost* presented in the pilot is just a bit thinner than the show we got in a way that could have quickly started to feel just a bit hollow.

---

*   He departed roughly a third of the way into Season One so he could go make the 2006 film *Mission: Impossible III*.

†   In "Walkabout," which is the subject of its own essay.

I love that we have the *Lost* pilot because it's a tremendous piece of television. But I'm glad that the show almost immediately started leaving it in the dust.

"TABULA RASA"

—

SEASON 1, EPISODE 3
ORIGINAL AIRDATE 10/6/04

On the Island: Jack tries to save the life of the US marshal who was escorting Kate, but ends up having to euthanize him when Sawyer's gunshot goes awry.

In the flashbacks: A fugitive Kate befriends a farmer, who alerts the authorities to her location in hopes of claiming a reward.

The first "regular" *Lost* episode after the two-hour premiere steps back from the Island's bigger mysteries—the monster in the jungle, the freaky French transmission, the polar bear—to ponder one of the smaller, more personal secrets teased in the pilot's flashbacks. We had already learned that Kate was a criminal in the custody of a US marshal named Edward Mars (Fredric Lane) on Flight 815. But just *how bad is she*?

"Tabula Rasa" doesn't establish exactly what Kate did. (That'll be teased out over two future Season One episodes.) This episode is more about establishing the template for *Lost* going forward in its first season, by balancing the larger story of the 815 survivors settling into their often-hostile new environment with a meaningful flashback to one castaway's past.

"Tabula Rasa" also introduces an idea that will continue to play out throughout the series, by suggesting that even a villain—if Kate can be called that at this point—can have redeeming qualities. According to the marshal, Kate is slippery and deceptive. But in the flashback, we see the genuine connection she has with a kindly-seeming Australian farmer; and even after the man says he's going to turn her in, she wrecks his truck but then costs herself valuable time making sure he's safely clear of the crash site. On the Island, meanwhile, when Kate offers to tell Jack about her crimes, he turns her down (establishing the precedent that on *Lost* no one ever asks about the things the audience is curious to know). He says that on the Island, for now at least, everyone gets to start fresh and be a new person.

But do they, though? A big part of "Tabula Rasa" is about Sawyer and Jack continuing to butt heads, as they establish the roles they're going to play on the Island in these early days. Jack: the conscientious hero. Sawyer: the selfish rogue. When the two of them meet in the plane wreckage at one point while scouring for supplies, Jack asks what Sawyer has found and he says, "Booze, smokes, a couple of *Playboys*. And you?" Jack replies, "Medicine." Sawyer: "Well that about sums it up." —*NM*

THE SALVATION OF JOHN LOCKE

"WALKABOUT"

—

SEASON 1, EPISODE 4
ORIGINAL AIRDATE 10/13/04

"Walkabout" is when *Lost* becomes *Lost*. For as groundbreaking as the series pilot was, any TV fan can think of plenty of shows—even very good ones overall!—with gangbusters pilots that never again hit that level. You can imagine the same happening to *Lost*, the goodwill earned by the pilot slowly dissipating as the show descends into *The Fun-time Island Pals*.

"Walkabout" perfects a formula that would serve *Lost* well across its run. It also introduces two key creative voices to the show: writer David

Fury, who would contribute several tremendous scripts to the first season, and director Jack Bender, who would direct this episode and the one following, then stick around with the show through the series finale, serving as its chief director throughout. The episode mixes a compelling character backstory pre-Island—namely John Locke's—with a concrete survival goal and a bit of eeriness. In the other storylines, the characters grapple with the significance of their situation, providing an emotional buffer from the weightier events of the episode.

"Walkabout" ends with a memorial service for the many who died in the crash of Oceanic 815, yet the scene never feels particularly heavy. The survivors of the crash are building a new life here on the Island, like it or not. For some of those survivors, like the previously paralyzed John Locke, the Island offers a fresh start. For others, like the hallucination-plagued Jack, it offers a chance to stew in their own traumas and misgivings.

At this juncture in the show's run, it is worth discussing the series as a post-9/11 show. The series debuted in the fall of 2004, in a TV landscape filled with programs that uneasily surveyed a country still attempting to process what had happened to it, even as the nation had embarked on two separate wars in the name of ill-defined justice.

Some series airing at the time, particularly Fox's *24*, leaned into the horror of being alive in America in the early 2000s, turning their storytelling into a paranoid funhouse, where every conspiracy theory you'd ever heard of, whether from the right or left, was true. Others, like the Sci-Fi Channel's *Battlestar Galactica*, used the distancing effect of genre television to directly consider the geopolitical questions of the times. Few shows were as forthright about the subtle ways torture destroys the torturer as well as the tortured as *Battlestar* was.

Then there's *Lost*. The show's most obvious 9/11 echo is in how it opens with a plane crash that offers a dark resonance with the events of that tragic day. But the echoes extend beyond that choice. The series occasionally nodded to the politics of its day. Sayid, for instance, is Iraqi, and he is known to engage in torture to get information. (Needless to say, having a member of the Iraqi Republican Guard be the show's primary torturer at a time when the United States' own torture program dominated headlines was a strange choice.) But for the most part, *Lost* aims to capture the vibe of the post-9/11 period. With the terrorist attacks fading in the rearview mirror and the wars in Afghanistan and Iraq facing ever more pointed scrutiny, the country had settled into a strange malaise. The desire for revenge that had so typified the America of 2002 and 2003 had subsided slightly, and while George W. Bush won reelection, it was by a closer margin than most wartime presidents enjoyed. It's in that uneasy grief where *Lost* resides.

It is easy to forget now that the show's biggest mysteries and reveals have been so thoroughly digested into the great pop culture subconscious, but the first season of *Lost* is positively suffused with a kind of sorrowful optimism. Yes, we are alive on this Island, and yes, we might come together to build a new society where things are more equitable, but still. A lot of people died, and we are living right next to endless reminders of their deaths. Even as this episode concludes with the burning of the airplane's fuselage as part of the memorial, the survivors continue to use items they scavenged from the wreckage. To survive is to walk atop the ashes of all who didn't. *Lost* literalizes that.

What makes any of this bearable is the centrality of Locke to the episode. A mysterious figure who barely speaks across the series' first several episodes, Locke draws the attention of viewers simply because he's played by the endlessly enigmatic and charismatic Terry O'Quinn. Tall and bald, O'Quinn was probably best known for the *Stepfather* horror films pre-*Lost*, but he'd spent much of the 1990s and early 2000s finding recurring roles on the most interesting genre series of the day. His work on *Lost* is immediately preceded, for instance, by his work on *Alias*. There, he played an assistant director of the FBI brought in to question the series' super-spy protagonist. Those sorts of authority figures were the characters O'Quinn was most often asked to play in the run-up to *Lost*.

What's fascinating about Locke is how the series utilizes all of O'Quinn's inherently commanding screen presence to create an archetypal figure of survivalist know-how, then spends almost its entire run undercutting that persona in a thousand tiny ways that ultimately add up to a distinct sense that the guy is full of it. "Walkabout," with its famous reveal that Locke had been in a wheelchair before he crashed on the Island, exemplifies this approach. Before he landed on the Island, Locke was a man who was sure he could be a great survivalist but never got a chance to put those skills to the test, for obvious reasons. Thwarted by a life that subjected him to humiliations from people who constantly underestimated him, Locke finds that the Island gives him the gift of being the self he always imagined he was.

Importantly, "Walkabout's" flashbacks don't paint Locke's wheelchair usage as his defining tragedy, which is how they narrowly evade the ableist trope of a disabled character suddenly rejoicing when they become able-bodied again. We learn, briefly, that Locke wasn't always in a wheelchair. Some incident paralyzed him, and that incident further curdled an animosity toward the world that seems to have been building across most of his life. Now, he's the butt of jokes from the awful middle manager Randy, and he imagines himself a great leader but only in a tabletop war game. He portrays himself as being in a relationship with a woman named Helen, but she's revealed to be a phone-sex operator.★ When he finally travels to Australia to go on the titular walkabout, he's told in no uncertain terms that someone in a wheelchair won't be allowed to participate.

Locke's life story pre-Island is perhaps the most purely tragic of the major survivors, which makes his embrace of all the Island has to offer seem almost a rational response to a fundamentally irrational situation. When the survivors run out of food, he offers to go and kill a boar, even as we come to learn that his hunting skills are more theoretical than real. Initially, he leads a little hunting party of Kate and Michael, but eventually, he heads off on his own, the zealot traveling to the heart of his faith. And the thing is, he's right. He kills the boar. He drags it back to camp. The survivors will have food to eat for another day or two.

And the Island seems to appreciate his worship—or at least the monster does. In a memorable sequence, Locke encounters the monster in the jungle, and it seemingly surveys him before moving along to other business, as if it has found him acceptable. Bender presents this from the point of view of the monster, letting the camera tower above Locke, so viewers never see the being's form.

Locke's zealotry also subtly nods to the show's post-9/11 allusions. Where others mourn and attempt to find a way to build community, Locke plunges on ahead, pursuing goals he insists are the correct ones but also ones only he can accomplish. He's a rugged individualist, and if

★ The name "Helen" in relation to Locke becomes even more important in later seasons.

that doesn't quite mark him as a proxy for the George W. Bush administration, it does allow the show to examine a particular response to the 9/11 attacks, one that insisted America had been chosen to weather a storm and only those who could see this fact could guide America through. Because Locke's enemies are only wild boars (at the moment), it's easy to miss this quality, but "Walkabout" shows that as the survivors mourn, Locke moves forward, then returns drenched in blood.

John Locke's existence across the run of the show will be typified by his headstrong certainty that he is the man to accomplish any given task and that the Island has chosen him as its avatar. Again, at every step of the way, the series will complicate this idea, but here, in "Walkabout," as he watches his wheelchair burn amid the flames consuming the fuselage, it's not hard to imagine him as everything he believes himself to be. And for viewers, the show also asks us not to get complacent. Nothing here is as it seems to be, not even the characters. —ESJ

"WHITE RABBIT"

—

SEASON 1, EPISODE 5
ORIGINAL AIRDATE 10/20/04

On the Island: The castaways struggle with a diminishing water supply until Jack (following Locke's advice) trails his father's ghost into the jungle and finds a spring.

In the flashbacks: Jack reluctantly travels to Australia to find his emotionally distant, alcoholic father Christian, who turns up dead.

Along with its characters and mythology, *Lost* is defined by its dialogue—and in particular certain key lines, which are repeated and referred to through the show's run. "White Rabbit" is an essential early *Lost* episode for multiple reasons; but its most critical contribution to the series is a warning from Jack, who tells his fellow 815 survivors, "If we can't live together, we're going to die alone."

Ironically, the rest of the episode is about how Jack himself has never really been a team player. The arc of the story in this particular hour is redemptive, ending with Jack giving his rousing speech, while also announcing that he's found a source for fresh water (thus ending the stress-inducing rationing of Oceanic water bottles). But in the flashbacks, we see Jack learning from his father at a young age that he's too "weak" to be a hero; and then we see Jack being guilted by his mother into retrieving Christian,★ as a kind of penance for going against the family in an incident as yet unseen.

It is to the writers' credit that this internal conflict in Jack never entirely goes away. He will remain a problematic protagonist throughout the series: short-tempered, self-serving, authoritarian, and very loose with his ethics. But it's also one of *Lost*'s fundamental flaws—shared with a lot of the entertainment of this era—that the show has more faith in Jack than Jack has in himself. It's woven into the fabric of the story that he must be the hero and that he has to learn to accept that destiny, because by the standards of the time he looked most like what heroes were "supposed" to look like: white, male, middle-aged, handsome, and from a comfortably privileged background. Plus, he's a doctor, a profession widely seen as inherently heroic. (He saves lives for a living!) From here on out, *Lost* will often contort itself to make sure Jack remains central, even when it doesn't make sense for him to be—and even when the character himself might prefer to be left alone. —*NM*

★ Although Christian Shephard appears occasionally in the first few *Lost* episodes as a kind of apparition, this episode delivers his proper introduction. It's the first time that he's played by John Terry, who will continue in the role all the way to the finale.

"HOUSE OF THE RISING SUN"

—

SEASON 1, EPISODE 6
ORIGINAL AIRDATE 10/27/04

On the Island: Jin and Michael squabble over a misunderstanding, Locke gets Charlie to trade his remaining heroin for his guitar, the castaways discover the bones of "Adam and Eve" in a cave, and Jack is surprised to find that not everyone wants to move away from the beach with him.

In the flashbacks: Sun's gangster father approves of her marriage to the working-class Jin, provided that Jin comes to work for him.

One episode after Jack insists that the 815 survivors have to "live together," they begin the first of many splits, as some follow Jack to the freshwater spring and cave and others decide to stay on the beach. Jack may have hoped that ending the water rationing would squelch the growing disharmony among the survivors, but they keep finding new things to argue about—including whether it's better to move farther inland to where "the monster" makes noises or to stay on the beach to keep a signal fire going for potential rescuers.

The biggest beef on the beach is between Michael and Jin, the latter of whom is enraged to see Michael wearing a watch that Jin had intended to deliver in Los Angeles on behalf of Sun's father. Because Jin can't speak English, Sun—who is secretly fluent—has to explain to Michael why her husband is furious. The bad blood there will linger for a while, with Michael distrusting Jin for suddenly attacking him and Jin distrusting Michael for being friendly with Sun.

"House of the Rising Sun" is ostensibly a Jin/Sun episode (The first one! The origin story!), and yet it doesn't reveal as much about the couple as it could. Their flashback feels slim, and incomplete. It puts across a simple idea: that the price Jin has had to pay for being close to the woman he loves has been an immersion into a criminal lifestyle that has, ironically, distanced him from Sun. But we don't really know these two yet; and it doesn't help that their on-Island scenes are surrounded by a lot of business unrelated to them. There is almost as much in this episode about Charlie's rock 'n' roll past—and the addiction that came with it—as there is about the episode's central characters.

Though what we do see of Jin and Sun is intriguing,★ and is framed by the episode's other power couple: the skeletons Locke and Jack find in a cave, with a pouch containing one white rock and one black rock. Our heroes don't know the deal with these two, so they start speculating—wrongly, as it will turn out—about who they might be. Presumption runs rampant in these early *Lost* episodes. But there's always much, much more to the story. —*NM*

"THE MOTH"
—
SEASON 1, EPISODE 7
ORIGINAL AIRDATE 11/3/04

On the Island: Charlie overcomes his heroin withdrawal by heeding Locke's self-help advice and by helping Jack escape a cave-in.

In the flashbacks: Charlie is pressured into becoming a rock star and a heroin addict by his brother Liam, who is insensitive to Charlie's doubts.

The metaphor of the moth in "The Moth" is the kind of old-fashioned TV storytelling gambit that *Lost* could do in Season One, before even the show's off-Island interludes became more about mysteries and mythology. The episode's premise is set up by Locke, who has convinced Charlie to hand over his remaining heroin, giving Charlie a choice about what to

★   It's also notable that just six episodes into its first season, *Lost* tested the network TV audience by producing an episode dominated by scenes in a foreign language, with subtitles.

do next. If Charlie asks for the drugs three times, Locke will give them back. Locke also shows Charlie a moth struggling to escape a cocoon and says that, like the moth, Charlie must free himself from his addiction on his own or he'll be too weak to survive.

The moth—or *a* moth, anyway—appears twice more in the episode. When Charlie accidentally causes Jack to get trapped inside a cave by falling rubble, he initially flees the scene, before returning and working himself inside to try and save Jack. After helping reset Jack's dislocated shoulder, Charlie discovers a way out of the cave by following the flight of a moth to an opening. And at the end of the episode, after getting his heroin back from Locke and tossing it into a fire, the two of them see a moth.

A bit heavy-handed? Sure. It all feels a little like a "very special episode" from the '70s or '80s, tackling the problem of addiction—like something *The Waltons* or *Lou Grant* might've done. It's not especially *Lost*-y.

But as with a lot of the early *Lost* episodes—as the writers and cast were still finessing the show's tone and style—"The Moth" works fine on its own merits, as a mini-drama with a poetic ending. And in the flashback scenes it works as a *Lost* episode too, in that we see a well-meaning young musician get pulled deeper and deeper into a terrible situation, by a bad influence who also happens to be a close family member. The tale of Charlie's rock 'n' roll rise and fall is very on-brand for this series about redemption. He must become the worst possible version of himself before he can start becoming someone better. —*NM*

"CONFIDENCE MAN"
—
SEASON 1, EPISODE 8
ORIGINAL AIRDATE 11/10/04

On the Island: Everyone's mad at Sawyer for hoarding supplies and medicine and endangering the asthmatic Shannon's life, but Kate is able to get close enough to him to find out about his troubled backstory as both the victim and perpetrator of long cons.

In the flashbacks: One of Sawyer's long cons unravels when he realizes that if he goes through with it, he will hurt a child.

The road toward Sawyer becoming one of *Lost*'s best characters begins in "Confidence Man," after he spends the first half-dozen episodes being a selfish, quick-tempered, bigoted jerk. It'll be a rocky road ahead, though, which at times will see Sawyer corrupting anyone who gets close enough to try seeing through his tough-guy facade.

Because Sawyer is a con man by trade—and thus always looking for an angle that benefits him personally—he has, ever since the crash, taken advantage of his fellow survivors' communal impulses and fog of confusion to grab whatever he could find, building up his own cache of useful items. Everyone therefore assumes that he has locked away the inhalers Shannon needs to survive; and when Sawyer refuses to let anyone look through his stash, he gets beaten by Jack and bound and stabbed by Sayid. (As we will continue to see in the episodes ahead, for the broken souls who crashed on the Island, violence is often Plan A.)

Kate is able to soften Sawyer by asking about the letter he keeps reading—a letter written to a crook named Sawyer detailing how he ruined one family's life—but he turns the moment creepy by asking for a kiss in exchange for the inhalers. When she complies, he admits that he never had the medicine in the first place. That's Sawyer in a nutshell: a bleeding heart and a bundle of raw nerves beneath a prickly exterior.

While all this is going on, in the off-Island flashbacks we see Sawyer running a scam that could net enough money to get him out of debt. But he hesitates, realizing that an innocent kid will be collateral damage; Sawyer himself was once hurt by a con man . . . named Sawyer. He took on the name and the occupation of the person he has spent his whole life trying to track down. So, we learn he has a righteous mission, and a tenderness beneath his flinty exterior. But that doesn't make him any easier to befriend. —*NM*

"SOLITARY"

—

SEASON 1, EPISODE 9
ORIGINAL AIRDATE 11/17/04

On the Island: Hurley finds some golf clubs and organizes a tournament to lighten the mood, while Sayid is captured and tortured by Rousseau.

In the flashbacks: Defying orders from his military superior, Sayid frees Nadia, a childhood friend he had been ordered to kill.

"Solitary" introduces two people who were living on the Island before Oceanic 815 crashed—although when the episode aired, viewers had no way of knowing the truth about one of them.

The known one is Danielle Rousseau, "the Frenchwoman" whose voice the castaways heard on the mysterious transmission they encountered back in "Pilot." When Sayid finds a buried cable leading into the ocean, he follows it back into the jungle where he is captured by Rousseau, who tortures him—just as Sayid, as we learn in his flashbacks, tortured others as an officer in the Iraqi military.

The flashback is about Sayid's final days as a soldier, when he risked his life and career to save Nadia (Andrea Gabriel), a childhood friend who grew into a woman he loved. Meanwhile, Rousseau tells Sayid that she was part of a scientific expedition that went awry after their boat crashed on the Island and her fellow team members were infected with a kind of madness. She says that she killed her team to stop the disease from spreading; she mentions a child named Alex, whom she has been seeking for years. Most importantly, she mentions that there are "Others" on the Island, whom she hears whispering in the jungle.

Sayid thinks Rousseau is probably being paranoid—although he too hears those whispers after he escapes her camp. But "Solitary" slyly introduces one of those Others, who will have his identity exposed in the next episode. Beyond our core group of heroes, through the early *Lost* episodes a few other survivors get names and some lines of dialogue.

One of these side characters is Ethan Rom (William Mapother), who appears for the first time in this episode as Locke's occasional hunting companion. Ethan, it turns out, is not who he appears to be.

This sets up the first big on-Island twist since the pilot, as once again the mystery of the Island itself and its hold on these characters moves back into the center of the narrative. —*NM*

THE CLAIRE CONUNDRUM

"RAISED BY ANOTHER"

—

SEASON 1, EPISODE 10
ORIGINAL AIRDATE 12/1/04

Casting a television show—especially early in its first season—is a little bit like constructing a baseball roster. The stars are the stars; and it's a given that any successful team is going to lean on its sluggers and aces. But you can't win consistently without some versatile utility players and a few breakout sensations. So, it behooves the people who do the hiring to throw a lot of people into the mix, and see who becomes essential.

Which brings us to Claire Littleton.

For those of us who were watching *Lost* weekly in 2004, Claire sure seemed like the kind of character who would go the distance. Her first flashback episode debuted in December, as part of the first eleven, before the holiday hiatus. "Raised by Another" also arrived right after the pivotal ninth episode, "Solitary," which introduced a hefty helping of *Lost* mythology, including the existence of the tragic castaway Danielle Rousseau; the idea that there are "Others" on the Island; the disappearance of Rousseau's daughter Alex; the idea that a "sickness" threatens the health of some people who wash ashore; and an Island map that includes the wreckage of the ship the *Black Rock*. In other words, "Raised by Another" follows an episode that really opened up the possibilities for this show, and where it could go next.

Which, again, brings us to Claire: a potential love interest for Charlie, who is smitten with her. She is also—and we will soon find out exactly why this is important—very pregnant.

And yet "Raised by Another" is the only "Claire episode" in Season One. (Warning: The spoiler-averse should skip this paragraph and the two that follow.) Claire will get another flashback in Season Two, another in Season Three, and then . . . nothing. The character leaves the story entirely at the end of Season Four and then comes back (in a way) in Season Six. On the whole, Claire's baby—Aaron—ends up mattering more to *Lost*'s plot arc than Claire.

None of this is Emile de Ravin's fault, understand. She's the perfect Claire, equal parts vibrant and vulnerable—the kind of person other people feel compelled to protect. During her time on the show, Claire had Charlie hovering around her with heart-eyes, determined to keep her safe and make her happy; and she had Locke acting as a kind of surrogate father, giving her life advice while building things for her. (Ironically, we will later find out that Claire's biological father, whom she never knew, had another child who is also on the Island.)

But perhaps because the character quickly came to be defined by what others thought of her, Claire never became a crucial part of the story *Lost* ended up telling. There's a moment in the "Raised by Another" flashbacks—after Claire's boyfriend Thomas (Keir O'Donnell) finds out she is pregnant, and after he has impulsively insisted that they could be good parents—when Thomas sees her puttering around their apartment in nesting mode and he becomes hostile to the very idea of spending the rest of his life with her and their child. Sometimes it feels like the *Lost* writers looked at her the same way, swinging from "It'll be great to have a pregnant lady in the mix!" to "But then again . . ."

All of that said, the episode is still a Season One high point, featuring scenes that remained important to *Lost*'s plot and themes long after Claire herself had been sidelined. The key figure in the flashbacks is a psychic, Richard Malkin (Nick Jameson), who gives Claire some conflicting—or, put more generously, evolving—advice. When she first visits him, he senses her pregnancy right away; and he gets such a bad vibe that he shoos her out. Later they meet again, and this time Malkin warns her not to give the baby up for adoption, no matter what. (Specifically he says, "Don't let him be raised by another.") But in their third and final meeting he flip-flops, telling Claire that he has found a couple in Los Angeles suitable to take care of the kid. He hands her a ticket to fly overseas . . . on Oceanic 815.*

What is so important about this baby? Did Malkin put Claire on a plane knowing that she and her unborn child would end up on the Island? Is he secretly working for the Others . . . or perhaps against them? (Should the title, in fact, be "Raised by an Other"?) How does all this tie into the nightmare Claire has on the Island at the start of the episode, where Locke† says that giving her baby away will cause unimaginable damage?

This all feeds into the episode's big twist—one of the first season's best. In the previous episode, "Solitary," Hurley had organized a makeshift golf tournament to try and lighten the mood on the Island, which was becoming increasingly tense. The 815ers had already splintered, with one group living on the beach where they crashed and another group living around a nearby cave. During Hurley's efforts at extending hospitality, we met a few new people around the two camps, including a man named Ethan (William Mapother). In "Raised by Another," after Claire gets attacked while sleeping,‡ Hurley decides to conduct a kind of census, making sure there's a record of everyone's name. After convincing the packrat Sawyer to give him the 815 manifest, he dutifully checks off everyone he can find. The only name missing? Ethan! An Other!

In a way, this is a big moment for Claire, confirming her suspicions that someone *was* after her and her unborn child. But it also confirms Rousseau's warning that the Others are everywhere on the Island, whispering and scheming. This marks the beginning of what will become a parade of new characters, entering the story and crowding

* Notably, when Claire tries to sign the contract with the adoptive parents, none of the pens work.
† In the nightmare, Locke's eyes are replaced by one black orb and one white orb, just like the black stone and white stone found on "Adam and Eve" in the caves.
‡ Prompting Shannon to sigh, "I am so not moving to the rape caves."

out some of the original castaways—though not before taking what they need. —*NM*

"ALL THE BEST COWBOYS HAVE DADDY ISSUES"

—

SEASON 1, EPISODE 11
ORIGINAL AIRDATE 12/8/04

On the Island: Our heroes follow Ethan to try and find Charlie and Claire, but are only able to rescue Charlie.

In the flashbacks: Jack subs in for his drunken father on a surgery that goes wrong and then tells the truth to the hospital's board when the patient's family sues.

For the most part Season One slowly reveals the Island's secrets, but from the moment we meet Rousseau, the show moves into narrative over-drive for a stretch, building momentum before the midseason break. These days, thanks to heavily serialized action-adventure shows like *Lost*, the term "midseason finale" has become a staple of network TV's self-promotion; but in 2004 these things came and went without much hype. Nevertheless, *Lost*'s writers structured "All the Best Cowboys Have Daddy Issues" to end on an emotional high and then a cliffhanger, giving their huge audience something to think about over the holidays.

This episode doesn't have the best reputation today, primarily because *Lost* is so glutted with "Jack episodes" that they retroactively seem less exciting. Even the title is something of a groaner, prematurely winking at a *Lost* theme that was quickly becoming a cliché.

Yet when watched as part of the three-episode run with "Solitary" and "Raised by Another," this is an exciting and crucial hour. The flash-backs close the loop on a story introduced in "White Rabbit," explaining how exactly Jack Shephard ruined his father's career, by being honest about Christian drunkenly botching a surgery. And on the Island, nearly all of the action involves a treacherous chase through the jungle, to find Charlie and Claire. The previous episode ended with Ethan confronting them both on their way to the beach, after which they disappeared, apparently abducted by the Others. The medical drama in the flashbacks carries over to the Island, as Jack finds a near-death Charlie hanging from a tree and is barely able to revive him. It's all very simple—and, sure, a bit corny—but thrilling, too.

And then, just as the episode is about to end—with Charlie safe but Claire still missing, and the awareness of the existence of the Others hovering over the camp like an ominous cloud—Locke and Boone stumble across something strange. Boone drops a flashlight and hears a clank. A little digging reveals a sealed metal hatch.

What's inside that hatch? It's going to be a while before we find that out. But one of *Lost*'s most defining and rewarding mysteries has entered the picture; and from here on out the show will subtly begin to change. —*NM*

"WHATEVER THE CASE MAY BE"

—

SEASON 1, EPISODE 12
ORIGINAL AIRDATE 1/5/05

On the Island: Sawyer and Kate find a locked suitcase that belonged to the marshal, and she and Jack try different tactics to persuade Sawyer to hand it over.

In the flashbacks: Kate is involved in a bank robbery that ends with her retrieving an envelope, which is later locked in the marshal's case along with his guns.

After a month-long hiatus, *Lost* returned with an episode that pulled back from all the mysteries bubbling up on the Island and instead told a fairly straightforward Kate story with some overly cutesy teases. Viewers who tuned in anxious to find out more about Claire's whereabouts, the Others, Rousseau, or the hatch were instead treated to an hour divided between Flashback Kate orchestrating a heist in New Mexico and Island Kate trying to retrieve and open a locked suitcase.

Neither half of "Whatever the Case May Be" is especially revealing, although the heist sequences are well-handled and there's some decent coyote-versus-roadrunner physical comedy in the scenes where Sawyer tries to open the suitcase while keeping it away from Kate. The connection between the two main storylines in this episode—and their larger connection to the series—becomes clearer at the end, when we learn what the case contains. It holds the marshal's guns, thus giving the castaways who know about the weapons access to deadly firepower and establishing yet again that there's a division among the 815ers between those who get to know the big secrets and those who don't.

The case also contains the envelope that was, effectively, the only "loot" from the heist in the flashback. The envelope was in safety deposit box #815. Its contents? A tiny toy airplane.

Naturally, these two details—815 and the plane—excited fans, who would keep spinning theories about the significance of this for the next several years, imagining some kind of mystical connection between the toy and Oceanic 815. Ultimately, the toy matters only to the next piece of Kate's backstory, coming toward the end of the season. The writers definitely intended to get viewers talking with this little airplane; but while it's fun to play, the guessing game will have meager spoils. —NM

"HEARTS AND MINDS"

—

SEASON 1, EPISODE 13
ORIGINAL AIRDATE 1/12/05

On the Island: Locke smears a psychotropic goo into a wound on Boone's head, sending the young man on a hallucinatory vision quest in which he realizes he needs to stop obsessing over Shannon.

In the flashbacks: Boone is tricked by Shannon into flying to Australia and giving her money to escape a bad boyfriend, and after he realizes she's been lying to him, the step-siblings have sex.

Lost fans differ on which Season One episodes are the best and which are the worst; but "Hearts and Minds" is a strong contender for the worst of the worst. The flashback is meant to be provocative but mostly comes off . . . well, icky. And the on–Island A-story relies on one of the most irritating storytelling conceits of the early twenty-first century, employed mostly for the purpose of tricking the audience. The end result of all this nonsense is an episode that has only a negligible effect on the season's larger story. Only two minor elements matter in the long run.

Let's start with the flashbacks, which confirm something that fans had suspected since the start of the series—but takes it further than expected. When we first meet Boone and Shannon, it's clear that Boone is smitten with his stepsister and that she uses his infatuation to manipulate him. In "Hearts and Minds" we see the full extent of that manipulation, as Shannon in the flashbacks fakes an abusive boyfriend—and not for the first time, we later learn—in order to get Boone to come to Australia and "rescue" her with their family's money.

She also seduces him, which . . . yeesh.

Now, these two are not biologically related, so their sexual encounter isn't really incest. But they've known each other since pre-adolescence, so it's more than a little creepy. Also, because Shannon hasn't had a full flashback yet, she remains at this point in the series an inexplicably mean-spirited femme fatale, who does not come off well in this episode ostensibly about Boone.

On the Island, meanwhile, Locke decides to play life coach for Boone the way he did for Charlie; but rather than using strictly psychological tactics he ties Boone up and smears a paste on an open head wound, inducing a psychedelic vision. For some reason, TV in the early 2000s was big on drug trips, spirit quests, and dream sequences. In this episode Boone has a vision of Shannon being killed by "the monster," which *Lost* viewers experienced at the time as actually happening . . . until Boone wakes up from his druggy dream, that is. Given that the audience was eager to see and hear more about the monster, the whole sequence came off as a cruel fake-out. It told us nothing about the Island that was relevant when the episode aired (although one could argue, given what we learn about the monster later in the series, that the Island here was speaking directly to Boone about secrets as yet unrevealed).

So, what can we take away from "Hearts and Minds"? Well, it shows how the Locke/Boone bond is strengthening, which matters in the episodes ahead. Oh, and in a seemingly minor subplot, Sayid tries to interpret Rousseau's maps with the help of Locke's compass but is flummoxed by how the tool shows that "north" is not where it should be.

Hmmm . . . —NM

UNANSWERED QUESTIONS

"SPECIAL"

–

SEASON 1, EPISODE 14
ORIGINAL AIRDATE 1/19/05

(Unlike most of the essays in this book, if you have never seen Lost *and want to remain unspoiled, then you should perhaps skip this essay, as it is impossible to talk about Walt without spoiling where the series goes with the character.)*

"Special" arrives in the first season's long middle stretch, when the show is simultaneously realizing everything it can do—and wondering whether it *should do* everything. This is an early inkling of the show appearing increasingly terrified at the prospect of running for multiple seasons with a premise seemingly designed for a miniseries or a two-season run at best. There may be no better sign of this than the mere existence of Walt Lloyd, source of the series' biggest unanswered questions—and also the show's single biggest missed opportunity, though not perhaps for the reasons fans might expect.

One of *Lost*'s real innovations was in how it presented the passage of time. True, it wasn't the first series to take place over a compressed period of time—its rough contemporary *24*, which debuted in 2001, famously compressed each of its eight seasons to a single day. However, *Lost*'s dedication to a gradually unfolding narrative, where each season took place over a matter of weeks, rather than paralleling the calendar year, granted it a grounded quality that helped sell the ridiculousness of its narrative. The flashbacks did open this storytelling up to some degree, granting the show access to the entire history of its characters' lives, but even those tended to follow only a few significant days in a character's life. The pacing—in both past and present—remained deliberate throughout.

Had the series kept the characters on the same timeline as the audience, then by this point, the characters would have been on the Island for nearly four months, which would make them finally deciding to pursue escape via a raft feel much too late in the game. By keeping the characters pinned to the aftermath of the crash, the show could explore in more granular detail how they tried to stay alive. Then, when the monster struck, its wrath felt of a piece with the other on-Island adventures because it was getting in the way of more-prosaic survival efforts. Notably, *Lost* had to train viewers to watch the show this way. Complaints about why the characters hadn't tried various methods of escape or explored certain corners of the Island were legion in Season One, despite the show's timeline then having covered only a few weeks.

Of course, if you're going to have a compressed timeline, then the absolute worst thing you can do is cast a kid. And perhaps an even worse choice than that would be to cast a kid on the cusp of adolescence, meaning that at any moment, you could have a teenager who seems to have gone through puberty in maybe two weeks.

"There should be a kid there" is a natural idea to have once you've come up with a deserted island show, but as with so many choices in early *Lost*, the decision seems to have been made with an eye toward a brief, glorious run and eventual cancellation. Once the show became a hit, Malcolm David Kelley quickly getting older than the character he played became a huge problem the show would have to solve.

All of *that* might have been fine if Walt had simply been another character on the Island. In that event, something like continually recasting the role with an ever-increasing number of preteens* might have worked. Yet from its earliest episodes, *Lost* has hinted that Walt boasts some manner of psychic powers, which this episode seems to confirm. In the early going of the show, Walt's nebulous powers and the Monster add a paranormal frisson to the proceedings. The survival drama half of the show *needs* the more genre-adjacent elements to stay entertaining just as much as the genre stuff needs the survival stuff to stay grounded.

So now, not only has the series painted itself into a corner with a child performer who will inevitably age, but it's also placed the weight of an extremely important plot element on his shoulders. What's admirable

---

*   This would have been similar to how *Mad Men* handled Bobby Draper.

about "Special" is how little interest it has in flinching from what Walt might be capable of. We already know he can seemingly manifest polar bears, but he can also make birds smack into windows. And he appears largely unaware of his abilities, too, leaving plenty of room for the show to evolve those powers.

It doesn't. Not to spoil where things are going overly much, but *Lost* never figures out what to do about its "kids grow up" problem. Walt simply disappears from the show after a while, and despite some half-hearted sops to figuring out some way to keep him around or to better explain his powers, the show mostly gives up. In terms of the biggest mysteries *Lost* never explains, the source of Walt's powers—or even what those powers are at all—is the biggest.

That lack of answers isn't the biggest missed opportunity with Walt, however.

When *Lost* aired, actor Harold Perrineau, who plays Walt's father Michael, spoke openly about how he felt the show not only betrayed his character but also the relationship he had with Walt. Fan backlash was swift, but Perrineau has continued discussing his issues with the show since the series run wrapped up, most notably in Maureen Ryan's 2023 book *Burn It Down*.

Walt and Michael are both Black, and Perrineau took great pride in portraying a relationship between a Black father and son on a huge hit TV show. TV had often treated Black fathers as negligent, propagating an awful stereotype.

Like most of the relationships that exist pre-Island on *Lost*, the relationship between Walt and Michael needs work, but across Season One, it seems as though the Island has given them space *to* work on it. "A parent and child become closer" is an almost universal story, but within this specific example of it, *Lost* had an opportunity to do something different from nearly every other show in TV history to that point.

It completely whiffed that opportunity. By finding a way to essentially take Walt off the board entirely, the show reduced Michael to a character who screamed his son's name a lot, then wrote both characters out. It's one of the biggest character failings across the run.

"Special," then, stands as an example of a show that could have been and never was. The flashbacks, which show a Michael who lost access to his son when Walt was very young, then found the kid abruptly thrust back into his life after the death of Walt's mother, set up a rich tapestry of elements the show could have drawn from if it had chosen to. It could—and arguably should—have told stories about Michael's struggles as an artist, Walt's adoptive father being white, and Michael's strained relationship with Walt's mom. It simply never did.

The on-Island action hints equally at how much potential this storyline had. Walt spends much of the first half of the season casting about for a father figure, understandably not trusting the biological father he's essentially just met. He finds one in Locke, which creates an interesting triangle of characters who want to get out of here (Michael), who want to stay (Locke), and who are just trying to figure themselves out (Walt). Michael and Locke's conflict over who should bear responsibility for Walt gives the on-Island action a connection to the flashbacks that doesn't always exist in the show's early going.

"Special" has some of the flaws of early *Lost* in its other plots. Charlie's struggles over whether to read Claire's diary hit the same beat over and over, and Claire simply stumbling back into camp at episode's end is a weak cliffhanger, deflating the impact of her disappearance. Yet the episode's portrayal of a father trying to figure out what's best for the son he just got back, only to realize he barely knows the boy, offers something the show could have made a meal out of if it had chosen to. Early *Lost* is littered with abandoned evolutionary paths, roads the show could have traveled down and chose not to, but few sting as badly as this one. —*ESJ*

"HOMECOMING"

—

SEASON 1, EPISODE 15
ORIGINAL AIRDATE 2/9/05

On the Island: Locke finds Claire, Ethan begins murdering castaways to pressure them to return Claire to him, and then Charlie kills Ethan.

In the flashbacks: The junkie Charlie tries to straighten up and become a photocopier salesman to impress a woman he likes, but he eventually relapses into drugs and theft.

Lost arrived toward the beginning of TV's prolonged antihero era, which more or less kicked off with *The Sopranos* and then reached its peak about ten years after *Lost*'s debut, when *The Walking Dead* was the most popular series on cable and seemingly every new prestige drama was about some physically strong but emotionally fragile dude (nearly *always* a dude) bending morals and ethics in order to achieve some righteous goal. These shows all feigned seriousness about their characters breaking rules and taking lives. (Sure, they got things done . . . *but at what cost?!*) But in interviews with the creators, it was usually pretty clear that the writers, producers, and stars openly admired anyone willing to ditch propriety and do serious damage.

That attitude is evident in "Homecoming," another meandering mid-season episode, notable primarily for Claire struggling to get back into the swing of camp life while in an amnesiac fog and for Ethan's campaign of terror (confirming that the Others are legitimately dangerous). Most of the rest of the episode is given over to Charlie, who goes on a journey from being an ineffectual loser in his flashback scenes to turning into a man of action on the Island.

The flashbacks are somewhat redeemed by Dominic Monaghan's gift for sad-sack comedy, which gives the scenes of a dopesick Charlie struggling to improve himself some welcome notes of dark humor. On the Island, however, Charlie's despair over Claire and his anger at the Others—coupled with his memories of all those times he has been told he's hopeless—ends with him shooting an already-captured Ethan, preventing Jack and Locke from questioning him. For *Lost* viewers, this was bad news; but for the writers it was very convenient to push any need to reveal the Others' secrets further down the road.

Mainly, though, Charlie's impromptu execution shows that even the meekest of our heroes won't flinch from killing and that on this show killing in and of itself doesn't mark a character as "bad." This is good to know, since we're going to see a lot more bloodshed in the years ahead. —*NM*

"OUTLAWS"
—
SEASON 1, EPISODE 16
ORIGINAL AIRDATE 2/16/05

On the Island: Sawyer, Kate, and Locke track a boar into the jungle.

In the flashbacks: In Australia, Sawyer looks for the man who ruined his life but instead finds only Christian Shephard and a guy who owes one of Sawyer's colleagues money.

During Season One's doldrum episodes—the long stretch between the midseason nail-biters and the intense finale—the writers fell into a bit of a formula. Both the Island story and the flashback story of any given episode would be simple and goal-driven, and would only touch glancingly on the show's larger mythology. But also—perhaps as a sop to the fans—something in the off-Island story would hint at a larger connection between the castaways of which they were, as yet, unaware.

Sawyer is at the nexus of a few of these moments of synchronicity. In "Hearts and Minds," Boone crosses paths with him in a Sydney police station; and in "Outlaws," Sawyer has a long conversation in Australia with Jack's wayward father Christian (whose "ah well" aphorism "that's why the Red Sox will never win the Series" is something Jack also says). Sawyer has at least two other connections to his fellow castaways too, both still unrevealed.

Is there a purpose to all this, or is Sawyer meeting Christian just another "Kate's tiny airplane" moment, meant to excite the audience without ever leading anywhere? The skeptics can point to the Island story in this episode, in which Sawyer—egged on by more of Locke's self-help tips—hunts for a boar that takes on an increasing metaphorical significance as it continues to elude him. This is "middle of Season One" *Lost* in a nutshell, advancing character development at the expense of plot. Sawyer's encounter with Christian and Sawyer stalking a giant animal . . . these both

41

directly affect Sawyer's personal growth, and not so much the story of this mysterious Island.

Still, both halves of "Outlaws" are entertaining; and there is an important takeaway from what happens in the flashback, where Sawyer is manipulated by an old colleague, Hibbs (Robert Patrick), into shooting someone he has mistakenly been led to believe is the con man who ruined his life. The sequence speaks to the way these characters so easily become the pawns in other people's games, which is central to the story of what they're doing on the Island, as we'll learn at the end of Season Five. —*NM*

"... IN TRANSLATION"

—

SEASON 1, EPISODE 17
ORIGINAL AIRDATE 2/23/05

On the Island: Jin is accused of burning the raft the castaways are building to get off the Island, while Boone tries to thwart the budding romance between Shannon and Sayid.

In the flashbacks: Jin takes a job with Sun's father, but he struggles with the expectation that he will have to hurt people.

Given how much flack the *Lost* producers would later take for underdeveloping their non-white, non-male characters, it's perhaps apt that one of the big thematic motifs in Season One involves Michael, Sayid, and Jin persistently being misunderstood—and misunderstanding each other, too. There's a reason why this theme recurs; and it's not entirely about urging the audience not to judge people by how they look. Throughout Season One, Lindelof and Cuse introduce an idea that will end up being crucial by the end of Season Six: The people who seem to be bad have some good in them; and the people who seem to be good have done bad things. No one is ever wholly who they seem to be. There are black stones and white stones, sharing the same game board.

". . . In Translation" is one of Season One's best episodes because it threads this message through two gripping stories: one of which takes the audience into its confidence and the other of which springs a genuine surprise.

The flashbacks finish the work begun in "House of the Rising Sun," retelling the story of Sun and Jin's blooming and rotting romance, but this time from *Jin's* perspective, focusing on the pressure put on him by her father Mr. Paik (Byron Chung) to become a more heartless and violent employee. To this point, Jin has been presented as cold, rough, and chauvinistic; but in this episode we're finally privy to details about Jin's past and Jin's plans that paint him in a different light. We meet the father whom Jin kept secret—and thus safe—from Mr. Paik. And we learn that the couple's trip from Australia to Los Angeles (via the Island, alas) was meant to be a reset for their marriage, with Jin finally realizing the job he took to win Sun's hand in marriage was driving them toward divorce.

On the Island, meanwhile, the castaways' raft is sabotaged when someone sets it aflame. Jin quickly becomes the top suspect because his hands are burned, so Sun is compelled to reveal her secret command of English to save Jin's reputation, telling everyone that Jin was actually trying to *save* the burning raft. Locke helps redirect everyone's attention by reminding them of the existence of the Others, although he knows that the real culprit is . . .

Walt. Sweet, innocent little kid Walt, who tried to destroy his best way of getting off the Island because he's not ready to leave. Everyone—*everyone*—has secrets to tell.

Add all this up and we have a powerful episode, which begins to shift *Lost* out of its midseason blahs and toward some meaningful action again. One signal that the stakes are changing? In the closing scene, Hurley's CD player—the source of several episode-closing reflective songs—runs out of batteries and dies. The days of lounging around on the beach are over. —*NM*

ANSWERS IN SEARCH
OF QUESTIONS

"NUMBERS"
—
SEASON 1, EPISODE 18
ORIGINAL AIRDATE 3/2/05

By the end of *Lost*'s run, its "built world"—all the different Island set-
tlements, camps, hatches, and temples—had become so vast and so grand
that when the show ended it almost felt like the end of an era for broadcast network television. Never again would something that aired on
ABC, NBC, CBS, or Fox have such a sweeping, ambitious narrative, or
look so . . . expensive.

It's strange to look back at the Season One episodes and rediscover them
looking so . . . small. Sure, the flashbacks hop all across the globe (while
mostly staying inside, in modest rooms actually shot in Hawaii); but on
the Island, for most of the season, the primary locations are a beach, a
cave, and various scenic clearings flanked by jungles and mountains.

So, what brought viewers back, week after week? Two things, primarily: the relationships between the characters and the promise that one
day—*one day*—the show would explain what the heck was going on.

By the time "Numbers" aired in March 2005—in the homestretch of
Season One—the character drama far outweighed the mystery. The construction of the raft was still leading to a lot of arguing and suspicion. Jin
was still freezing out Sun. Sayid and Shannon were tentatively flirting.
Locke was turning rendered animal fat into glue to build a cradle for
Claire, who was struggling to remember what had happened to her when
she was kidnapped by the Others.

But it was hard to ignore that *Lost* had fallen into a minor rut by the
middle of Season One, offering character flashbacks that added little to our
understanding of our heroes, Island action that smacked of time-killing

melodrama, and only the occasional glimpse of a polar bear, or a broken compass, or an Other, or Walt's magic powers to remind the audience that the woo-woo was still out there, waiting to be unleashed.

And then "Numbers" came along, delighting fans by introducing another of *Lost*'s main characters: 4, 8, 15, 16, 23, and 42.

The episode features the first Hugo Reyes flashback and, given that the show had been deploying Jorge Garcia primarily as comic relief,* "Numbers" was itself intended to lighten the mood. The flashback scenes in particular play as a kind of escalating farce. First, Hurley's grandfather dies of a heart attack at the press conference announcing Hurley's huge lottery win. Then his mom snaps an ankle while he's taking her to see her new dream house—which promptly burns down. Hurley gets arrested due to a misunderstanding with the cops. He sees a man falling out of a high office building window while he's getting the news from his accountant that a hurricane in Florida helped boost the price of his stake in orange futures. In short . . . He's rich, but cursed.

"Numbers" puts a poignant spin on the whole Hurley tragicomedy. The flashback is sparked by our man looking through Rousseau's papers and seeing page after page of the same repeating numbers—4, 8, 15, 16, 23, 42—that Hurley used to win the lottery. The numbers had been stuck in his head ever since his time in a sanitarium, when one of his ward-mates, Leonard Sims (Ron Bottitta), would repeat them incessantly. When Lenny learns Hurley played them in the lottery, he warns him that he's opened "the box" and tells him to track down the man in Australia who gave Lenny the numbers. It turns out that the man, Sam Toomey, died under mysterious circumstances, though his widow Martha (Jayne Taini) is still around to tell Hurley he got the numbers from a stray radio signal. (Sound familiar?)

On the Island, Hurley's bad luck continues. Determined to go see Rousseau and hear what she has to say about the numbers, he takes off through the jungle, alarming Sayid, Jack, and Charlie, who doubt him and condescend to him—even after they see him barely duck one of Rousseau's traps, while claiming, "I'm spry." (These kinds of charming and vulnerable character moments are a big part of why *Lost* became an instant hit.)

---

* Remember when Hurley got diarrhea?

Finally, he stands face-to-face alone with Rousseau and speaks for *Lost* viewers everywhere when he delivers a rant: wondering about whether the numbers are cursed; making reference to all the weirdness on the Island ("That thing in the woods, maybe it's a monster . . . I don't know"); and demanding, "I want some friggin' answers!"

Us too—but what kind? When *Lost* neared its end, Damon Lindelof was often asked about some specific pieces of the show's lore, as fans hoped for explanations before the series wrapped; and in an interview with *Entertainment Weekly*'s Jeff Jensen, Lindelof said about the numbers, "For fans waiting for an advanced dissertation on the mythic significance of the numbers, I direct them to Qui-Gon Jinn's speech to Shmi Skywalker regarding midichlorians and pose the following question: Happy now?"

For those not versed in *Star Wars*–ese, Lindelof is referring to the way George Lucas filled the *Star Wars* prequels in the '90s with made-up scientific jargon meant to apply wonky space-physics to esoteric concepts like "The Force." Or in other words: Perhaps some things don't need an explanation. Perhaps they can just be freaky for their own sake.

In the featurette "The Genesis of *Lost*" on the Season One DVD set, one of the show's original staff writers, Jeff Pinkner, said that an initial inspiration for the show—clearly evident in "Numbers"—was video games. He said, "The exploration of this place was a mystery and adventure to itself. . . . The Island in itself could be, in a way, a dramatic version of a video game. You could find the hatch, but it could take you several weeks before you had the proper tools to be able to open the hatch."

Answers were never supposed to come easy. Getting around the Island was never supposed to be easy. The viewers, like the characters, were supposed to pick up little tidbits here and there, to be stowed in our inventory until needed. The numbers are a prime example of this. With the numbers as a new tool in our kit, so many seemingly minor details on the show took on new significance. (Oceanic Flight *815*, you say? Oh ho ho!)

Along those same lines, after being told by everyone that Hurley's worries about curses are "crazy," Rousseau puts his mind at ease just by acknowledging that she too thinks the numbers are cursed. It doesn't matter why they're spooky. It only matters *that* they're spooky. As if to drive that home, the episode ends with a shot of the concrete hatch Locke found near the beach, on the side of which is carved 4, 8, 15, 16, 23, and 42.

This recurrence of the numbers (the first of many, many more) encourages viewers to keep looking closely, to see how the scattered narrative pieces connect.

By this stage of *Lost*'s larger story, this too was enough for many fans—just the occasional acknowledgment that between all the interpersonal drama on the Island and all the backstory spilled in the flashbacks, *Lost*'s creators didn't want us to think that all the spine-tingling tidbits were random or coincidental. For all of us who were already poring over every episode for hidden clues and deeper meanings, with "Numbers," the show was reassuring us, whispering, "You're not crazy." —*NM*

"DEUS EX MACHINA"
—
SEASON 1, EPISODE 19
ORIGINAL AIRDATE 3/30/05

On the Island: Locke has a vision that sends him and Boone into the jungle, where they find a small airplane in a tree; Boone investigates because Locke's legs are balky, which ultimately leads to Boone being critically wounded.

In the flashbacks: Locke finally meets his birth mother and birth father, who work a con together to get him to donate a kidney.

Nearly every 815 passenger has a tragic backstory, but John Locke's past rivals Job. On the Island, he seems so confident and wise: a man of many useful skills, sensitive to other people's needs yet willing to employ some tough love. But each new flashback reveals a man who up until the plane crash had been treated very unfairly by life: abandoned, abused, exploited, and underestimated. (To Locke, being underestimated is the deepest insult.)

The parallels between the pathetic off-Island Locke and the heroic on-Island Locke become stronger as the series goes on, as our man suffers serious setbacks in the present-day storyline. Those setbacks begin with "Deus Ex Machina," an excellent episode that partially serves as a corrective to all those drippy Season One episodes where Locke tries to "fix" one of his fellow castaways. Here, Locke takes his disciple Boone on an excursion—provoked by a vision of a small airplane's wreckage—and everything goes awry. Locke's legs begin to fail him, suggesting that his mystical connection to the Island is wavering. Then the plane falls off a cliff with Boone inside—badly, but not fatally, injuring him.

The flashbacks in "Deus Ex Machina" fill in central pieces of the Locke canon. We get our first look at his birth mother Emily (Swoosie Kurtz), who it turns out has been paid by his sociopathic criminal mastermind father Anthony Cooper (Kevin Tighe) to nudge Locke toward meeting his dad and donating a kidney to him. As soon as both parents get what they want, they ditch their son again. (Cooper will go on to be a recurring nemesis to Locke in his flashbacks; and he ultimately has a part to play in *Lost*'s larger narrative, too.)

But it's the disastrous expedition in "Deus Ex Machina" that has the most immediate impact on the Season One story and reverberates deep into Season Two as well. Boone's crash doesn't just have tragic consequences; it also sours Locke's previously solid reputation with the 815ers, sowing seeds of distrust. And there's more! Before the crash, Boone uses the radio on the plane and ends up contacting someone who says, "We're the survivors of Oceanic Flight 815," setting up a new mystery to be resolved. The plane, it turns out, is carrying Virgin Mary statuettes filled with baggies of heroin, which before long will provide some fresh temptation to Charlie. The plane also carries a corpse in priest's clothing,★ whose identity will be revealed in Season Two. And after Boone is injured, Locke despairingly pounds on the outside of the seemingly impossible-to-open hatch . . . and in reply, he sees a light in the hatch's window.

So, Locke's a mess. But he may be on the verge of a breakthrough. The airplane, the hatch . . . some kind of god could be working within these machines. —*NM*

★   A literal deus ex machina?

"DO NO HARM"

—

SEASON 1, EPISODE 20
ORIGINAL AIRDATE 4/6/05

On the Island: Jack scrambles to save Boone's life but lacks the resources, while Kate helps Claire have her baby, with assistance from Jin and Charlie.

In the flashbacks: Jack prepares to marry Sarah, with advice from his father.

Inconvenient labor is the kind of TV cliché that even the smartest writers can't seem to abandon. "Do No Harm" would be an eventful episode even if Claire didn't give birth to her baby, Aaron, at the end of it. We have Jack trying to save Boone's life by donating his own blood (with the help of an improvised hypodermic made from a sea urchin spine, courtesy of Sun and Jin). We have Shannon missing out on all of the chaos surrounding her stepbrother because she's on a date with Sayid. And then, in the middle of all that, Claire goes into labor, and has to rely on Charlie and Kate (with remote instructions from Jack) to get through it.

Given that the birth is such a big *Lost* moment, one might expect the episode's flashbacks to be Claire-centered. But no, we're back to Jack for the third time this season (or fourth, counting the multi-character flashbacks in "Pilot"), to get the story of his marriage to Sarah (Julie Bowen), a former patient whose life he saved. It's a sweet enough little tale, with a surprise appearance from a pre-Australia Christian Shephard, giving Jack some fatherly advice about writing his vows—coupled with a cautionary observation about Jack's inability to let things go. This ties back into Jack's ultimately futile attempt to save Boone's life, where he puts his own health at risk—until Boone tells the doctor to let him die. (He also tells Jack about the hatch he and Locke found, which . . . well, to be continued.)

49

But while this episode is plenty intense, its most important action has nothing much to do with its main character. The real story here is that Boone dies and Aaron is born. The Island giveth and the Island taketh away. —*NM*

"THE GREATER GOOD"

—

SEASON 1, EPISODE 21
ORIGINAL AIRDATE 5/4/05

On the Island: The castaways are all convinced that Locke is responsible for Boone's death, and only Sayid is willing to give him the benefit of the doubt.

In the flashbacks: While searching the world for Nadia, Sayid ends up in Australia, where he's enlisted in a scheme to entrap an old friend, now in a terrorist cell.

The United States officially invaded Iraq in March 2003; and by the time *Lost* debuted in September 2004, the initial overwhelming public support for the war had begun to fade, and many questioned whether the Bush administration had a proper exit strategy.* This growing feeling of ambiguity about the occupation itself didn't necessarily manifest as a forgiving attitude toward the Iraqi military, though; so, it was a decidedly bold choice for *Lost*'s writers to put a veteran of the Iraqi Republican Guard into their primary cast of characters, and not as a villain. From the start of the series, *Lost* was clear that our "good guys," seen in a different light, could be read as bad guys.

The flashback scenes in "The Greater Good" show the dire outcome when people don't get a second chance. Having escaped his Iraqi military commitments, Sayid finds himself working with Australian and American secret agents in Sydney to stop a suicide bombing; and he tries

---

* Some *Lost* fans would later feel similarly uncertain about Lindelof and Cuse.

to convince his handlers that the would-be bomber, Essam (Donnie Keshawarz), could be coaxed into surrendering before doing anything illegal. Instead, the agents have Sayid goad Essam into procuring explosives; and when Sayid tries to prevent the situation from getting any worse by telling his friend what's up, Essam kills himself. Even when he tries to keep old friends and old enemies safe, the nature of global politics in the early 2000s sours the deal.

That's what makes Sayid such a strong choice to anchor an episode that is primarily about how the 815 survivors turn against Locke—who had been one of the few among them that seemed, until recently, unambiguously heroic. Given Sayid's past and given how the castaways *and the TV audience* might be inclined to regard an Iraqi at the time, he embodies the idea that no one is exactly who they seem to be on the surface.

Does the widespread distrust of Locke seem a bit abrupt and perhaps even over-the-top? To some extent, yes—especially when it leads to Shannon urging her new boyfriend Sayid to prove his commitment to her by exacting some revenge against Locke. At this point, no one even knows what actually happened to Boone and to what extent Locke is responsible. They're just sure that he's lying.

And he is, of course. Sayid doesn't try to kill Locke but he does make Locke walk him through the steps of what happened to Boone; he gets Locke to come clean about the airplane in the jungle and, eventually, about the hatch. He gives Locke the benefit of the doubt—goodness knows he's needed that himself a few times. —*NM*

"BORN TO RUN"

—

SEASON 1, EPISODE 22
ORIGINAL AIRDATE 5/11/05

On the Island: While one set of castaways looks for a way to open the hatch, another puts the finishing touches on the raft and suffers another act of sabotage when Michael gets poisoned.

In the flashbacks: Kate reconnects with a childhood friend, but becomes acci-
dentally responsible for his death while fleeing from the police.

While the other 815ers' backstories are told in Season One either in
chronological order or by bouncing back and forth across long stretches
of time, Kate's initial run of flashbacks go backward and follow a fairly
direct and tightly packed timeline, with each new Kate episode revealing
something that retroactively illuminates the one that came immediately
before. In "Tabula Rasa," we see Kate at the end of her fugitive days, just
before she gets nabbed by the marshal in Australia. In "Whatever the
Case May Be," we learn that Kate is the subject of an international
woman-hunt in part because she robbed a bank to retrieve a toy airplane.
And then in "Born to Run" we learn the significance of the airplane.

It seems that in the past, on a trip back home to visit with her dying
mother Diane (Beth Broderick), Kate reconnected with her childhood
friend Tom (Mackenzie Astin), with whom she had once buried a time
capsule containing Tom's toy plane. Her connection to that plane is tied
to her connection to Tom—and to her guilt over his death, after she
drove his car through a hail of police bullets with him in the passenger
seat. It's a sad tale; and while it's not the last major Kate flashback (we still
need to find out why she was on the run from the law in the first place),
it tells us most of what we need to know to understand the previous two
Kate episodes. She has done terrible things . . . but for good reasons.

Kate's criminal past is partially exposed on the Island by Sawyer, who
tells the 815ers what he knows about her to distract attention from himself when Michael accuses him of slipping poison into his water bottle.★
Sawyer suggests that Kate is scheming to grab a spot on the nearly completed raft and leave the Island under an assumed name. All the hubbub
here speaks to the rising level of tension on *Lost*, pre-finale. Part of *Lost*'s
popularity was that in its best stretches it induced a familiar kind of
anxious excitement in audiences—that feeling of eagerly tuning in to
find out what was going to happen next, while also nervously muttering
"oh god," knowing that the next hour could be a rough ride for our
heroes. —*NM*

★ The actual culprit is Sun, who was trying to poison Jin's water, to keep him from
  leaving on the raft.

ABRACADABRA

"EXODUS"

—

SEASON 1, EPISODES 23, 24 & 25
ORIGINAL AIRDATES 5/18/05 & 5/25/05*

At its best, *Lost* is like a magic trick pulled by a magician who, despite explaining every step of the trick, still manages to dazzle you. Especially this early in its run, the show leaves little to the imagination, but it frequently finds ways to pull its many storylines together that still surprise.

Case in point: At the end of "Exodus, Part 1," the three-episode† finale of *Lost*'s first season, the castaways launch the raft Michael has been working on for much of the back half of Season One. If you are at all a TV fan, you know that most likely, the raft will set off to sea with Michael, Walt, Sawyer, and Jin on board. (It does.) The show needs its characters to be competent people who succeed from time to time. Yet you also know that, most likely, some trouble will befall them, and they will end up right back on the Island. (It does.) A show about castaways on a (somewhat) deserted island needs to keep its characters on the Island. You can see every beat of this storyline coming from a mile away.

So, here's where the magic trick happens: The raft launch is inexplicably one of the most moving sequences in the entire run of a show crammed full of moving moments and possibly in the history of

---

*   The second and third episodes of the finale aired together as a two-hour event on May 25 but were produced as separate episodes of television, both for syndication purposes and in keeping with Hollywood union guidelines around per-episode pay for those who made them.

†   By now, the show was such a massive hit that it could get away with essentially anything it wanted. It could convince ABC to give it a three-episode finale because the network wanted as many episodes as it could get.

53

television.* This big, sweeping sequence detailing an effort that we intellectually know is doomed still becomes so grand and full of life that we start to think, "Hey, maybe they'll pull this off after all." Most of that is on execution. The scale of the sequence is unlike much else TV had done to that point; director Jack Bender included many pulled-back aerial shots showing the raft floating out to sea. What's more, most of the cast is present for the scene, along with a bunch of extras, lending the moment a feeling of culmination.

But mostly, it's the dog.

See, as the raft heads off into the Pacific, Vincent the dog paddles along after it, trying to catch up to Walt, the boy who has been caring for him these last few weeks. Walt calls out to him to go back, and still Vincent keeps paddling away, the camera just above water level to watch him as he swims. Finally, Walt convinces the pup to return to shore, and he turns around and paddles back. It should be cheap to rely on a trope as corny as this, but *Lost* understands very well that this kind of earnest sentimentality can be enormously effective when deployed well, especially in contrast to the harshness of the show's life-and-death stakes. The raft sequence needs that little extra spice to push it over the top, and it finds it in one of the oldest stories there is: a boy and his dog.†

Across its run, *Lost* gained a reputation as a show full of twists, where the story would turn in unexpected directions regularly. That perception is often true. This show, after all, put a polar bear on a tropical island. Watch "Exodus," however, and you'll realize that what made the show so successful was how the unexpected was almost always used as an interesting flavor off to the side of the main dish. And the main dish was often made up of some of the oldest storytelling tricks around.

I have occasionally described *Lost* as a massive stew filled with essentially every American pop culture trope from the twentieth century, blended in a way that simultaneously reminds you why you loved those tropes and recontextualizes them to make them feel *just* new enough. That "everything and the kitchen sink" approach to storytelling can be

---

* I'm allowing for your personal taste. I *absolutely* think it's somewhere in the top 100 most moving TV moments.

† I'm struggling not to tear up at the thought of poor Vincent trying to catch up to Walt as I write this. He's such a good dog!

exhausting without a keen sense of when too much is too much. But in Season One, *Lost* almost always landed on the right side of that line.*

The storytelling is also elegant in its simplicity. In "Exodus," the characters have two main goals: Launch the raft before monsoon season sets in, and protect baby Aaron from the Others, who Rousseau insists are coming to kidnap the little guy. Everything follows from those two ideas. Why are Jack, Locke, Hurley, and Kate hiking to the mysterious "Black Rock"† to get dynamite? They need to blow open the Hatch so that they can hopefully find space within it for the castaways to hide. Why does Charlie come across the drug smuggler's plane full of heroin that can so sorely tempt him? He's on the trail of Rousseau, who has taken Aaron to try to make a deal with the Others. Every plot point in the episode follows logically from something the characters might do to achieve their goals, while also providing some degree of surprise and suspense.

After *Lost*'s first season proved such a smash, TV networks would spend years attempting to replicate what made it such a hit. Almost all these shows would fail, and even the ones that succeeded for a time‡ failed to match the long-running success of *Lost*. These shows usually tried to start in such a big, all-encompassing place that the audience lacked anything to grab hold of. Either there were so many characters that none of them stood out or viewers were dropped into the mythological deep end. *Lost*'s elegance stands out in comparison. Now at the end of Season One, we still don't really know who the Others are, nor have the castaways done much to explore the Island. Yes, Jack and Locke get the hatch open, but famously, they don't find out what's inside. Come back next season, folks!

Mostly, those other shows forgot the dog. By that, I don't mean that they all should have had a dog.§ I mean that they don't have those tiny-but-significant moments of sentimentality and feeling, which buy the

---

* Stay tuned for future seasons to see if this remains true!
† It turns out to be a nineteenth-century slave ship washed up far inland on the Island, in another reminder of how skillfully the show deploys the unexpected when need be.
‡ Particularly NBC's superhero series *Heroes*, which ran for four seasons from 2006 to 2010 and which briefly seemed like it had out-*Lost*-ed *Lost* before it succumbed to an endless slew of boring, go-nowhere plots.
§ Though all TV shows should have a dog.

audience's goodwill and allow the series to keep pushing into darker, weirder territory. A viewer will forgive a show for a lot if they get to see a moment like Vincent swimming after the raft. *Lost* understood that, but too many of its imitators did not.

In rewatching the series for this project, I've found myself coming back to a quote from Patrick Somerville, in reference to his miniseries adaptation of the novel *Station Eleven*. Somerville worked closely with *Lost* co-creator Damon Lindelof on the HBO series *The Leftovers*, and in trying to explain why his *Station Eleven* adaptation so often went for the heart above all else, Somerville said he had learned from "Damon Lindelof's school of twists." He said:

> People don't want twists. What they want is to be told four times
> that it's coming, and then for it to come. Because then different
> kinds of watchers are prepped. Some people can get out ahead of
> it and know it's coming. Some are still surprised, but subconsciously,
> it's a warmer embrace of a turn. It's not quite a surprise, but it's a
> hope that you are falling towards, just like water over a waterfall.[*]

When you're telling a story, surprise is good. Twists are good. The unexpected is good. You want to keep the audience guessing on some level. But an audience doesn't want to guess forever. For a story to feel satisfying, sometimes it needs to leave us on the precipice of revelation, staring down into a just-opened Hatch. When given a choice between revelation and a dog swimming after a raft, *Lost* usually chose the dog. That tendency came back to bite it more than a few times, but in episodes like "Exodus," it made for a show that felt incredibly familiar and also incredibly singular. —*ESJ*

---

[*] From "How 'Station Eleven' Told a Pandemic Story That Didn't Depress the Shit Out of Us," *Rolling Stone*, January 13, 2022.

FURTHER READING: CANON FODDER? CONSIDERING *LOST'S* BOOKS, GAMES, AND "MOBISODES"

On November 1, 2005—about six weeks after *Lost*'s Season Two premiere—Hyperion Books published *Endangered Species*, a novel about an Oceanic 815 survivor who hadn't been featured on the show. The book followed the basic format of a *Lost* episode, alternating between flashbacks and Island action to tell the story of Faith Harrington, a herpetologist who in her first few days on the Island is struggling with guilt, after discovering just before boarding the airplane that her boyfriend had used her collection of deadly venoms to attack a social activist.

Endangered Species was followed in January '06 by *Secret Identity*, about a college student who had assumed a fake persona before 815 crashed; and then in March '06 by *Signs of Life*, about a scandal-plagued artist whose paintings took a dark, portentous turn on the Island.

Then, in May '06, Hyperion published the mind-bending *Bad Twin*, a book that isn't about an 815 survivor but rather *by* one: a writer named Gary Troup, who according to *Lost* lore was the man sucked into the jet's roaring engines during the mad scramble on the Island right after the crash. Troup's *Bad Twin* manuscript was later discovered by Hurley and read by Sawyer—in an actual aired-on-ABC Season Two episode, "Two for the Road."

Of these books, *Bad Twin* made the biggest impression on the *Lost* fandom. A detective story about two wealthy brothers with very different personalities, *Bad Twin* speaks to Lost's love of dualities: Man of Science versus Man of Faith, Jacob versus The Man in Black, et cetera. The book also directly references people and concepts far more relevant to

Lost than some random herpetologist, student, or artist. "Gary Troup" (whose name is an anagram for "purgatory," and who in real life was the novelist Laurence Shames) wrote about the Widmore Corporation, the Hanso Foundation, Paik Industries, Oceanic Airlines, and Mr. Cluck's Chicken Shack. *Bad Twin* also mentioned the Oceanic flight attendant Cindy Chandler (one of the 815 "Tailies"), who in the larger *Lost* reality was Troup's fiancée.

Do you need to read any of these books to get a "complete" picture of *Lost*'s story? According to the show's head writers, absolutely not. In a 2008 *Variety* article, Carlton Cuse said, "Our criteria is, everything you need to know about *Lost* is contained in the mother ship." Besides, while *Bad Twin* was a bestseller, Lindelof and Cuse reportedly weren't happy with how it incorporated—clumsily—many elements from the show that hadn't yet been fleshed out on *Lost* itself.

And yet simultaneously with the release of *Bad Twin*, ABC and *Lost*'s broadcasting partners in the UK and Australia collaborated on "The *Lost* Experience," an alternate reality game that combined physical media, websites, and TV ads into a kind of interconnected playing field, littered with hints at *Lost*'s deeper lore. *Bad Twin*, flaws and all, was a big part of this game, which was primarily about the corruption of the Dharma Initiative's primary benefactor, the Hanso Foundation. Some of the game's clues even pointed to Gary Troup's out-of-print nonfiction book about "the Valenzetti Equation," a math formula containing Hurley's "numbers"—and, according to Hanso and Dharma, a possible key to a global apocalypse.

The game spilled out into promotional appearances for *Lost*. Lindelof and Cuse fielded angry questions from an actor playing as a Dharma-Hanso conspiracy theorist at the 2006 San Diego Comic-Con. On his ABC late-night television talk show, Jimmy Kimmel interviewed another actor playing a gruff and defensive Hanso spokesman. All of this made *Lost*'s ancillary products seem awfully important at the time, no matter what Lindelof and Cuse would later say.

"The Lost Experience" wasn't the only time the promotional teams for the show used the internet to give fans more to explore. ABC was behind an "official" Oceanic Airlines website that contained sly references to the show if visitors poked around enough. The UK's Channel 4 helped promote *Lost* in its early days with a site called "*Lost*: The Untold," which mostly introduced the series' main characters and plot but did also contain some goodies—like an Oceanic 815 passenger manifest—unavailable anywhere else. ABC's Oceanic site returned in modified form in 2007 to become part of "Find 815," another alternate reality game, designed to fill out some of the backstory behind the discovery of Oceanic 815's wreckage in Season Four.

The core *Lost* creative team generated a lot of bonus video content themselves, too. Between Seasons Three and Four, ABC released a series of two-minute "mobisodes" (episodes made for mobile devices), under the title "*Lost*: Missing Pieces." Unlike the sparse and largely useless deleted scenes on the *Lost* DVD, these Missing Pieces were designed to be evocative vignettes, filling in some of the gaps in the main story. Christian Shephard was at the center of a couple of its spotlight moments, which suggested—for the first time, really—his larger importance to the narrative. Walt's time with the Others was brought up and described, answering some of the fans' nagging questions about what happened after he was kidnapped.

Lost also inspired a video game, *Lost: Via Domus*, released in early 2008, right as Season Four began. Plotted out by Lindelof and Cuse, the game follows an amnesiac 815 survivor named Elliott Maslow, who interacts with several of the show's main characters and explores some of the show's already-revealed locations. The primary value of *Via Domus* for die-hard fans was the opportunity to linger for a while in spaces like the Black Rock and the Hydra station, to take a longer look around. (The same opportunity was afforded by a series of jigsaw puzzles released by TDC Games, which when completed showed fans things they couldn't see so clearly on television.)

Lostpedia, an online wiki for the show, files most of this under the category of "deuterocanon." The term refers to material that supports the show's story, but which doesn't add anything essential—and in most cases is dismissed as non-canonical by *Lost*'s creators. (Lindelof and Cuse have said that they're fine with "The *Lost* Experience" but that they don't really consider "Find 815" to be part of their universe; and that despite their involvement with *Via Domus*, only its locations are canon, not anything the characters do or say within them.)

Still, for some *Lost* fans, watching the show as it originally aired, playing these games, and watching these videos was as much a part of the true

"*Lost* experience" as reading weekly recaps on various websites and theorizing in the comment section. These fans were participating in a concept defined by scholar Henry Jenkins as "transmedia," described on his website Pop Junctions as "a process where integral elements of a fiction get dispersed systematically across multiple delivery channels for the purpose of creating a unified and coordinated entertainment experience."

The advantage of consuming *Lost* as a work of transmedia was that it extended the thrill of discovery beyond the one hour a week in which ABC aired the show (in the days before streaming and binge-watching made it easier for fans to immerse themselves in this world). Describing the excitement surrounding *Bad Twin* in his book *The Meaning of Video Games: Gaming and Textual Studies*, scholar Steven E. Jones wrote about the strange delight of seeing Sawyer read a book on *Lost* and then seeing it again outside the show's TV frame—as though the world of *Lost* were overlapping with our own. For those who enjoyed following *Lost* into every new media channel it entered, the endeavor often made them feel more fully informed than the average viewer.

But *were* they? *Lost*'s core creative team were generally—and understandably—hesitant to consign to a game or a website anything critical to their show's larger narrative. None of the new characters in these ancillary products crossed over to the TV series; and most of the new details about the likes of Dharma and Hanso proved trivial. Even worse, for some fans: By not making the transmedia uses of, say, Hurley's numbers canonical, *Lost*'s creators perhaps inadvertently belittled their viewers' fascination with these mysteries.

Scholar Jason Mittell put it best in his 2012 essay "Playing for Plot in the *Lost* and *Portal* Franchises," published in the *Journal for Computer Game Culture*. He wrote, "The transmedia versions of the map detach it from Locke's character motivations and the core island narrative events, making it a potentially fun puzzle to play with, but offering little storytelling payoff despite the promise of hidden mysteries and revelations," and "One of the great contradictions of *Lost* is that the series built as robust of a mythological universe ever devised for television, but then undermined the importance of its own mythology by relegating many of its mysteries to transmedia extensions that it deemed as 'bonus content' rather than core storytelling."

The highs and lows of *Lost*'s transmedia efforts are both fully evident in what has to date been the last bit of proper *Lost* content overseen by Lindelof and Cuse, made to be watched—and debated—after watching the series finale, "The End." (For people watching the series for the first time while reading this book, you might want to skip the rest of this paragraph.) "The New Man in Charge" is a twelve-minute epilogue included on the Season Six DVD set, featuring a couple of adventures of Hurley and Ben, from their years as the Island's co-protectors. In one scene, Ben tells a few remaining Dharma Initiative employees that their mission is over and then shows them a video that answers some of their—and our—lingering questions. In another scene, Ben and Hurley reconnect with Walt and offer him some long-delayed closure on his Island experience.

Removed from the hubbub of weekly *Lost* episodes and conversations, the tying-off-loose-ends quality of "The New Man in Charge" makes the fans' fascination with some previously unsolved mysteries—like the purpose of Room 23, or the reasons why there were polar bears on the Island—seem petty. But as the first bit of new *Lost* story in months, the epilogue satisfied a deeper need: to spend time with these characters and this world again.

Ultimately this was the real purpose of all books and games: to give *Lost* fans more *Lost*. —NM

SEASON TWO

ACHIEVEMENTS UNLOCKED

There is a tendency among *Lost* fans to romanticize the first two seasons. The story was slowly unfolding, the world was gradually expanding, and nearly every episode partially functioned as an emotionally involving, character-driven stand-alone drama. The conventional wisdom is that Season Three is where *Lost* started to stall, as Lindelof and Cuse began running out of stories that wouldn't start advancing the overall narrative toward an ending that ABC didn't yet want.

But Seasons One and Two have plenty of doldrums too, especially compared to the final three seasons, when the plot chugs along like a freight train. For the most part, these early episodes are charged with mystery and packed with action and drama. They're good TV. But there are undeniably times that Seasons One and Two venture into negligible backstory and abstract spiritual quests, too. Such are the complications of producing over twenty episodes in a calendar year. It can test the limits of television writers' imaginations, even as it also allows them the freedom to explore the world they've created and the people who live there.

So let's quickly note the elements of *Lost*'s second season that haven't held up well so that we can focus more on what still works like gangbusters. The biggest issue is that the conflict between Jack and Locke over the nature of the Island and how to react to its myriad wonders becomes increasingly shrill, at times making both characters tougher to be around. In general, *Lost*'s characters begin communicating more via shouting and sarcasm. As the situation on the Island intensifies, either the writers or the actors (or both) reveal that they're shakier at generating straight melodrama than they are at low-boil adventure and left-field weirdness.

There are also plenty of Season Two flashbacks that doodle around the margins of a picture we've already seen. Sure, it's entertaining—and even poignant—to return to Hurley's last day before he won the lottery, or to the time that Jin first met Sun. But we're seeing and hearing these stories while on the Island there are gun-pulling standoffs and jungle cat-and-mouse games. The tone, at times, can feel discordant.

But just at times. For the most part, what connected in Season One still hits in Season Two. And one of the big reasons why fans remember Season Two fondly is that this is when Lindelof and Cuse primarily shift from merely teasing audiences with the Island's history and secrets to actually serving up moments that are, quite often, completely and delightfully unexpected.

It all starts with the season premiere, when the 815ers finally get to see what's inside the Hatch. Fans speculated wildly all summer, imagining something that would explain one of the Island's many mysteries: the polar bear, the numbers, the Monster . . . anything! Instead, our heroes found a guy in a jumpsuit: **DESMOND HUME** (Henry Ian Cusick), who would later explain that he had been living down there for years, keying 4, 8, 15, 16, 23, and 42 into a computer every 108 minutes* to prevent "the end of the world." This is a twist that no *Lost* fan could've predicted.

Unfortunately, Desmond doesn't know much about how or why these numbers work, so he can't really give the castaways or the home viewers the answers they want—at least not yet. He does, though, introduce what at the time seemed like the most important new piece of the *Lost* mythology: the Dharma Initiative, a hippie-dippy scientific research community that had built this hatch (dubbed "the Swan") and several other "stations" around the Island, for reasons only partially revealed in the incomplete fragments of Dharma's orientation films that remain on the Island.

So, this is what Season Two is really about: adding pieces to a puzzle that still remains, fundamentally, a puzzle. Throughout the season we

---

*   As *Lost* fans quickly figured out, $4 + 8 + 15 + 16 + 23 + 42 = 108$.

learn more about the Dharma Initiative, without really finding out who they were or what happened to them. (There is a reference in one of the orientation films to an "incident.") We see the castaways get into more confrontations with the creepy "Others," who mostly remain in the shadows—and who were presumed by many viewers to be the surviving remnants of Dharma. (The truth, revealed a few seasons later, would prove to be much more complicated.)

Lindelof and Cuse take more chances with the storytelling in Season Two, including a few episodes where the flashbacks take place on the Island, in the recent past. And although some ABC executives had anxiously urged Lindelof and Cuse to minimize the freaky stuff, the writers kept introducing wild new concepts into nearly every episode, perhaps without always knowing their purpose . . . or at least not yet. Just as they had thrown together a bunch of characters in Season One without knowing which ones would stick, in Season Two they started stockpiling ideas, figuring they could always decide later which ones were essential.

They trotted out new heroes and villains, too. While some of the original group of 815ers get killed off (or go missing, like Walt . . . a creative choice dictated by Malcolm David Kelley's teenage growth spurt), new people literally start coming out of the jungle. Early in the season, the group that tried—and failed—to leave the Island on a raft in the Season One finale is captured by a group they believe to be the Others. It turns out instead that these are also 815 survivors, who were in the plane's tail section and landed on the other side of the Island, where they have been regularly tormented by the Others.

Some of these "Tailies" would play a significant role in the rest of this season and beyond, including

ANA LUCIA CORTEZ (Michelle Rodriguez), a prickly former police officer who is fiercely protective of her fellow Tailies and distrustful of any strangers.

LIBBY SMITH (Cynthia Watros), a psychologist and peacemaker who has mysterious off-Island connections to multiple characters.

MR. EKO (Adewale Akinnuoye-Agbaje), a former drug-trafficker who became a priest, and who even more than Locke seems spiritually bonded to the Island.

BERNARD NADLER (Sam Anderson), a kindly dentist whose wife **ROSE HENDERSON** (L. Scott Caldwell) landed on the beach with the Season One 815ers, and had been a minor character throughout that season.

CINDY CHANDLER (Kimberley Joseph), an Oceanic flight attendant, who takes a special interest in protecting two young kids who had survived the crash (before getting abducted by the Others).

The biggest addition to the cast in Season Two is a character who was originally going to have just a short arc, before the writers fell in love with the actor's portrayal. A man calling himself "Henry Gale," caught in one of Rousseau's traps, claims to have been stranded on the Island with his now-dead wife while hot-air ballooning. Sayid, though, can sense right away that this newcomer is lying. He turns out to be **BENJAMIN LINUS** (Michael Emerson), the leader of the Others and one of the primary antagonists for the rest of the series.

With each new character—from Desmond to Ana Lucia to Ben—Lindelof and Cuse would tease viewers with the possibility that these people might be able to give us the information about the Island we were eager to learn.

Emphasis on "might." By the end of the season, it became clearer that we had just met a bunch of folks who were just as much in the dark about the Island's nature as our original cast of characters—or, for shady nefarious reasons, were inclined to lie about what they really knew. —*NM*

DOWN THE HATCH

"MAN OF SCIENCE, MAN OF FAITH"

—

SEASON 2, EPISODE 1
ORIGINAL AIRDATE 9/21/05

In the *Lost* Season Two DVD featurette "Secrets from the Hatch," Damon Lindelof said that the concept of the Hatch existed before the show's first episode was shot, even if he and J. J. Abrams didn't yet know what the Hatch actually was. "Finding the Hatch and discovering the Hatch and going into the Hatch are the very first things that J.J. talked about at the very first meeting that I sat down with him. . . . And I said 'Oh, that's incredibly compelling. What's inside?' And he said 'I don't know. We'll figure it out later.' But you know, eventually, later comes."

Lost's Season One finale frustrated some devoted viewers when it ended without showing what—or, as we would soon find out, who—was inside the Hatch. But with the Season Two premiere, "later came," so to speak; and the episode made up for Season One's lapse, in spades.

Ask just about any *Lost* fan to cite some of the show's most memorable moments—the ones that made their spines tingle, made them lean forward, and made them head to the internet as soon as the credits rolled to theorize—and nearly everyone's list will include Season Two's cold open, when we first meet a long-haired Scottish hunk who lives in an underground bunker.★ It's one of the cleverest and most surprising few minutes of TV from the 2000s: watching a man wake up, tap a few keys

---

★   We first meet him by seeing his eye open, just as the Season One premiere began with a shot of Jack's eye.

on a computer keyboard, put on Cass Elliot's "Make Your Own Kind of Music," make a smoothie, and do some exercise. We don't know where we are. We don't know *when* we are.[*]

But then we hear a boom, and after the man's barracks stop shaking, we get our first sense that we're somewhere related to the Island. In a series of quick cuts, we then see flashes of images that don't yet have much meaning: the Dharma Initiative logo, a medical case filled with inoculations, an armory. So it will go throughout this episode. At various times, in and around the hatch—aka the Swan station—we see a QUARANTINE sign, a key drawn toward a wall that seems magnetized, a mural featuring words and drawings related to parts of the Island mythology we had yet to encounter. It was as though Lindelof and Cuse were providing viewers with a map from the opening pages of an epic fantasy novel—you see it all, even if you don't yet know what "it all" is, or means.

Season One's phenomenal success gave the writers the freedom to start building like this, revealing a level of ambition beyond anything most fans had anticipated.[†] Lindelof and Cuse seemed determined to come up with solutions to story problems that completely defied prediction, and which often opened new avenues to explore. Sticking a button-pushing/world-saving Desmond inside the big mysterious hatch is one example. But so is the Dharma Initiative itself, which was, in part, a way to explain how the castaways stayed fed. (The answer: a seemingly limitless supply of shelf-stable Dharma-branded foodstuffs.)

"Man of Science, Man of Faith," though, is notable not just for introducing Desmond and Dharma but for ramping up a conflict that had been raging since Season One. Throughout their first month-plus on the Island, Jack (the "man of science") had taken on the practical day-to-day responsibility of keeping everyone safe, focusing primarily on the essentials: shelter, food, protection from anything hostile in the jungle, and making plans for some future escape and/or rescue. Meanwhile, Locke (the "man of faith") had encouraged anyone who would listen to him to embrace the mystery and secrets of this strange land.

---

[*] That computer looks pretty vintage!

[†] The success also apparently freed up more money for the budget; the sets and the cinematography become more noticeably eye-catching.

But discovering Desmond doesn't really settle any of Jack and Locke's ongoing arguments. On the one hand, Locke is right that there is something more to the Hatch than simply a possible hiding place to avoid the Others. But to find a confused guy in a jumpsuit, and a bunch of outdated technology . . . Well, that's "man of science" stuff, isn't it?

Our heroes don't actually meet Desmond until the end of the episode. Before then, the action is more about the clash between Jack and Locke, who argue about whether they should explore the Hatch right away or wait until daylight. Locke, joined by Kate, ignores Jack's orders and grabs some exploratory supplies. Jack meanwhile struggles to calm the castaways, who in his absence have been bickering over whether the Others actually exist and have been getting angry that more and more of their own people are dying. And while Jack may be a leader, he's also much pricklier and more cynical than the soulful Locke, who tends to have a disarming tone even at his most fanatical.

At one point Hurley asks, "What's that thing where doctors make you feel better, just by talking to you?"—before telling Jack he lacks it. That's one of the cues for this episode's backstory, which is Jack-focused. We get a look at one of the most important moments in his life—from back in the '90s, when he had floppy hair. That's when he met Sarah, who rolled into his hospital's emergency room after a car accident that left her with a busted spine. He's certain she'll never walk again—displaying that utter lack of a bedside manner Hurley noted—but after meeting a stranger who says he is in training for a race around the world, Jack starts to understand that maybe part of his job is to offer people a little hope. When he gets back to the hospital, Sarah—his future wife—is wiggling her toes.

And who was this stranger, who says goodbye to Jack after their brief encounter with a cheery, "See you in another life, yeah?" Well, that was Desmond, of course—because nearly everyone drawn to the Island seems to be connected in some way, even if they never really knew each other back in the outside world.

Jack is about to see this firsthand when he finally goes down the Hatch after Locke and Kate, who haven't returned as quickly as he'd expected. And the *Lost* audience is about to see it, too. We don't get a good look at Desmond at the start of the episode; so when he pops up in Jack's flashback, his face doesn't ring any bells. But as Jack is exploring this underground bunker, he gets stopped in his tracks by the gun-toting

Desmond; and as Jack and the TV viewers see the Dharma-suited Desmond in full, Jack says, "You?"*

Now . . . is it reasonable to expect that Jack would recognize a person he spent about five minutes with many years ago? Maybe not. But that's not the point of this episode. The point is that as much as Jack had liked to write off all the Island woo-woo as coincidence, at the end of "Man of Science, Man of Faith," he's face-to-face with a walking, talking example of something well beyond coincidence.

Season Two's premiere had effectively issued a declaration: Yes, this Island is magical, in ways neither the characters nor the viewers could ever imagine. The surprises were just going to keep coming. —*NM*

"ADRIFT"

—

SEASON 2, EPISODE 2
ORIGINAL AIRDATE 9/28/05

On the Island: In the wake of the Others' attack on the raft, Sawyer and Michael try to find a way back to shore. Meanwhile, Kate and Locke descend into the Hatch, dovetailing with the events of "Man of Science, Man of Faith."

In the flashbacks: Michael's ex, Susan, tries to get him to sign away his parental rights to Walt, something he eventually, reluctantly does.

"Adrift" is a messy episode of *Lost*, one hampered by a production that originally planned to center on Sawyer flashbacks but swerved to Michael flashbacks at the last minute. It is ridiculous to think anyone would have

---

* More from "Secrets of the Hatch," about when the writers started figuring out what should be in there: "Our hard and fast rule was: As soon as we found the hatch on the Island, we had to have some idea of what was inside. If a light was going to go off inside, then we had to have an idea, at least physically, you know, what was causing that light to go on. And it started to feel to us that the most logical explanation was going to be that there was somebody inside there. So, the question became: Who was it? How did they get there? What was there?"

wanted to center this episode on a character other than Michael in the first place, and maybe if the episode had been written with him in mind from the outset, it would have worked better.

As it stands, the episode we have feels—perhaps fittingly—like it's treading water. Sawyer and Michael, adrift at sea, do eventually pull it together enough to figure out a way to fend off a shark, then make it to a pontoon that will help them float more effectively. Yet when it comes time for them to make their way back to shore, it happens largely through no effort of their own. The waves simply carry them back.

The flashbacks are more effective, underlining why Michael gave up his parental rights to Walt in the first place as a way to derive even more poignancy from Walt's disappearance from the raft. As with many Season Two flashbacks, these feel less like new revelations and more like filling in tiny gaps in a story we already know, but Harold Perrineau plays the scenes beautifully. He's especially effective in a scene featuring the last time Michael ever saw Walt before going to collect him in Australia. He stoops down beside a toddler, hands that toddler a teddy bear and effectively conveys how much this decision guts him but also how he hopes it will be all to Walt's betterment.

In the Hatch, *Lost* begins experimenting with a form of storytelling it will eventually perfect—here, it's still very much in its incipient stages. After Jack walked in on Locke being held at gunpoint in the season premiere, this episode rewinds to Kate and Locke's descent into the Hatch in the first place. The show knows how much we want to see inside the Hatch, but this retread doesn't give us anything like new information.

It's all worth it for the cliffhanger, though. As Michael and Sawyer make it to shore, Jin races toward them, stalked by shadowy figures. "Others!" Jin calls. "Others!" Cut to title card. —*ESJ*

"ORIENTATION"

—

SEASON 2, EPISODE 3
ORIGINAL AIRDATE 10/5/05

On the Island: After Desmond accidentally shoots a computer in the Hatch, he claims the world will end unless it is fixed soon. Sayid is pressed into computer repair, while Locke finds a film that explains who built the Hatch. Meanwhile, Sawyer, Jin, and Michael, now held in captivity, meet a woman named Ana Lucia—whom viewers will remember from the Season One finale.

In the flashbacks: Locke's embittered relationship with his father jeopardizes his new connection with a woman named Helen.

When pressed to answer "So what's up with this Island anyway?," *Lost* comes up with a sneakily ingenious way to avoid having to answer its biggest questions: the Dharma Initiative.

A group of scientists who converged on the Island in 1970, Dharma worked to understand the Island's mysteries and use its strange properties for their own research. They built the Hatch—and possibly brought polar bears to the Island (if a brief glimpse of them in the orientation video Locke watches is any indication)—but now, it seems, they've mysteriously disappeared, leaving behind a massive infrastructure that just might be necessary to save the world.

The characters' having to push a button every 108 minutes to avoid catastrophe—even though they don't know what the button does—is a terrific motivator for a tense, involving episode of television. Sayid's desperate race to fix the computer in time provides just enough plot momentum to allow for the long expositional infodumps that make up much of the episode's running time. Whether pressing a button every 108 minutes can motivate any episodes beyond this one is the much larger question.

In flashback, Locke's anger at his father has already entered a well-worn groove, even if few actors can play this kind of harsh bitterness as well as Terry O'Quinn. Helen, played by Katey Sagal (at that point still best known for *Married . . . with Children*), makes for a wonderful foil for him, however, even if it's never precisely clear why she's romantically interested in Locke.

"What does this woman see in this guy, exactly?" is one of those perpetual *Lost* flashback questions. You can largely explain the lack of a clear romantic throughline here with the fact that the flashbacks only portray the most emotionally fraught moments in the characters' lives. Still, on a show that occasionally has trouble giving even its lead female stars inner lives, it's not a great sign that Helen seems to exist mostly to tell Locke he's great.

Meanwhile, over on the other side of the Island, the remaining raft trio find themselves trapped in a very different hole in the ground. Michelle Rodriguez remains nervy and compelling as Ana Lucia, here making her debut as a regular cast member, but it is perhaps telling that *Lost*, at this point a monster hit, is already starting to tell stories about people who are trapped by circumstance and don't see a way out. —*ESJ*

"EVERYBODY HATES HUGO"

—

SEASON 2, EPISODE 4
ORIGINAL AIRDATE 10/12/05

On the Island: Hurley finds himself tasked with overseeing the food stores the Dharma Initiative left behind in the Hatch, a task that fills him with increasing anxiety. On the other side of the Island, Ana Lucia and her group reveal themselves as fellow plane crash survivors.

In the flashbacks: Hurley's lottery winnings irreparably begin to change his relationships with people he cares about—especially his best friend.

Lost's relationship to Hurley's weight is one of the aspects that has aged the most poorly. Jorge Garcia, who plays Hurley, is a bigger guy, and

Hurley is subjected to frequent jibes about his weight, mostly from Sawyer. Those watching the show even got in on the cruel jokes—during its original run, articles and blog posts about the show would jokingly suggest one of its "unanswered questions" was why Hurley hadn't lost any weight.

"Everybody Hates Hugo" at first seems like it's going to be about Hurley's weight. When the survivors who know about the Hatch put Hurley in charge of distributing the food, he freaks out, and we might anticipate a weight-loss PSA. Instead, the episode zags into something more poignant: examining Hurley's relationship to the wealth he had prior to arriving on the Island and all the misfortune that came with it.

To be sure, the storytelling here takes some leaps. It never feels like Hurley's mental distress is so great that he would consider blowing up the Hatch's pantry with dynamite. Still, his foolhardy plan leads to a lovely scene with Rose where she gets him to open up about all he lost (i.e., his nine-figure bank account). Finally, Hurley realizes that the food is never going to last this many people all that long, so he throws a feast, cementing him as the group's morale raiser.

The flashbacks follow the pattern of the last few episodes, shading in some of the details around the stories told in Season One. But seeing Hurley and his friend Johnny (DJ Qualls) have a great time, even as Hurley knows all his newfound wealth is going to change everything, offers a glance at Hurley's great capacity for friendship before he even arrived on the Island. If the Island is a mystical place that enhances our most innate qualities, for good and ill, then Hurley's willingness to take people as they come and have a good time with just about anybody is invaluable.

Over on the other side of the Island, Sawyer, Jin, and Michael learn something the audience almost certainly figured out in the previous episode: Ana Lucia and her group are survivors from the tail section of Oceanic 815. But the plot does confirm that Rose's husband, Bernard, is still alive, which lets viewers anticipate one more heartwarming reunion to come. —ESJ

"... AND FOUND"

—

SEASON 2, EPISODE 5
ORIGINAL AIRDATE 10/19/05

On the Island: The tail section survivors embark on a journey to reach the beach camp we already know and love. On the way, Michael takes off to find Walt on his lonesome, and Jin and Mr. Eko pursue, nearly being captured by the Others. Back at the beach camp, Sun looks for her wedding ring and worries about having to grieve Jin.

In the flashbacks: Jin is told he will soon find love, and Sun starts seeing a guy she likes, as the story of the two's first meeting is told.

The first third of *Lost* Season Two is a bit slow, but it's effective. The series has drastically expanded its scope by introducing concepts like the Tailies and what's inside the Hatch. Consequently, it's giving viewers a chance to get used to those ideas as it drills down into the characters we already know and love. "A character loses her wedding ring" isn't the sort of plot that most genre shows would turn to; that *Lost* tells a story this small and personal amid its chaotic overarching plot is part of what makes it such a good TV series.

What's more, the journey of the Tailies and the three raft castaways across the interior of the Island beautifully captures the unknowability that encompasses much of this still-unexplored territory. When Jin and Eko crouch in the underbrush to hide from a procession of Others—who include a child dragging a teddy bear among their ranks—the moment captures both the mystery and the dread that typify some of *Lost*'s best moments early in its run.

The trip back to the beach camp also allows the show to fill in some of the other characters among the tail section survivors, especially Mr. Eko and Libby. Eko's combination of peaceful thoughtfulness and sudden ruthlessness immediately mark him as a character worth paying attention to, while Watros gives the less-defined Libby a warmth that stands out against the Tailies' grim circumstances.

Sun attempting to find her wedding ring is a plot that's barely a plot—she ultimately finds it when she stops looking, just as Locke suggests she will—but it gives Yunjin Kim and others a chance to play some poignant scenes. In particular, the scene between Kim and Evangeline Lilly lets both women play their nagging uncertainty over what happened to the guys on the raft—even if the scene leans too heavily into the question of how Kate feels about Sawyer versus Jack.

The flashbacks are slight but similarly effective. As a series, *Lost* relies a lot on coincidence and the feeling that the Island is manipulating events toward its own ends. Yet any good love story—and Sun and Jin have a great one—will be filled with moments of serendipity and fate tipping its hand. We already know Sun and Jin are good together; this flashback gives us a chance to feel like they're also destined to be together. —*ESJ*

THE SHANNON STORY

"ABANDONED"

—

SEASON 2, EPISODE 6
ORIGINAL AIRDATE 11/9/05

After *Lost*'s first season, ABC's publicity team announced that some new cast members would be joining in Season Two, and they noted that most of these characters would be 815 passengers from the plane's tail section—immediately dubbed "the Tailies" by fans. The news sparked speculation about how the show was going to integrate these castaways into the story. When and how would they meet up with the folks we'd been following for twenty-five episodes?

The question nobody asked? Which of these Tailies would shoot and kill Shannon Rutherford.

"Abandoned" is a cruel title for what is, for all intents and purposes, *Lost*'s final Shannon episode. At the start of the series, both Shannon and her stepbrother Boone were very much presented as "types"—two spoiled rich kids ill-prepared for roughing it. But before Boone was killed in Season One, he was starting to show some personal growth, under Locke's tutelage. And Shannon? She had become more integral to the series' larger design by the start of Season Two. She had a budding romance with Sayid;* and she was seeing ominous visions of a soaking wet Walt, who had been abducted by the Others. Both of these subplots—the Sayid affair and the ghostly Walt visitations—loom large in "Abandoned."

The title actually refers to what happens in Shannon's flashbacks, which reveal her as a much happier and less embittered person, in the days surrounding her father's death in a car accident. She is all set to pursue her dream of studying dance in New York City, until her stepmother Sabrina (Lindsay Frost) cuts off her access to the family fortune. She asks Boone for help, only to find out that he had taken a job working for his mom—abandoning Shannon, in other words.

The larger point of this flashback is to suggest that Shannon was never really a spoiled brat—despite Sabrina reacting to Shannon's insistence that she'll be working sixteen hours a day on her dance internship by scoffing that the only thing her stepdaughter has ever done for sixteen hours straight is "sleep." Punished by her stepfamily, Shannon chooses to become the selfish slug Sabrina already imagines her to be—and she chooses to make Boone pay for failing her. In classic film noir femme fatale fashion, Shannon starts living down to her reputation.

Which brings us back to the Tailies.

A good chunk of the Island action in "Abandoned" isn't about Shannon at all, but is rather about the remaining survivors of the tail section—the ones who haven't been taken by the Others, that is. They are making their way through the jungle to the beach, escorting Michael, Jin, and a wounded Sawyer. It isn't a happy journey. Sawyer intentionally irritates Ana Lucia, in retaliation for the way her group held them captive when

---

* In the Season Two DVD "On Location" featurette, Naveen Andrews said that the idea was for Sayid and Shannon to end up together. ("What would really shock Middle America?" Andrews said. "What if Sayid was to have a relationship with a woman that looked like Miss America?")

they first met. When the frustration boils over, Michael finally asks what happened to these people to make them so damned disagreeable?

The Others happened. As Ana Lucia describes it, the Others took three of the Tailies on the first night of the crash, then came back two weeks later to abduct nine more. "They're smart," she says. "And they're animals. And they can be anywhere at any time." As if to prove her point, before the traveling party reaches its destination, the 815 flight attendant Cindy is abducted, as the unnerving sound of whispering in the jungle intensifies.

Ana Lucia's story about how there "used to be" twenty-three* in her group sparked another round of second-guessing and theorizing among *Lost* fans. Ana Lucia initially came across as a high-strung character, and maybe not entirely trustworthy. What if she were lying about the Others?† Maybe the Tailies had destroyed each other, because—unlike Jack's group—they didn't stay united. This is a show about dichotomies, right? Good versus evil, science versus faith, "live together or die alone" . . . the same Island, experienced and exploited in a variety of different ways. Maybe this new hero is no hero after all.

This isn't to say that life back at the beach is . . . well, a day at the beach. In "Abandoned," we see how the splintering of the tribe that began in Season One—when some moved to the caves and some didn't—has been accelerating ever since discovering the Swan station. Some castaways are taking advantage of the Hatch's modern conveniences, like its washers and dryers. Others are still hand-washing their clothes and hanging them on a line. Even the romance between Sayid and Shannon has its bumpy moments, largely due to his skepticism about her actually having seen Walt. (More than anything on *Lost*, what these characters most need is confirmation from an outside party that they are not crazy.)

Worried that Sayid will "abandon" her—there's that word again—like everyone else, Shannon coaxes him into joining her on a Walt-hunt, out in the jungle. And what do you know? They both see the apparition of Walt this time, shushing them as the sound of whispers reverberates around them. Shannon chases after the ghost and bursts into a clearing,

---

*   One of Hurley's numbers!

†   Spoiler alert: She's not.

where she stumbles across the Tailies. Ana Lucia, certain she's an Other, shoots Shannon dead.

That's a powerful twist, even though it comes at the expense of yet another original character—pushed out of the show, almost literally, by one of the newbies. But give credit to the writers—led by the episode's credited writer, Elizabeth Sarnoff—for giving Shannon's death meaning, even if it's just to heighten *Lost*'s many ironies.★

In the flashback, for example, while in the Los Angeles hospital with her dying dad, she briefly passes by Jack. It turns out that her father's accident was the same one we saw in the Season Two opener in Jack's flashbacks. Faced with two critically wounded people, Jack chose to save Sarah, whom he'd later marry and divorce, rather than Adam Rutherford. That choice would lead to a miserable marriage for Jack and the loss of a family fortune for Shannon. Fate, as always, is not her friend. —NM

US VS. THEM

"THE OTHER 48 DAYS"

—

SEASON 2, EPISODE 7
ORIGINAL AIRDATE 11/16/05

Many of the best episodes of *Lost*† immerse viewers in a world different from the one they have become used to, only to send that world crashing up against the series' already-established cosmology. "The Other

---

★ Damon Lindelof, in the "On Location" DVD featurette: "We knew that Shannon was going to die before we started Season Two. Shannon's death served a number of story purposes, the most important being that we wanted the tail section people, and our core group of castaways to be sort of forced to merge under incredibly uncomfortable circumstances."

† And television in general!

48 Days" is by far the most radical exploration of that storytelling idea across the first two seasons, and it serves as a signpost for where the series is going. *Lost* has always been many small stories adding up to one larger one, with all the survivors' backstories intertwining with and commenting on each other, but "The Other 48 Days" suggests that the series could become many different *TV shows* adding up to one larger show. It's a bravura episode and easily one of the best of the show's second season.

It also inevitably prompts one question: Why don't the Tailies mesh with the show, as established so far, all that well?

Lost expanded its ensemble in ways small and large with every new season, sometimes adding new performers to the regular cast from the jump (as happened with Michelle Rodriguez at the start of Season Two) and sometimes waiting to see which recurring characters popped before adding them to the ensemble (as was already happening with Henry Ian Cusick's Desmond, not yet in the main cast). Constantly bringing in new characters served two main purposes for the show, one plot-related and the other thematic.

On a plot level, the series needs fresh meat to chew through with each new season. The show has a high body count, and if it's going to continue killing off characters, then it constantly needs to find new ones to add to the ensemble. Since the series is set on a not-so-deserted Island, the show must contort itself into some very strange pretzels to justify new characters, which adds even more fuel to the plot engines. If the survivors of the 815 tail section crashed in a different part of the Island, what might they find there? Could they bump into some of the mysterious inhabitants of the Island's interior? And so on.

On a thematic level, however, *Lost* is often a series about how people are mysteries to each other and occasionally to themselves. In the most obvious way, the *Lost* characters can say basically anything about their lives before the Island and be trusted. Goodwin can be one of the Others and still worm his way into a leadership position within Ana Lucia's little society, simply because he portrays himself as a helpful asset to the community.

On a less obvious level, the series constantly sets up us vs. them dynamics designed to destabilize the characters' status quo. Yet when it comes time for viewers to dig into the pasts of the characters in question, we inevitably learn they're more complicated than they seem, and the show encourages us to have empathy for even its most despicable figures. That doesn't mean we're asked to support the evil things they do; instead, we are asked to see everyone on the show as human, first and foremost. For instance, we see Sawyer's cons and how they can hurt people, but we also see the deep pain that underlies his motivations. He is a person who has done bad things, not an outright villain.

"The Other 48 Days" is perhaps the first big test of this conceit. From the moment that Sawyer, Michael, and Jin meet the Tailies, their relationship is driven by paranoia and conflict. The survivors of the tail section have *been through it*, and they treat every single interaction with anybody they meet as a potential battle. When they finally make contact with the survivors whom we've spent most of the show with, they accidentally kill Shannon in an incident the Island itself seems to egg on, via the mysterious whispers that occasionally fill the jungle's darkness. When we get to "The Other 48 Days," then, we are primed to see these characters as violent reactionaries, tackling every problem with brute force.

"The Other 48 Days" pulls back from the fatal first contact and returns to the events immediately following the plane crash, when the tail section survivors find themselves having a much rougher time. Almost immediately, the Others start taking members of their group, and Ana Lucia's already-edgy leadership style grows understandably more and more paranoid. Mr. Eko kills two Others and immediately takes a vow of silence, a girl Ana Lucia vowed to protect disappears, and a survivor named Nathan might *actually* be one of Them, whoever They are.

One of the virtues of *Lost*'s flashback structure is that it can subtly change its genre when it needs to, and "The Other 48 Days" suggests a kind of metatextual take on the TV cop show versus the medical show. Where Jack Shephard is a doctor who seems intent on creating a community where people care for each other, even if he frequently fails at the task, Ana Lucia is a cop who sees enemies around every corner and hiding behind every tree. Yet she's not *wrong*, either. The Others really do seem to have focused their efforts on the tail section survivors first and foremost, and the paranoia that resulted twisted the screws on Ana Lucia's already frazzled nerves. You'd probably lose it, too.

It's instructive to look at how similarly Ana Lucia and Jack are introduced. Both run around the crash site, pulling survivors to safety and providing emergency medical care to those they can help. Ana Lucia even gets a big hero moment when she coaches Bernard to reach over and grab a tree branch before the airplane seat that he's still strapped into tumbles from the tree that it landed in. She is presented as strong and capable and ready for anything, but she isn't ready for the Others. Then, who would be?

"The Other 48 Days" comes the closest the show has so far to something that is purely horror-driven. It sets up a scenario where literally nobody can be trusted, one that is reminiscent of *The Twilight Zone*, among other sci-fi and horror anthologies. "Who's the real enemy here?" was a major question of genre TV of the time, with the robotic Cylons on *Battlestar Galactica* playing a similar role in that series to the Others here. Both shows underlined the ways in which never knowing whom you could trust would eventually cause you to lose some essential part of your humanity.

These ideas coalesce in the scene where Ana Lucia confronts Goodwin. The show's efforts to keep viewers from guessing that Goodwin is the villain are halfhearted, but in many ways, casting the oily Brett Cullen in the part already raises the hackles just a little. He and Ana Lucia dance around the topic of his allegiance before he finally comes out and admits his Otherness. What's more, he says, the reason all those people kept disappearing is because they were "good people." Those left behind were *not* good people, and Ana Lucia would have realized that sooner or later.

As you go deeper into the show's run, the more this little speech makes sense. But in the immediate context of "The Other 48 Days," it plays as borderline religious fundamentalism. Goodwin and the Others have cracked the code on what it means to be "good," and now they will judge everyone else who comes across their path. He and Ana Lucia fight, and she gets the best of him, as viewers know she will. We saw his body atop the wooden spike in an earlier episode.★

★   One complaint about this episode: The "remember all this stuff?" speed-run through the season so far that concludes the episode is very, very clunky. It's a remnant of the show's status as a broadcast network TV series, which viewers had to watch week-to-week, and it's hard to imagine a modern version of *Lost,* especially one on a streaming service, making the same choice.

Yet if you ponder the episode for a few moments more, you might consider that the Others sometimes seem to function almost as mirrors of the 815 survivors. Ana Lucia, too, makes split-second judgments on the people she meets, and sometimes those judgments are drastically, dramatically wrong. When the stakes are not life-and-death, that's not a problem. But when they are, the wrong person (aka Shannon) might die.

The tail section survivors likely struggled to mesh with the show's tone because the series they were in was subtly, incompatibly a *different* one from the series we'd been watching. Had we started with Ana Lucia and company, we'd surely have found the introduction of Jack and his friends similarly jarring. But since we're just meeting the tail section survivors now, there's nothing the show can do to make them seem less like paranoid husks. We can understand *why* they are the way they are, but we perhaps can't cross the gap to truly sympathize with them. And if it's us vs. them, well, you're bound to pick "us" every time. —ESJ

"COLLISION"
—
SEASON 2, EPISODE 8
ORIGINAL AIRDATE 11/23/05

On the Island: In the aftermath of Ana Lucia shooting Shannon, the survivors meet the Tailies, and integration between both groups seems like it will be complicated, to say the least, especially after Ana Lucia takes Sayid hostage. Jack and Kate treat a badly wounded Sawyer.

In the flashbacks: When Ana Lucia discovers her fellow police officers have found a man who shot her during a burglary attempt, she pursues her own form of justice—and kills him in cold blood.

When Season Two of *Lost* aired, Ana Lucia Cortez received much of the season's criticism from fans. She was too brusque, too angry. She shot first and asked questions later. The original castaways we'd gotten to know in Season One weren't exactly cuddly, but the show built a warmth around them and their camp that viewers had come to love. The Tailies' harder go of it left fans jumpier and more paranoid; to viewers, that energy didn't mesh.

When we watch the show now, however, Ana Lucia stands out as a character the show instantly had a bead on from the word go. In her first showcase episode, the series even seems to anticipate many of our 2020s conversations about "copaganda"—shows that exist mostly to suggest the police are stalwart good guys, standing up against a dark, crime-ridden world, and solve the vast majority of crimes they come across. *Lost*, unusually for its time, subverts this style of storytelling.

Michelle Rodriguez's performance evokes a jumpy anxiety that filters out of the screen and into the audience, with how ready she seems to bolt into the jungle at any given moment, but it's hard to suggest she *shouldn't* behave that way, given all she's seen. Even when she was an LAPD member, Ana Lucia wasn't a good cop. When given the opportunity to put a man who shot her behind bars, she instead pursued her own justice, which is to say she pursued vengeance.

That type of character is an unpredictable element to introduce into the show's ensemble, and "Collision" turns her arrival at the beach camp into a wrecking ball that scatters the pieces the season has built thus far. *Lost* Season Two is twenty-four episodes, meaning this marks the end of its first third, and the concluding montage of reunions between those who've been torn apart from each other—particularly Sun and Jin, and Rose and Bernard—would be an effective way to close this chapter.

But the show doesn't end there. It ends on Ana Lucia and Jack warily regarding each other. They've both seen things they've had to fight back against, and they've both made some hard decisions in that time. Where Jack seems tortured by his need to be important, however, Ana Lucia just assumes she is, an attitude that can be dangerous when applied with the wrong amount of force.

"Collision" gives us a glimpse into what drives her, and we might not like what we see. That doesn't make Ana Lucia a bad character; instead, it makes her all the more vital to the story the show is telling. —*ESJ*

"WHAT KATE DID"

—

SEASON 2, EPISODE 9
ORIGINAL AIRDATE 11/30/05

On the Island: After Kate comes across a mysterious horse in the jungle, she comes to worry that the spirit of her deceased father has possessed the convalescing Sawyer. Meanwhile, Eko and Michael learn of the Hatch. Eko has footage to splice into the orientation film, but it's Michael who discovers the computer can seemingly make contact with others on the Island—others who might include Walt.

In the flashbacks: Kate kills her abusive father, then attempts to go confront the man she believed was her biological father, with Marshal Edward Mars in pursuit.

Most characters on *Lost* have father issues, and a few have mother issues. Only Kate Austen really has *both*. The man she believed to be her biological father abandoned her to an abusive stepfather—only for her to learn her stepfather was her biological father all along. Then, after she killed her abuser (by blowing up his house!), her mom ratted her out to the feds. Can you blame her for constantly being on the run?

Kate's fear of staying anywhere or with anyone for too long drives the best episodes about her—of which this is one—but also sits at the center of why the show's writers seemed particularly bedeviled by trying to write strong material for her. Because Kate's past involves being on the run and because Kate's present tends to involve whether she will end up with Jack or Sawyer, the show too often conflates her fear of being trapped with a fear of commitment.

Kate's disinterest in choosing one of her suitors might have some qualities in common with her need to escape an abusive household. Still, it feels a touch dismissive of the very real pain she's suffered to conflate the two so easily.

What's more, the on-Island plot of this episode doesn't really center Kate as much as it could. She's *there* in most of the major plotlines, but even the deeply moving funeral for Shannon doesn't actually feature her. (She's taking a shift at the Hatch. Later, she apologizes to Sayid for missing the funeral.) She does get some poignant scenes talking about her past, as well as a touching monologue. In an episode where she was more integrated into the action, you might get a sense of her finally putting some painful aspects of the past behind her.

Both the flashbacks and Evangeline Lilly hold up their ends of the bargain. The dark secrets Kate has been carrying around have a tragic weight to them, and Lilly is fantastic in the most emotional scenes she's had on the show yet. Still, when the on-Island action keeps circling back to an idea of a Kate who just can't settle down, it feels a little churlish on the part of the show. The woman *exploded her father* because he abused her. If anyone deserves a little time on a magic Island with a mysterious salvation horse to be her boon companion, it's Kate. —*ESJ*

"THE 23RD PSALM"

–

SEASON 2, EPISODE 10
ORIGINAL AIRDATE 1/11/06

On the Island: When Eko learns that Charlie totes around a statuette of the Virgin Mary, he destroys said statue—revealing the heroin within it. He and Charlie go on a quest to find the smugglers' plane, encountering the Monster on the way. In the Hatch, Michael continues his conversations with the person he believes to be Walt.

In the flashbacks: Eko's past as a Nigerian drug runner comes to light, particularly via his relationship with his brother Yemi, who is a priest.

One of Season Two's strengths is how casually it reveals major information. So it is with this episode, in which we first get to see the true form of the Monster—a long, sinuous tendril of black smoke that flashes and makes terrible noises. When you come face-to-face with it, as Mr. Eko does, visions of everything you've ever done flicker and dance among its clouds, as if you are being judged. The show reveals not only the Monster's form, but also a retroactive argument for the flashbacks' relevance to the on-Island plot. (And since this episode was the first to air after a six-week break, the Monster—henceforth the Smoke Monster—gave the series a big reveal to get fans buzzing about the show again.)

"The 23rd Psalm" is one of Season Two's best episodes and a fantastic first showcase for Mr. Eko. *Lost* has always been very smart at pairing up characters to allow for strong storytelling possibilities, and this episode's decision to send Charlie and Eko off into the jungle together is inspired. Charlie needs someone to lead him; Eko is ready to learn what it means to be a leader.

Lost is streaked with religiosity, but Eko—who seems to be a priest when we first meet him—is core to what is probably the show's most religious season. That this episode pulls off an ending like Eko and Charlie quietly reciting the titular psalm together as the plane that bore Eko's brother (and a cache of drugs) burns before them reinforces just how willing *Lost* is to get deeply, painfully sincere in its explorations of faith.

What's more, Eko's relationship with God also helps sell the incredible coincidence that his brother—an actual priest, unlike Eko, who simply poses as one to help smuggle drugs—was in the plane that crashed on the Island and proved so central to Season One's endgame. Yes, a magical Island surely drew these characters to some sort of reckoning, but the added dose of deep and abiding faith in God helps sell the idea. From birth, these brothers have been in one crucible or another. What's the Island in the face of that?

As American television episodes written by white writers about the political situation in Africa go, "The 23rd Psalm" could have been a lot worse. It leans on easy stereotypes, to the degree that you might roll your eyes when you learn Eko was a drug runner. But in its portrayal of the love between Eko and Yemi—a love that is tested but never broken—it finds something heartfelt and true.

Plus, there's that Smoke Monster. Think about the first time you heard the monster out in the jungle. Now, the show has revealed its form. Would you ever have guessed it would look like *that*? Even when it seems to be settling into a routine, *Lost* can still surprise you. —ESJ

"THE HUNTING PARTY"

—

SEASON 2, EPISODE 11
ORIGINAL AIRDATE 1/18/06

On the Island: Michael plunges off into the jungle to find Walt, and Jack assembles a group to go after him, cutting Kate out of the process. The Others meet Jack's group in the jungle, then show their strength, prompting him to contemplate a more aggressive response.

In the flashbacks: A woman and Jack become too close as he prepares to operate on her father's spinal tumor. After her father dies, the woman and Jack kiss. He pulls away, but the indiscretion ends his marriage to Sarah.

We are entering some rough territory.

The second half of *Lost* Season Two is very much an up-and-down proposition. It ends extremely well, and there are a lot of good episodes along the way. But the trilogy of episodes from "The Hunting Party" to "The Long Con" might be the most directionless the show ever felt. It's here that a viewer can really start to feel how difficult it is to build an entire season around conflicts that *might* come to fruition. There are only so many times the characters can wonder what happens if you don't push a button or only so many times Michael can think about going after Walt before the audience wants something new already. *Lost* will very soon find that something new, but for now, the storytelling feels stuck in a rut.

Some of this stems from the flashbacks. Season Two hasn't used the flashbacks to provide the audience with radically new information, but it has often used them to show us the same characters from slightly new angles. It's becoming very difficult to do that with Jack, whose savior complex has defined him both on and off the Island. As such, his flashbacks take a turn toward overt melodrama, which sometimes works, but rarely with Jack, one of its more straightforward, bullheaded characters.

Michael's plot in this episode similarly underlines how the series has painted itself into a corner in many ways. If the Others are holding Walt and nobody knows where they are, then the story ultimately becomes very binary: Does someone (probably Michael) try to find out more information, or do the castaways just write off Walt as an inevitable loss? The series has essentially avoided the implications of this dilemma, leading to a rudderless Michael. The show understands he misses his boy, but it doesn't want to really explore the pain around that loss. So he races off into the jungle, as though he were some other show's problem for a while.

The ending of this episode, at least, promises a direction forward: With Ana Lucia's help, Jack is going to build an army to take on the Others. Even here, however, you might find yourself wondering who will be in that army. Yes, the castaways have guns, but are they ready to potentially die for what still feel like very nebulous goals? *Lost* seems unsure of the answers to those questions.

Still, the sight of the Others lighting up their torches in the darkness of the jungle as a show of strength is a deeply unsettling image. The show can still bring its best when it needs to, which is an encouraging sign as we drift through these doldrums. —*ESJ*

"FIRE + WATER"

—

SEASON 2, EPISODE 12
ORIGINAL AIRDATE 1/25/06

On the Island: Charlie becomes convinced that Aaron is in danger and attempts to protect the child, both physically and spiritually, via baptism. His actions create division between him and Claire. Locke confiscates Charlie's stash of heroin-filled Virgin Mary statuettes—despite Charlie insisting he was going to destroy them. At episode's end, Mr. Eko baptizes Claire and Aaron at her behest.

In the flashbacks: Charlie's brother, Liam, endangers his relationship to both his family and the mother of his child thanks to his drug habit. Charlie attempts to help him but struggles to do so.

Charlie is the major character *Lost* has most struggled to find something to do with him in Season Two. The Season One finale introduced the idea that his addiction would come back in a major way, and Season Two has flirted with making this a more central plot. But an addiction storyline can really only travel in one direction on a TV show. The character with that addiction will get clean, then relapse, then get clean again, over and over. It's a sine wave storyline.

In the case of *Lost*, where a magic Island frequently tempts the characters with exactly what they want, it also lacks the tension of asking where Charlie might get his next score. You know that once he works through the drugs he found in the crashed airplane, the Island will contrive some other reason to give him more. On the one hand, this reflects the Island's love of tempting the castaways to indulge in their worst selves; on the other, it's awfully convenient that this aircraft is full of Charlie's drug of choice, no?

As such, "Fire + Water" becomes a slog, the characters working through the beats of an addiction storyline in a medium (network television) that can never make the nature of Charlie's addiction as explicit as it perhaps needs to be. Charlie's dreams are occasionally potent on a visual level—especially a piano floating out to sea with a baby squalling inside of it—but the ways in which he endangers Aaron become so over-the-top that you wonder how Claire could ever speak to him again, on a show where you know she will eventually take him back with open arms.

However, the episode's climax offers some positive qualities. Charlie makes one final bid to baptize Aaron, having become convinced that's the only way to protect the child, only for Locke to interrupt him, take the baby, then punch Charlie repeatedly in the face. It's a brutal, hard-nosed climax to a story that never goes quite as far as it needs to.

Metaphorically, the episode ends with Claire forgiving Charlie already. Eko baptizes Claire and Aaron, which was Charlie's whole desire in the first place (albeit a desire he developed at Eko's suggestion). The sequence is visually stunning, and it continues Season Two's flirtation with Christian iconography (and its intriguing suggestion that Charlie is more religious than he lets on). Yet it remains a tiny island in an episode that is very much underwater. —*ESJ*

"THE LONG CON"

—

SEASON 2, EPISODE 13
ORIGINAL AIRDATE 2/8/06

On the Island: Sawyer undertakes an elaborate long con to gain sole access to the stash of guns the characters found in the Hatch. To do so, he gets Charlie to fake a kidnapping of Sun and makes his fellow survivors suspicious of each other. Meanwhile, Sayid and Hurley fix an old radio to see what signals they can receive.

In the flashbacks: Sawyer cons a divorcée named Cassidy, in the process entering what feels like an authentic relationship with her, even though he ultimately betrays her.

Why does Sawyer do anything he does in "The Long Con," and why do the other castaways simply put up with it?

Don't get me wrong: The *plot* reasons for everything that happens in "The Long Con" are quite clear. The show needs to effectively take the guns off the table for a little while, especially as the plan to form an army to take on the Others ramps up. The best way to do that is to put the guns in the hands of a character we already know but don't always trust. Sawyer is the obvious call.

On a *character* level, however, it's not clear why he does any of this at this point in the show. If he were motivated by his building attraction for Kate or a simmering jealousy of the way others simply treat Jack as the leader or just about anything other than naked ambition, the show might make sense of his actions. Indeed, Charlie's part in the whole scheme, driven as it is by his addiction and his desire to humiliate Locke, more or less makes character sense. Sawyer's role doesn't, not really.

Lost is fascinated by con artists and the ways they pull one over on their marks, and it often loves turning the audience into the mark. Sawyer might seem the perfect character to tell such a story with, as he actually is a con. Yet this deep into the show's run, we've gotten to know him so well that his concluding line—"I've never done a good thing in my life"—doesn't have the resonance it should, where the audience, who is aware of several good things Sawyer has done, knows Sawyer better than his crippling guilt does.

Even worse, the other characters' protest at Sawyer's successful con is simply too weak. It's as though they know that his plan has to work if the plot is going to keep on the tracks it's already on. It would be tempting to write most of them off as rubes at this point.

Fortunately, the small story of Sayid fixing the radio at Hurley's request features some of that vintage mysterious beauty *Lost* is so good at. When the two sit on a starlit beach and listen to Glenn Miller's "Moonlight Serenade," which might be a signal beaming to them from the past, it makes for a wonderfully lovely *Lost* moment. —*ESJ*

"ONE OF THEM"
–
SEASON 2, EPISODE 14
ORIGINAL AIRDATE 2/15/06

On the Island: Rousseau captures a mysterious man in one of her traps, turning him over to Sayid, who brings him back to the Hatch and interrogates him. His name is Henry Gale, and he says his balloon crashed on the Island, but it's unclear if he's telling the truth. Meanwhile, Hurley and Sawyer search for a frog.

In the flashbacks: American soldiers press Sayid into their service to torture an Iraqi CO into revealing the location of a downed pilot. Afterward, Sayid vows not to torture again.

It is truly remarkable *Lost* has gotten this far without an antagonist.

Yes, it has found ways to turn the castaways against each other, and yes, the Island itself functions as an antagonist, and yes, there's a Smoke Monster right there. But when it comes to the sort of human-to-human conflict that drives a TV show like this, *Lost* simply doesn't have anywhere to turn. Jack and Locke can only yell at each other about believing in the Island so many times.

Enter "Henry Gale," who is not yet an antagonist but who has the *shape* of one. At present, we have no reason to distrust him, other than Rousseau's insistence that he is one of the Others. We might believe Rousseau—who, after all, has had more intimate contact with the Others than our castaways have—or we might not. But the simple fact that we don't immediately understand Henry's motivations provides a shot in the arm to a show desperately in need of one. He's a question mark masquerading as a character, to some degree, but in the hands of actor Michael Emerson (at this point most famous to TV fans for an Emmy-winning guest arc on the legal drama *The Practice*), that question mark is more than enough to propel the drama.

He's also a perfect foil for Sayid, whose experiences with the US military leave him understanding a bit of what it is to feel caught in the middle of a war you don't entirely understand. Not only does this complicate the series' politics around the Iraq War a bit more, it also leaves plenty of room for ambiguity around Henry's identity. What if he really is just some poor guy whose hot-air balloon crashed and whose wife died? If that's true, then finding himself suddenly a pawn in a much larger battle must be deeply horrifying.

Lost provides little in the way of clarity at this point, but it might be offering a nod toward what it's doing over in the B-plot, where avuncular Hurley and increasingly antiheroic Sawyer track down an annoying chirping frog. Hurley successfully gets Sawyer to stop making fat jokes about him—at least for the length of the search—and when the two find the frog, Hurley offers to release it at a beach just distant enough from the castaways' beach to not bother them anymore. Instead, Sawyer crushes it in his hand.

It evokes the old parable of the scorpion and the frog, and it suggests that if Henry isn't who he says he is but is, instead, one of the deceptive Others, the castaways just might not have the upper hand after all. —*ESJ*

"MATERNITY LEAVE"

—

SEASON 2, EPISODE 15
ORIGINAL AIRDATE 3/1/06

On the Island/In the flashbacks: An on-Island flashback details Claire's time in the captivity of the Others in Season One. A health crisis with Aaron prompts her to turn to Libby to unlock Claire's memories of that time, and she is successfully able to recall a time among the Others that suggests they have surprisingly sophisticated medical facilities, a time that ended only because a teenage girl freed her. Meanwhile, Henry Gale, in conversations with Jack and Locke, seems to be subtly turning them against each other.

In the 2000s, a whole host of genre dramas suddenly discovered the storytelling possibilities of memories suppressed due to trauma, then told stories that utilized this very real phenomenon. (Most notably, *Battlestar Galactica* used the "I've repressed these traumatic memories!" gambit to motivate the robotic Cylons.) After all, the idea that you might suddenly start remembering things you didn't know you had experienced, in brief, horrifying flashes, has big horror undertones. There's a reason so many genre stories function as metaphors for trauma.

As genre stories from the 2000s about traumatic memories resurfacing go, "Maternity Leave" is one of the better ones. Its portrayal of how Libby helps Claire get her memories back is a little simplistic, but in a season that has been so heavy on stories about the guys, having a story centered on the quintet of Claire, Libby, Kate, Rousseau, and Sun feels like a moment of respite. Plus, "What happened to Claire" is an on-Island question that should have a relatively straightforward answer, even if it spins off a million other questions.

Indeed it does. The on-Island flashbacks are appropriately eerie, and when Kate, Claire, and Rousseau find their way to the facility where Claire was held captive, it has a perfect haunted-house quality to it. Claire's memory is patchy, and she remembers this facility being more like an actual medical clinic than the abandoned place it seems to be.

Yet Kate finds what seems like a costume in one of the lockers. Perhaps these Others are putting the castaways on, misleading them for purposes that aren't yet clear.

Claire's flashbacks also capture the loopy paranoia of a third trimester, when even those who aim to help seem like they might hurt you. The last few months of a pregnancy can be isolating, unnerving times for some people, who might feel as though their bodies have suddenly become something other than their own. The Others' smiling faux-friendliness in these scenes becomes all the more deeply disturbing in that light.

The Henry Gale storyline once again offers an intriguing counterpoint to the episode's other storyline. If the Others are much more sophisticated than they let on, then everything he's saying might be part of an elaborate con. Why he might need to infiltrate our group of survivors isn't immediately clear, but he, too, has a folksy friendliness that he uses to make Locke question just why Jack is in charge. At this point, it's clear someone on *Lost* is playing the long game, but it's also becoming clear that someone isn't one of the characters we've come to know so well. —*ESJ*

"THE WHOLE TRUTH"
—

SEASON 2, EPISODE 16
ORIGINAL AIRDATE 3/22/06

On the Island: Sun and Jin's relationship becomes more fractious, just as Sun learns that she is pregnant. Jin is overjoyed, but Sun is forced to tell him something: The reason they hadn't been able to conceive off-Island is due to him, not her. Meanwhile, Ana Lucia interrogates Henry Gale and gets a map to his downed balloon.

In the flashbacks: Sun and Jin's struggles to have a baby are detailed, even as her affair with Jae Lee is further explored. Sun learns their fertility problems rest with Jin, not her, but the doctor told them it was her fault to avoid Jin's wrath.

Anytime *Lost* needs to downshift to a lower gear to build up momentum for a big push forward, it can reliably turn to Sun and Jin. The second third of Season Two—"What Kate Did" through this episode—has been a bumpy ride for the characters and the show, but this episode serves as a perfect respite from the paranoia that increasingly defines the series and its characters. We'll come to appreciate this little pause as the action grows more heated in the episodes ahead.

"A married couple gets pregnant" is too often a story that TV shows turn to out of desperation. To be sure, lots of married couples *do* have children, but raising a baby is rarely a great way to generate stories for most TV shows. Not so with *Lost*. In *Lost*, having a baby on a magical Island—one that sure seems like it's not very hospitable to pregnant people even *beyond* the lack of state-of-the-art medical facilities—raises the stakes substantially. When baby Aaron gets sick one episode prior to this, it is quite potentially a matter of life and death.

Balancing these fears against Sun and Jin's struggles to conceive off the Island is a smart way to tell a pregnancy story, and because the passage of time on *Lost* is so deliberate, it might take several seasons before Sun gives birth. Plus, the fact that Jin was the cause of the couple's fertility struggles—and the implication that Sun might have conceived with Jae Lee instead—adds a delicious twist of melodrama to an already-potent stew.

That said: It is very silly that the emotional climax of this story, in which Sun insists to his face that she did not cheat on Jin, is Jin saying "I love you" in English. That's an emotional climax for the presumed English-speaking audience, not the characters.

The Henry Gale story is less well-integrated into everything this time, but it does allow for a stronger Ana Lucia episode than the last few. Given what we know about her anger issues, it's fascinating to see her in a room with a man who seems very good at sticking his finger in the castaways' wounds. That she eventually backs down from seriously injuring him and asks for further evidence suggests she, too, is growing and changing on the Island.

Of course, as Henry says, while munching on cereal, he might have been leading her and the others into a trap. "You guys got any milk?" he asks to end the episode, turning a simple request into an instantly iconic *Lost* moment. —*ESJ*

"LOCKDOWN"
—
SEASON 2, EPISODE 17
ORIGINAL AIRDATE 3/29/06

On the Island: Mysteriously, the Hatch goes into lockdown, leaving Locke with his legs pinned beneath one of the heavy blast doors, necessitating a temporary alliance with Henry Gale to push the button. When it seems Henry has failed, Locke sees an enormous map of the Island, painted on the blast door, rendered in paint visible only under black light. At episode's end, Ana Lucia's group returns with big news: A Henry Gale crashed on the Island all right, but this Henry is not him.

In the flashbacks: Locke's relationship with Helen progresses to a new level, and he prepares to propose. Once again, however, his horrible father returns to screw everything up.

"Lockdown" firmly pushes *Lost* Season Two into its third act. There will be some episodes in this final stretch that don't contribute to relentless plot momentum, but for the most part, everything that happens from here on out points toward the season finale and some major shifts in the status quo.

Thus, "Lockdown" features two big revelations. The first is one the audience has surely suspected for weeks now but which the show has done a surprisingly effective job of keeping us from definitively concluding: Henry Gale is not who he says he is. Yes, there is an enormous balloon on the Island, and yes, there is a grave beneath it. But the grave does not hold Henry's wife. It holds Henry himself, a Black man from Minnesota and very much *not* the Henry we already know. (Who buried him? Who knows!)

Sometimes, *Lost* gets too far behind its audience, which is very good at figuring its puzzles out. Here, the audience likely knows that Henry is one of the Others, but the show *knows* the audience knows. The characters themselves also suspect, but they don't entirely know what to do.

If they have one of the Others in their custody, what does that even *mean*, precisely?

Locke, for one, has come to mostly trust Henry. After all, the man clambered through some vents to push the button on the computer that might end the world. *Lost* has pushed the button to the back burner in recent episodes, perhaps having tired of it as a plot device as much as the audience. But "Lockdown" pulls it right back into the foreground again, smartly escalating what happens by showing a time when the button *isn't* pushed within 108 minutes—even if it is eventually pushed before things get too bad.

That's where the second revelation comes into play: His legs pinned beneath the door, helplessly waiting to see if Henry betrayed him, Locke looks upon an enormous map of the Island, painted there by an unknown person. It's the sort of thing that feels more like a gift to the audience than the characters—there's even a detailed shot of it for the freeze-framers out there—but at this point in the season, the die-hard fans will almost certainly take it.

Even the flashbacks have more purpose. Yes, we're watching Locke fall for his father's cons yet again, and we're watching his inability to say no to his dad tank yet another good thing in his life by destroying his relationship with Helen. But given the way the episode gets him to trust Henry, only to brutally pull the rug out from under him, the flashbacks remind us of one big point: On the Island, Locke might seem like he has it together, but he's always been just another mark. —*ESJ*

TWISTS AND REVEALS

"DAVE"

—

SEASON 2, EPISODE 18
ORIGINAL AIRDATE 4/5/06

"Dave" is often held up as one of *Lost*'s weaker outings, an episode that relies heavily on a twist that is too easy to guess and a series of extremely dated portrayals of both disordered eating and mental health.

I, however, kinda like it, so let me make a halfhearted case for it.

I will start with the complaints I mostly agree with. The show's portrayal of someone who is overweight and struggles with binge eating has an incredibly cringe-y quality to it, one that feels straight out of a "You can overcome your weight with the power of your mind!" diet book.

In one section of the episode, Hurley destroys the food he's been hoarding, in a slow-motion montage of potato chips and peanut butter flying everywhere, only for a Dharma drone to drop another pallet of junk. The moment plays not as a darkly funny turn but almost as a Looney Tunes gag, where Hurley is Wile E. Coyote and "food" the Road Runner. The undercurrent of all of this—especially the scenes where Hurley talks about his disordered eating with Libby—places the weight of what Hurley's going through subtly on his shoulders. He just hasn't tried hard enough to stop binge eating!

The episode's portrayal of a mental health institution is also deeply dated, though in this case, the show seems to know it is. To its credit, the show doesn't cast a bunch of guest stars to come in and play over-the-top mental illness caricatures. Yet it also doesn't have the space to do anything nuanced, leaving its portrayal of the hospital as a series of scenes where Hurley hallucinates a guy (the titular Dave) while extras wander around in the background, acting stereotypically "crazy," but, y'know, not *too* "crazy."

The criticisms I can't get on board with, however, involve the very heart of the episode—the relationship between Hurley and Dave, his hallucinated best friend, played by a very good Evan Handler.

The episode exists within a solid genre TV tradition: What if this weird story is all just somebody's hallucination?* Naturally, more than a few fans of the show had guessed that the Island might be something one of the characters was dreaming up in some capacity. "Dave" fits solidly into that trope and seems designed to poke holes in it.

Yes, if you watch "Dave" solely as a story that asks "Is all of this a hallucination?," then it's pretty bad. The twist that Dave isn't real lands with a thud, because you've surely already guessed that he's a manifestation of Hurley's mental health issues. What's more, "Is this a hallucination?" is a fan theory that doesn't really require a response because "It was all a dream!" would be a pretty lousy place to take a story like this. The show has Sawyer smartly puncture that idea. If all of this *were* a dream, he says, then would Hurley have hallucinated dozens of other people, all with their own lives, concerns, and storylines? Probably not!

All of that said, I prefer to read what happens with Dave not as a twist but as a reveal. Where a twist takes everything you thought you knew and turns it on its ear, a reveal confirms a suspicion you might have had in a way that deepens the emotional stakes for the characters involved. Twists are generally bad if they're guessed ahead of time; reveals sometimes gain power from the audience getting ahead of them.

The distinction between a twist and a reveal sometimes depends on the individual, so take my musings with a grain of salt. Yet, the reveal of Dave's nonexistence occurs roughly halfway through the episode, and by the time it arrives, the audience has surely concluded that he is a literal imaginary friend. By letting us get ahead of Hurley to this degree, "Dave" allows us to build empathy for how little of his pain he lets show through his happy-go-lucky demeanor. It might be a cheap trick to get at the depths the character possesses—depths the show will plumb in other, better episodes—but it also underscores just how lonely and empty Hurley can feel, even on the Island.

---

* Not just genre TV, however! The final episode of the 1980s hospital series *St. Elsewhere*, for instance, memorably suggests the entire series was hallucinated by a minor character.

Think of Dave not as a bad storytelling device but instead as a manifestation of the tragic events Hurley can't let go of, and the episode snaps into place. Suddenly, it's not a story about whether the Island is a hallucination but, instead, a story about the kind of person who would dissociate into the idea that nothing he is going through is real, which describes a great many people both on the Island and in the audience. The very quality that allows Hurley to stay a wisecracking fan favorite who says "Dude" a lot is also at the source of his pain.

The scene where he reveals in therapy that he can't let go of his guilt over a balcony collapse for which he holds himself personally responsible, even as the doctor assures him that he is not at fault, provides a core nugget for Hurley that informs so much of what happens with him going forward.★

And you know what? The scenes with Libby and Hurley, while sometimes clumsy, are performed with surprising gravity, as we come to understand the romantic connection that is building between the two has everything to do with how similarly they've processed their tragedies. The episode doesn't boast the show's strongest script, but it has a lot more going on than it generally receives credit for.

If nothing else, the episode works as a marvelous two-hander for Jorge Garcia and Handler, who have a fun chemistry you could imagine working week after week. "Here's this really important guy you don't know about" is always tricky for a guest star to handle, but Handler's nervy energy provides a perfect counterpoint to Garcia's more laconic jokester persona. Every time I watch "Dave," I'm struck all over again by how much fun these two actors seem to be having with each other, and I almost wish Dave had stuck around as yet another manifestation the Island brought back a few times.

Will I go to bat for this as one of the very best episodes of *Lost*? No. There are too many stronger hours across the show's run. Will I go to bat for it as a surprisingly rich text about the weight of trauma, the legacy of guilt, and the ways we all dissociate away our pain just a little bit?

★   Mild spoiler: If you think about where his character arc ultimately lands, this scene is even more satisfying.

Absolutely. The haters have it all wrong. "Dave" isn't one of the show's triumphs, but it *is* triumphantly mid.★ —*ESJ*

THE OTHERS

"S.O.S."

—

SEASON 2, EPISODE 19
ORIGINAL AIRDATE 4/12/06

Early in the first season of *Lost*, the series established that forty-eight people survived the crash of Oceanic 815. Some of those characters became cannon fodder, deaths meant to underscore the harsh realities of Island life—getting sucked into a plane engine here, getting eaten by a Smoke Monster there. Most hung out in the background of scenes, extras filling in the moments around the characters audiences knew and loved.

In Season Two, the series brought in even more survivors, revealing the twenty-two survivors from the tail section of the plane and charting their harrowing journey after infiltration by the Others. Yes, many of these characters died as well, leaving the series as largely un-mourned extras, but even after those deaths, the show had access to several dozen crash survivors it could have turned into characters. Instead, it mostly stuck to the fourteen series regulars established in Season One[†] and the three new regulars added from the tail section.[‡]

★   Some part of me wonders if this episode might have had its cake and eaten it too by having Hurley remember that Libby had also been in the mental hospital, then starting to wonder if he was having a *Wizard of Oz* experience where, say, he started remembering the other characters as also being present in the hospital. Equally cheap? Probably. I do wonder if this would have given extra shading to Libby, however, which is something the episode—and the series at this point—needs.

†   Jack, Kate, Locke, Sawyer, Charlie, Sayid, Hurley, Michael, Walt, Sun, Jin, Boone, Shannon, and Claire.

‡   Ana Lucia, Mr. Eko, and Libby.

"So, who are all these other people wandering around?" is a natural question to ask of the show, but it's also one the show can't really answer effectively. It occasionally feints toward adding a guest star or two who can be one of the non-regular crash survivors and can then move toward more prominent status. Yet, it usually ends up treating these characters as cannon fodder as well.*

In truth, the further *Lost* gets from the pilot, it feels cheap to continue introducing side characters we haven't heard much about despite being in the background all this time. We'll see just how hard it is for the show to pull this off very soon,† but in "S.O.S." we get a closer look at the two characters it *has* managed to elevate to "crash survivor who's important but not central to the story" status: Rose and Bernard.

Rose is an interesting amalgamation of character arcs that were meant for other characters and that are suggested naturally by the show's themes. The more the series divides itself along "science vs. faith" or "rational vs. irrational" lines, the more those two poles apply specifically to the Island itself. Yet we know that plenty of people in our reality have faith in things that aren't a mystical Island. The show is lousy with characters who work in more-rational spaces, but when it comes to characters who have a deep faith in something *other* than the Island, the first season essentially had only Rose, a devout Christian, to turn to.‡

When the show needs Jack to have a crisis of faith in Season One, it can't very well have him turn to Locke, whose fervent belief in the Island is set up in direct opposition to Jack clinging to rationality by his fingertips. Thus, the doctor has a sit-down with Rose, who might not have faith in the Island but does have faith that God has preserved her husband's life, that he is somewhere else on the Island.§

---

* RIP, Arzt, we hardly knew ye.
† As soon as Season Three!
‡ In Season Two, of course, it added Mr. Eko, though there are wrinkles to his devotion. Sayid is Muslim, and the series occasionally presents Charlie as a lapsed Catholic, but it is only fitfully interested in either man's spiritual life.
§ The "my husband survived the crash and must be somewhere else on the Island" is a character arc meant originally for Kate, but once Jack steps firmly into the role of "leader of the survivors," Kate has most of what was distinctive about her sanded off. More on this in a later essay.

He is! In Season Two, we meet Bernard as one of the tail section survivors.* In keeping with the show's ethos, he is presented as levelheaded and eminently rational, and in this episode, we learn that, yep, he's the man of science to Rose's woman of faith, even if he's willing to indulge in tracking down a faith healer in Australia for the woman he loves.†

Rose and Bernard are not characters we see every week, and in some ways, we don't need to. They form a relatively simple dialectic, and their marriage is uncomplicated and happy in a way viewers likely don't want to see threatened. Whereas Sun and Jin are effectively separated before the crash, and the Island brings them back together, the only thing separating Rose and Bernard is physical distance, and once that's collapsed, there's not much story left for them.

However, you can tell a lovely short story about them, and "S.O.S." suggests an evolutionary path *Lost* could have (and arguably should have) followed, one where every few episodes, it becomes a pseudo-anthology series with a short, meaningful side story about a character whose bearing on the central narrative is less pronounced but still present. It also reminds us of a central issue the show needs to revisit every so often: Just what are these people doing to get off the Island?

Not much, as it turns out, and Bernard is determined to change that. He begins by building a massive SOS symbol out of rocks on a beach. After all, if Dharma airdrops keep coming, that suggests planes fly over the Island. If they see a message of distress written on a beach somewhere . . . mightn't they send out rescuers? It's a fair notion, but it's also one that we the audience know isn't likely to work, even as Bernard, as a character, cannot.

As the show goes on, the harder it has to work to ever justify why the characters would want to leave. Leaving cuts against the very existence of the show. The writers will figure out better ways to exploit this tension going forward, but the ways in which the show struggles to maintain some of what made it so compelling in Season One fuels both the tension and creative missteps of Season Two. If the Island is full of creepy Others, shouldn't one want to leave?

---

* Technically, we "meet" him on the other end of the radio transmission Boone sends late in Season One, but he's not identified as a crash survivor, given a name, or played by Sam Anderson.

† Remember: Rose had cancer, and the Island appears to have cured it.

Well, on *Lost*, the solution to nearly any story question is "Have we got a love story for you!" "S.O.S." details the love between Rose and Bernard, from the moment they first meet in the middle of a snowstorm to when they decide to stay on the Island because they know Rose's life-threatening cancer is gone here where it might recur back in "the real world." The scene where Bernard proposes to Rose even though she's let him know she's dying is deeply moving, and it's bookended by a scene where the two realize they have more time than they ever expected thanks to the crash.

Presumably, there are dozens of smaller stories like this scattered across the Island, but the audience can only hear so many variations on "the Island is a terrible curse, but it gave me a beautiful gift" before all those stories start to blend together.★ "S.O.S." is one of the warmest and most beautiful episodes of *Lost*, and its mere existence speaks to the creative risks *Lost* was taking even as it settled into being an Emmy-winning hit show.

Do I want more from Rose and Bernard now? Yes. But also, do I want to see their newfound bliss threatened by, like, a Monster? Absolutely not. That sea of extras might be filled with great stories; it also might be filled with people just trying to live their lives who have little room for Jack and company's nonsense. —*ESJ*

"TWO FOR THE ROAD"

—

SEASON 2, EPISODE 20
ORIGINAL AIRDATE 5/3/06

On the Island: Henry attacks Ana Lucia, leaving everyone reeling. Michael, freshly back from the Others' camp, says that they live worse off than those at the beach camp. Ana Lucia seduces Sawyer to gain access to his gun, then goes to the Hatch to shoot Henry. She can't do it, so Michael offers to

---

★   The main characters' arcs also follow this "beautiful gift" idea but on a more dramatic scale. Kate is no longer going to jail, Locke can walk, and Hurley just might have broken his curse. They're the main characters, so the stakes are raised.

do so—but instead, he shoots Ana Lucia, then Libby, who has come to the Hatch to get blankets for a picnic with Hurley, killing both women. He opens the door to Henry's cell, then shoots himself in the arm.

Off the Island: Ana Lucia's mother questions her about her shooting of an unarmed man (in "Collision"). Ana Lucia then quits the police force and travels to Sydney to work as private security for one Christian Shephard.

Plot twists don't always need to be justified if they're well-executed enough. The writers may later feel obligated to fill in the gaps around that twist, but as it's happening, the twist itself can be enough to keep an audience on the edge of their seat. "Two for the Road" features such a twist.

Sometimes, we see the seams in *Lost*'s plotting; here, they're successfully hidden beneath an examination of Ana Lucia trying to make restitution for her past sins and Michael's return to the camp. Both feel sufficiently weighty in a plot sense, and Ana Lucia's seduction of Sawyer complicates the series' central love triangle so satisfactorily that we never guess what's coming.

When you do know where "Two for the Road" is going, an already good episode kicks up another notch. Sure, after you've seen Michael free Henry from the room he's locked in, you've probably guessed that the Others have turned Michael somehow, in exchange for Walt's freedom. But that doesn't make the grim inevitability of what happens to Ana Lucia and (poor!) Libby any easier to bear.

Reportedly, Michelle Rodriguez only ever wanted to commit to *Lost* for a single season, and as such, the show gave her a memorable exit. It's easier to quibble with Libby's death, both because the audience knows so little about the character and because this is a show that has a huge gender disparity in its cast. After the shock of the episode wears off a bit, one might be tempted to wonder if *both* women had to die for the episode to have its impact.

At the time, Libby's death was justified by the fact that a certain portion of the audience didn't much like Ana Lucia and would be happy to see her go. Therefore, the producers reasoned, another character the audience *did* like had to die as well. Hence, Libby. Now, however, it's hard to watch this episode and not feel a great deal of sympathy for Ana Lucia, a woman who simply wanted to return home and seek some sort of atonement with her mother. Ana Lucia brought a different energy to the beach camp, and "Two for the Road" offers a grim reminder that for those who die on this Island, their stories are over—leaving their business on- and off-Island unresolved on- and off-Island.

"Two for the Road" is an episode that all but begs you to keep watching if you're binge-watching. Can you see the seams a little more with successive rewatches? Yeah. But who cares? This episode gives a huge jolt to a season that can otherwise feel a little sleepy. —*ESJ*

STATION TO STATION

"?"

SEASON 2, EPISODE 21
ORIGINAL AIRDATE 5/10/06

Next to Desmond, the most important new "character" in *Lost*'s Season Two premiere is the Dharma Initiative. The organization gets a proper introduction in "Orientation," with the short, explanatory film that introduces Dharma scientist Dr. Pierre Chang (François Chau), going under the alias of Marvin Candle. The film offers a mini-history of the Initiative: funded by Alvar Hanso and founded by the University of Michigan grad students Karen and Gerald DeGroot, with the intention of studying everything from weather to animals to sociology to psychology to parapsychology to "the unique electromagnetic fluctuations" of the Island. Dr. Chang also mentions an "incident" that necessitated the creation of the Swan—and notes that the Swan is "Station 3," suggesting more stations are still undiscovered.

In fact, nearly every time Season Two starts to get a little dreary, with the plot stuck in low gear and one too many Jack/Locke smug-offs, the castaways would find another piece of the Dharma Initiative puzzle, rewarding the fans' faith.

"?"—which features the first appearance of Station 5, "The Pearl"—is actually an episode all about faith, focusing on two of Oceanic 815's most devout survivors. Early on, Mr. Eko has a dream about his late brother Yemi (Adetokumboh M'Cormack), who warns him that Locke is in a funk and needs a mission. So Eko asks Locke to take him to "the question mark"—the spot on a hand-drawn map in the Swan that may contain a Dharma station. It turns out to be a spot Locke knows well: the location of the small plane containing Yemi's corpse, which was also the source of the heroin-filled Virgin Mary statuettes and the place where Boone was mortally wounded.

Thanks to more dreams and visions—plus a climb up one amazing-looking giant tree—Locke and Eko are able to find the Pearl under that plane, at the center of a patch of scorched grass in the shape of a question mark. Inside, they find surveillance equipment and logs, as well as another orientation film, hosted by "Mark Wickmund" (actually Dr. Chang again*), who quotes Karen DeGroot in touting the importance of "careful observation." All these artifacts and clues point to one conclusion. Back in the heyday of the Dharma Initiative, the Pearl was staffed by people whose job was to spy on the workers at the Swan, to see if they would keep entering the codes and pushing the button—suggested here to be a menial task of no real importance.

"?" arrives at a pivotal point in Season Two, as the tension and action start ratcheting up for the finale.† Michael has just shot Ana Lucia and Libby, and freed Henry Gale. With the whole of *Lost* fandom on the edge of its collective seat, what did the writers give us the next week? "?," an entertaining and thematically rich episode that also cools down a story that had been building up to a pretty good boil. Locke and Eko are meant to be chasing after Henry when they change plans and embark on their spiritual quest; and by ditching that mission entirely, they

---

★   Dr. Chang's aliases (which also include "Candle" and "Halliwax") suggest that he came up with the names on the spot while looking at a menorah. Pierre Chang's real name, meanwhile, is a nod to the actor who plays him, François Chau, whose name also combines French and Chinese.

†   Fun fact! Originally this episode was going to be directed by Darren Aronofsky, until he got too busy. Later in 2006, his epic fantasy movie *The Fountain* would be released, exploring some very *Lost*-like themes about faith, science, and human need.

ostensibly allow the prisoner to get away and return to the Others, which will have a profound effect on how this season ends.

Meanwhile, back with the castaways, Michael is alarmed to learn that Libby is in critical condition but still alive. There's some delicious tension when he has to sweat out whether she's going to spill the beans— and a haunting moment when he cleans up the blood of the people he attacked. The drama intensifies when Jack manipulates Sawyer into revealing where he has been stashing all the camp's guns and medicine. Jack, tossing his Hippocratic Oath aside—not for the first time, and not for the last—suggests that he's willing to let Libby suffer excruciating pain unless Sawyer allows Kate to follow him to where his secret supplies are.

The flashbacks show Mr. Eko, back in the days when he was a priest, assigned to visit Australia to investigate a possible miracle. The flashbacks are far too short, but they matter to the episode's larger thrust. On the Island, we have Michael stewing in his own lies and Locke learning that the whole button-pushing operation may be pointless. And the flashbacks depict a moment when Eko has to decide whether a fantastical story about a drowned girl springing back to life is actually true, or if the people involved faked the whole thing. Complicating matters for *Lost* fans is that the girl's father is Richard Malkin, the psychic who told Claire not to let her baby be "raised by another"—and who now confesses to Eko that he is a complete fraud.

So . . . Claire's psychic is a liar, and the Dharma Initiative may have been manipulating the Swan's employees into pushing a meaningless button every 108 minutes. Is anything about this seemingly magical Island and its many supernatural and technological wonders legit, or is it all just stagecraft and bluster?

Surprisingly, Eko's takeaway is that it is now *more* important than ever to push the button at the Swan. While a frustrated Locke is starting to doubt everything—and, tellingly, finding it harder to walk as he becomes more skeptical—Eko insists that the existence and purpose of the Pearl are clarifying. He tells Locke that he now believes pushing the button is incredibly important work, because it proves their faith.

And the thing is . . . Eko's not wrong. A few episodes from now— warning: spoilers ahead—we'll find out that the pneumatic tubes in the Pearl lead to a dumping ground in the jungle, implying that the reports filed by the Pearl's workers were meaningless; and that perhaps *they* were the subjects of a Dharma experiment, not the people at the Swan. And in the season finale, we'll learn that *not* pushing the button *does* cause a catastrophe. By the end of the series, we'll know that the real guiding forces of the Island are in fact testing *everybody*, to see if they're worthy.

Part of the experience of being a *Lost* fan when the show was originally airing was the hunger for "answers" to all the little questions and mysteries the writers scattered around the Island. But "?" answered the ones that really mattered—even if we didn't know it at the time. —*NM*

NO TEAM IN I

"THREE MINUTES"

—

SEASON 2, EPISODE 22
ORIGINAL AIRDATE 5/17/06

"Three Minutes" refers to the amount of time the Others allow Michael Dawson to spend with his son Walt before they send him on his mission to free "Henry Gale." It's the mission that will end with Michael shooting Ana Lucia and Libby in "Two for the Road," after which he will lie to his friends in order to lure them into the Others' trap. The title is tinged with tragedy. Michael sacrificed so much, and for what? Just three minutes.

But there's another moment in this episode—untimed, but also lasting roughly three minutes—that hits even harder. After the drama at the bunker, Michael returns to the beach for the first time since he stormed off on his search for Walt two weeks earlier.* He's warmly greeted first by Claire and Charlie, and then Jin and Sun. But while

★   Or ten episodes ago, for *Lost* viewers.

he's feeling that love from his old friends, Michael gets distracted by something he sees in the distance: graves being dug for the two women he killed.

When it debuted, "Three Minutes" was, for the most part, a transitional episode, doing the necessary work of filling in some of Season Two's gaps while also setting up the two-part finale, which aired in full the following week. Perhaps born of that necessity, the episode takes some real chances, starting with its structure. For the third time in the show's run,★ the flashbacks circle back to cover events that happened recently on the Island, rather than before the crash. Also like those previous episodes, "Three Minutes" provides an alternate perspective on characters and moments we've already seen.

Specifically, we're taken back to the events of "The Hunting Party," when Jack, Locke,† and Sawyer tried to find the AWOL Michael and were thwarted by Mr. Friendly and the Others, who had captured Kate. While all of that was going on, Michael was nearby, listening with a pained expression as his friends were being scared half out of their minds. Already, he was feeling guilty over the people who had been hurt by his mission to find his son—and that was *before* he was taken to the Others' crummy-looking seaside camp and told that in order to be fully reunited with Walt he'd have to betray Jack and company yet again.

During that scene out in the jungle, though—the one where our heroes are surrounded by a ring of the Others' fire, demonstrating their enemies' strength—Michael is reassured by Alex that her traveling companions have no intention of hurting Kate or anyone else. Alex then peppers Michael with questions about Claire, whom she met and helped in "Maternity Leave." (Alex asks, excitedly, if Claire had her baby.) This is a fleeting moment, primarily intended to reinforce the audience's awareness of Alex, who will be a significant character in the series going forward. But it also speaks to an essential storytelling and character-building

---

★   After "The Other 48 Days" and "Maternity Leave," both from earlier in this season.

†   You will recall that Michael escaped Locke in that episode by knocking him on the head—something that seems to happen to Locke a lot. Which raises a question: How do the people on this Island know how to hit each other in just the right spot with the right force to induce unconsciousness?

element on *Lost* throughout its run—especially in its first three seasons. By now, the people on the Island could largely be grouped into two sets: the Oceanic 815 survivors★ and the Others. But within those groups, a lot of people have their own agendas and secrets that they are not sharing with their comrades.

This is evident throughout "Three Minutes." Early on, as Michael tries to assemble a crew to pay a visit to the Others, Hurley shames them all by reminding them that Ana Lucia and Libby are still lying dead on the floor. Elsewhere in the episode, Eko moves into the Hatch to focus on pushing the button, abandoning his plans to build a church alongside Charlie (who in response to Eko's snub ends up staring long and hard at his heroin-filled Virgin Mary statuettes, before deciding to fling them into the sea, as a disengaged and dispirited Locke looks on silently). Sayid, meanwhile, deduces from Michael's tone and body language that he has been "compromised," and so he tells Jack he's planning to shadow Michael's upcoming expedition—while also telling Jack not to let anyone else know what's up. (Whatever happened to living together or dying alone?)

There is not much levity in "Three Minutes," though there is a thematically on-point semi-comic moment in the flashbacks to Michael's time at the Others' camp. There he meets Ms. Klugh (April Grace), who hands him the list of people Michael is supposed to bring back with him. Michael looks at the list and wants to know who James Ford is. He's been living with Sawyer for months and still doesn't know his real name. Hilarious. And sort of sad.

Much of the action in this phase of *Lost* is driven by that kind of petty irony. Everyone still thinks that they can keep information to themselves and squeak by. The result is a mounting death toll.

To be fair, though, these characters are in some ways just following the lead of their creators. As soon as the castaways start having more face-to-face encounters with the Others in Season Two, the viewers see more of what's *really* happening on the Island. We get teases . . . but no concrete information. We're aware that the Others have a "list" of selected

---

★   And those survivors can be subcategorized: the beach-dwellers and the cave/Hatch colony; the Tailies and the group we met in the pilot; the people anxious to leave the Island and those who love it there; and so on.

815ers (Jack Shephard, Kate Austen, Hugo Reyes, and James Ford), but we don't know for a while who's on it or why. The list Michael gets from Ms. Klugh is one piece of a larger puzzle. When the Others' goon Danny threatens Michael with violence, Mr. Friendly tells him to back off because they "need" Michael. Undoubtedly there are more people who are important to the Others—or to whomever the Others answer to—than just Jack, Kate, Hurley, and Sawyer.

And what of Walt? What did the Others want from him?

That's the big question, and it's a nagging one, too. It's a question that makes certain episodes weaker in retrospect, once we know we're never going to get a proper answer. Even here in "Three Minutes," as the *Lost* writers are preparing to send Michael and Walt off the Island—one temporarily, one permanently—they're still emphasizing how special the child is. Even as Ms. Klugh is ducking Michael's inquiries into who the Others really are, she's also grilling him for information about Walt's birth and boyhood.

The Others are amazed by Walt. (But why?) Yet they're about to let him go. (*WHY?*)

Once again, competing agendas come into play. Viewers at the time wanted the writers to tell us more about Walt and the Others. The writers wanted to tell a story about a good man who gets manipulated into doing terrible things. That tension between what some people want and what they actually get carries over into one of *Lost*'s most eventful season finales. —*NM*

OUR MUTUAL FRIEND

"LIVE TOGETHER, DIE ALONE"

—

SEASON 2, EPISODES 23 & 24
ORIGINAL AIRDATE 5/24/06

Some of the most memorable moments, lines, and images in *Lost*'s entire run occur in the Season Two finale, "Live Together, Die Alone." Let's tote 'em up!

The giant four-toed foot!

As Michael leads Jack, Kate, Sawyer, and Hurley—everyone on the Others' list—to an uncertain fate, a distrustful Sayid sails along the coast in Desmond's boat, with Jin and Sun's help. As the sailors pass by parts of the Island they've never seen before, Sayid spies the remains of what must once have been a towering statue. All that remains is the foot, which has only four toes. This is a new piece of Island mythology, well outside the Dharma drama we've encountered up to this point—and something that will remain unaddressed by the show until Seasons Five and Six.

The Pearl tubes!

While walking through the jungle, Michael's party find a pile of plastic messenger tubes, filled with the handwritten logs from the Pearl station. This unmanned clearing in the middle of nowhere, it seems, was the intended endpoint of all the records kept by the Dharma staffers at the Pearl—thereby confirming the theory that the psychological experiments were being performed *on the Pearl team*, and not on the button-pushers at the Swan.

The Others' fakery!

Earlier in the season, in "Maternity Leave," Kate stumbles across a locker at a Dharma medical outpost containing tattered clothes and stage makeup, suggesting the Others were merely pretending to be some kind of rough-hewn survivalist community in order to confuse and frighten our heroes. In the Season Two finale, the ruse is more widely exposed. When Sayid and company arrive at the Others' camp that Michael was taken to in "Three Minutes," they discover not only that it is empty but that much of it is phony. It's a Potemkin village, slapped together to deceive Michael. Elsewhere on the Island, after Jack and company are captured by the Others, Mr. Friendly removes his fake beard because he knows the 815ers have figured out the truth.

"We're the good guys, Michael!"

Fans were frequently frustrated throughout the first two seasons at the castaways' apparent incuriosity regarding the Island's hostile inhabitants. During their brief encounters with the Others, our heroes never seemed to ask enough questions about who these people were; and on their own, the 815ers didn't talk much about their mysterious opposition. (Only Sawyer seemed interested in the Others, as an audience conduit who theorized that the Others could be ex-Dharma . . . or space aliens.) We don't get any real clarity in the Season Two finale, either, although before Michael and Walt leave the Island,★ the man going by the name of Henry Gale says three notable things: (1) that his real name is Benjamin Linus; (2) that he has lived on the Island his whole life; and (3) that his people are "the good guys." The first is true, the second is a fib, and the third . . . well, that's kind of what the rest of the series is about.

The Hatch implodes!

When a despondent Locke tries to prove that Mr. Eko is wrong about the importance of pushing the button, he locks his former friend out of the Swan's computer room and allows the clock to wind down. What happens? Absolute mayhem. The clock switches from numbers to hieroglyphics. Metal objects start flying about or crumpling. The whole structure shakes. And then Desmond slips into a crawlspace below the room with a special key, which vents the energy beneath the Swan manually—with an earsplitting whine and a blinding flash of white light. When all is said and one, the Swan is destroyed, several people are unaccounted for, and . . .

★ Ben provides precise coordinates for Michael to follow in his boat to escape the Island's "mystical pull." And then as a final humiliation as Michael is leaving, Ben tells him he won't be able to come back and that the stain of what he did to escape will be indelible.

"ELECTROMAGNETIC ANOMALY DETECTED!"

As a stinger to the episode, we see two men manning some kind of arctic base, who receive an alert with the Island's current coordinates, signaled by the destruction of the Swan. They call Desmond's true love Penny, thus setting in motion a sequence of events that will culminate in Season Three's dramatic ending (and then the lengthy repercussions in Season Four).

So yeah . . . "Live Together, Die Alone" is essential *Lost* viewing. It's also a chore at times.

It didn't feel that way when the episode originally aired, to be clear. All of these aforementioned moments were jaw-droppingly exciting back then—and for the most part still are. But rewatching the end of Season Two, having seen the whole series, a lot of what happens seems like busywork, moving characters around the Island as gradually as possible to delay the big finish. Some of the machinations are pretty contrived, too: like the way Jack and Michael have to convince Hurley to come along on their trek to the Others' camp because he's on the list of 815ers they demanded to see. Ultimately, after they arrive, Ben just has Hurley carry a message back to the beach explaining what happened to Jack, Kate, and Sawyer—which doesn't sound like the kind of job that *only Hurley* could do. Of course, the real reason Hurley goes to see the Others is the same reason that Charlie helps Mr. Eko try to dynamite open the Swan: because these are major characters on the show, and they need something to do.*

In an A.V. Club interview with Lindelof and Cuse, Lindelof said that when it comes down to storytelling versus plausibility, he believes storytelling always comes first. But some of the storytelling decisions that make sense for a TV show—meant to be seen by people once a week for an indefinite amount of time—don't make as much sense for a complete 121-chapter narrative that people can sit down and watch in big chunks. For example: the way the Others' disguise themselves as ragamuffins. That's for the viewing audience's benefit, to keep us guessing, more than for the castaways. Again: busywork.

What keeps "Live Together, Die Alone" from feeling too labored is the flashbacks focusing on Desmond Hume, which cover a character

---

* Hurley's presence does also lead to strange moment when a giant bird swoops overhead and appears to say his name. This moment won't be fully paid off until the series' epilogue episode, "The New Man in Charge."

whom fans had been anxious to learn more about since the Season Two premiere. And it says something about the popularity of Desmond—and the way he becomes integral to the overall *Lost* narrative, whether the writers originally intended him to or not—that he *feels* like a Season Two regular, even though he disappears not long after the premiere and doesn't return until the finale.

Lindelof and Cuse and company don't waste a minute of Desmond in "Live Together, Die Alone." We see a little bit of his pre-Island story, beginning with how he left prison with only two personal effects: an unread copy of Charles Dickens's *Our Mutual Friend* and a photo of himself with his arm around a woman. We meet the woman: Penelope Widmore (Sonya Walger), whose relationship with Desmond angers her father Charles (Alan Dale), a powerful industrialist. (These two will also be major players in *Lost*'s endgame; and although viewers had no way of knowing that at the time, by this point in the series fans had gotten into the habit of seeing every new character as significant.) And then, to close the loop on how Jack first met Desmond, we see our Mr. Hume at the stadium in Los Angeles, training for a boat trip—sailing a vessel he borrows from Hurley's future almost-girlfriend Libby!—that he hopes will impress Charles Widmore.

The boat crashes on the Island, where in an impressively stylish, trippy sequence, Desmond is saved by Kelvin Inman (Clancy Brown), a Dharma dead-ender who—alongside a colleague named Radzinsky—kept pushing the button at the Swan long after the rest of the Initiative was wiped out. The flashbacks connect a lot of Season Two's dots, vis-à-vis our heroes' first encounter with Desmond and their confounding early experiences inside the Hatch. Kelvin says to Desmond a lot of what Desmond would say to the 815ers when they met him. (When asked why they're pushing the button, they both respond, "Just saving the world.") And in the flashbacks, we learn who was responsible for the edits in the Dharma orientation film and for the invisible ink map on the blast door. (Radzinsky, in both cases . . . though Kelvin took over after his partner killed himself.★)

★   There's a nice bit of dark, sick humor when Kelvin points to the brown stain that Radzinsky left behind when he shot himself, and then ruefully says he only had 108 minutes to bury him.

But what really makes the Desmond scenes so effective is that they subtly mirror the main question being asked in the present-day Island storyline: How much of what our heroes have been told about or experienced firsthand on the Island is "real"? Are the Others phonies? Does the button do anything? Are the people who have ended up stranded on the Island there for a reason?

The Desmond scenes offer evidence for both sides. In the present day, he tells Claire not to bother tapping Dharma's supply of special vaccines for Aaron,★ because in the flashbacks he noticed Kelvin's protective hazmat suit had a rip in it, meaning the air on the Island is fine. But also: While looking at the Swan records that Locke and Eko printed out at the Pearl, Desmond notices that on the one day he was late pushing the button, Oceanic 815 crashed. And in the flashbacks, we see that when Desmond was in his depths of despair, considering shooting himself, his life was saved by hearing Locke (equally despairing at the time) pounding on the outside of the Hatch. These can't just be coincidences, right?

And then, of course, there's the beginning of the episode, where Desmond—who earlier in the season had tried to leave the Island on Libby's sailboat—finds himself drifting back to the beach because the Island won't let him leave. He drunkenly howls at the 815ers that they're all in a "snow globe" and that he didn't come back on purpose.

Of course, Penny might note that Desmond *is* responsible for where he finds himself, because he didn't have to set sail in the first place. Perhaps it was his own stubborn hubris that led to him washing ashore, so many years ago.† This will be another theme in the *Lost* seasons ahead, especially in stories involving Desmond and Penny. Is it possible to opt out of Island drama altogether? Or will the forces that control this strange place just keep grabbing whomever they want, and never letting go? —*NM*

★ Also, when Sayid is making plans to ambush the Others, Desmond calls them "the Hostiles," adding another piece to *Lost*'s mythology and establishing that our heroes really have no idea who these people are or how long they've been around.

† Well, that plus the coaxing of an interested stranger. But we'll get to that in Season Three.

FURTHER READING: ON KATE AUSTEN

When you think about the characters of *Lost*, you can surely think of a signature episode or two for all of them. Whether it's Locke and "Walkabout" or Desmond and "The Constant" or Sawyer and "LaFleur," the show created standout hours of TV that deserve their place in the pantheon. And those hours also cemented the show's characters as all-time greats.

And yet—how many of those standout episodes are about women? And to get more specific, how many of them are about *Kate*, the purported female lead?

In Abrams and Lindelof's original conception of *Lost*, Kate Austen was to evolve into the series' hero. Jack would have died at the midway point of the pilot, leaving the survivors without a leader, and Kate would have stepped up to take charge and lead them forward. All the while, she would be seeking her husband, who had been seated in the tail section of the aircraft and who she believed was still alive. Considering that Abrams's two previous TV successes were *Felicity* and *Alias*, it made sense for him to once again center a show around a (presumably) young woman[*] in an unfamiliar situation.

Yet Abrams and Lindelof were talked out of killing Jack, and the big shocking death at the pilot's midpoint instead went to the airplane's pilot, which wasn't as surprising as killing off the supposed protagonist but did increase the survivors' feeling of being trapped. Meanwhile, Kate's "looking for her husband" backstory was taken from her and given to the recurring character of Rose instead. That left Kate without an obvious

---

[*] We don't know that this original conception of Kate was meant to be a woman in her twenties or thirties. Obviously, that rough description could describe a woman in her fifties or sixties. But c'mon. This is television. She would have been as young as possible while still being believable as a married woman.

plot hook. The series' solution was to make her a recently apprehended criminal, being brought back to the United States from Australia. So far, so good. The Island needed a few more reprobates among the original cast.

The problem quickly becomes obvious in the show's second episode: Because Kate is one of the show's leads, she can't be *too* bad of a person. The series rapidly begins to sand off the implied edges of her criminal past, and by the time we find out what she was guilty of,★ the show has mostly turned her into a young woman who got in over her head and turned to a life of crime. That's fine as a character background, but it leaves Kate with very little engagement in the larger mysteries of the Island. Where most of the other characters have something to gain or learn about themselves on the Island, Kate mostly doesn't have to go to jail. What's more, she doesn't really have anything she wants to get back to either. Compared to some of the other, richer character stories, it's a bit limp.

Had Abrams stayed with the show past its first few episodes, he might have had better success with the character. *Felicity* and *Alias* demonstrated his skill for writing young women who acted before they thought and (at least in the case of *Alias*) could do a roundhouse kick to their problems. In Abrams's absence, the series placed the characters in a state of constant existential struggle for their souls. Kate, a character of immediate, visceral action, didn't fit the paradigm of the show as it developed. She became an Abrams character stranded in a Lindelof show.

On some level, the version of Kate we meet was not reconceived well enough to develop beyond the pilot. Evangeline Lilly possessed endless charisma but was very much learning on the go in her first major role and couldn't immediately command the audience's attention like the more experienced actors. The result was a character who sometimes felt like she belonged in another show entirely. By the first season's midpoint, Kate's reason for being on the show largely derived from her position in a love triangle with Sawyer and Jack. She became so defined by that love triangle that Lilly herself commented on the matter. "I felt like my

---

★   Murdering her abusive father.

character went from being autonomous—really having her own story and her own journey and her own agendas—to chasing two men around the Island, and that irritated the shit out of me," she said to the *Lost Boys* podcast in 2018.

Plenty of TV shows evolve past their original, main characters, but must keep them around for various reasons.* Arguably, *Lost* got to that point with *both* Jack and Kate, but the show had turned a corner on Jack by its final season. It never really got there with Kate, to the degree that when Noel and I discussed what *the* Kate episode was . . . we couldn't think of one.

So why not just write Kate out if the character's function had largely been subsumed by others? That brushes up against one of the biggest problems with *Lost*: The portrayal of its woman characters is pretty awful.

Lost was a show predominantly written, directed, and produced by men. Women were involved in the production, to be sure, particularly Elizabeth Sarnoff, who served as a writer and producer on the show for its second through sixth seasons, but the show centers largely on men and stereotypically masculine adventures and drives. As a proto action heroine, Kate should fit nicely within that milieu, but nearly every one of her character traits is doubled by several other (mostly male) characters in the show, which means that the series decides that her main function becomes a romantic one. Even her backstory is predominantly defined by men, whether evil (abusive dad), good (beloved childhood best friend and possible true love), or both at once (her cop ex-husband). Kate's crime involved a man, her tragic backstory involved a man, and her time on the Island involved men. It's no wonder Lilly grew frustrated.

But if Kate weren't in the show, it simply wouldn't have anything like a woman lead. The three other female Season One regulars—Yunjin Kim's Sun, Maggie Grace's Shannon, and Emilie de Ravin's Claire—are also largely defined by their relationships with men.† Kim, especially, finds a way to build Sun out from the rather paltry place in which she

---

*   Often contractual.

†   Sun, her husband; Shannon, her stepbrother; and Claire, her would-be lover Charlie and her eventual son.

starts, but that's almost entirely thanks to her (terrific) performance. The other characters didn't make quite the same impact.

Arguably, the show doesn't establish a compelling, autonomous female character until Season Three when Elizabeth Mitchell joins the cast as Juliet.★ Yes, Juliet's on-Island story is largely concerned with which guy she will side with, but her motivations are driven (at least at first) by her desperate need to get off the Island and back to her beloved sister. She always has her own agenda. And even after the addition of Juliet, the show continues to add memorable guys (Daniel Faraday and Frank Lapidus in Season Four) and much less memorable women (Charlotte Lewis also joins the cast in Season Four and barely makes a blip). When the show's women became vital parts of its ensemble, it was usually because of the actors' compelling performances, as with Kim and Mitchell. Yet the show's default was ultra-masc in a way that occasionally trapped even Juliet and Sun in romantic plotlines from which they couldn't escape— Sun is tossed into a love triangle in Season One, and she's *married*.

Lost ultimately reflects the time and place in which it was made. While the 2000s proved to be one of the greatest eras in American television, it was also an era when the viewpoint of the white, cis, straight guy was constantly elevated over others. Among those men are some of the most compelling TV characters ever, and some of them are on this very show. But the assumption of these shows—and often the people making them— was that the most interesting story to tell was that of a man who could brood artfully over a troubled, difficult life. Unless you had world-class writers, directors, and actors, it was too easy for the women surrounding them to be lost in their shadows. *Lost* wasn't always guilty of this, but few other dramas in its weight class of that era had as much of a problem with their women being eclipsed by their men: Carmela Soprano stands up admirably with Tony Soprano, Peggy Olson is a wonderful counterpart to Don Draper, Skyler White is a terrific foil for Walter White, and both *Deadwood* and *Battlestar Galactica* are lousy with great women characters. Really, only *The Wire*—arguably the greatest show ever

★   I might make an argument for Michelle Rodriguez as Ana Lucia, but she only joined the show for a single season, and the series struggled to know what to do with her for much of that season.

made!—has a similar problem to *Lost* when it comes to women being overshadowed by men.

There is nothing wrong with a show being more interested in its men than its women so long as it understands its limitations. The ideal, of course, is a show with many compelling, nuanced characters of all genders, but not every show can be the ideal. *Lost* featured a bunch of amazing men. It had some women characters, too, and that was just how it was. You might not have noticed—or you might not have cared. But isn't it a glaring issue to make one of your show's most-significant female characters also one of its biggest ciphers? —*ESJ*

SEASON THREE

THE END OF THE BEGINNING

Lost wasn't the first fantasy television series to try and tell a complete epic saga across multiple seasons. But the shows that came before tended to be smaller-scaled productions, aimed at niche audiences—and they often aired on cable channels and UHF stations. *Lost*, on the other hand, had a huge price tag; it defied expectations by becoming a massive, Emmy-winning hit. Had it struggled to draw decent ratings, *Lost* likely would've been canceled long before its story was anywhere close to being complete. Instead, the *Lost* team faced the opposite problem. So long as ABC was raking in money, the executives saw no reason to hustle their customers toward the exit.

In a way, this dilemma was an extension of a divide that had existed between *Lost*'s producers and ABC from the start. The network had long been nervous about the show becoming too serialized. Ongoing stories about Island romances and personality conflicts? Totally fine. A complex narrative in which airplane crash survivors become embroiled in a long-simmering conflict between a team of idealistic scientists and an ancient tribe of protectors in a mystical land? No, no, no.

But Lindelof and Cuse were uncommonly attuned to what their fans were saying. They knew that if they kept moving their story's pieces along too slowly for too long—and especially if they kept moving further and further away from any kind of resolution—they would lose what their core audience thought was special about *Lost*. Fans loved the show's characters, but what excited them more was the mythology of the Island;

and at some point, the jagged puzzle pieces of that lore needed to start fitting together.

Season Three offers both the best and the worst of *Lost*, all born of the writers proving—intentionally or not—that ABC needed to allow them to set an end date.

The first six episodes were uniquely frustrating to devoted viewers. After the huge developments and cliffhangers of the Season Two finale, the show settled into an exhausting storyline that saw Jack, Kate, and Sawyer imprisoned by the Others at the Dharma Initiative's Hydra station, on a smaller island near the main Island. Because *Lost*'s serialized nature meant that viewers had less patience for the traditional network TV scheduling model of that time—where a couple of weeks of new episodes would be followed by a repeat—ABC smartly decided to lump the season's first six episodes together into a bloc, airing them on consecutive weeks in the fall and then holding the rest of the season to run with no breaks starting in February.* So Lindelof and Cuse intentionally structured these six episodes as a mini-arc, setting the Jack/Kate/Sawyer love triangle against their first prolonged encounter with the Others.

But alas, nothing much happens at the Hydra beyond a lot of yelling and very little new information about the Others (or *from* them, regarding the history and nature of the Island). Meanwhile, back on the Island, the only major development is "the Monster" killing Mr. Eko (reportedly because Adewale Akinnuoye-Agbaje wasn't interested in sticking around beyond the one season he was originally contracted for). When the show returned in February, the viewership numbers dropped significantly for the first time, from around seventeen million a week to around twelve million a week. And while the storytelling improved from the seventh episode onward, there were several episodes that drew the ire of fans.

Some of these—like the experimental "Exposé," designed to answer the question of what the less-important 815 survivors had been up to all this time—are far better than their initial reputation. Others—like the pointless "Stranger in a Strange Land," which dedicates an entire flashback to how Jack got his tattoos—are notable primarily for being so dire that they helped convince the ABC executives that maybe they should

---

* This has become standard procedure now, with networks adopting new terminology like "midseason finale" or "winter finale" to cue the hiatus.

finally let Lindelof and Cuse start steering this ship toward the harbor. (The Season Three ratings drop also surely played a role.)

And yet, ask the average *Lost* lover to name some of their favorite episodes and you'll undoubtedly hear a healthy number of titles from Season Three, including the mind-blowing final three: "The Man Behind the Curtain," "Greatest Hits," and "Through the Looking Glass"—all of which were written after ABC gave Lindelof and Cuse the green light to map out the rest of the series, and thus have an added sense of urgency.

Season Three introduces only a few significant new characters, the most important of which is **JULIET BURKE** (Elizabeth Mitchell), a fertility specialist recruited by the Others and then kept on the Island against her will by Ben, who has a crush on her. Given how much time is spent with the Others this season, several other Others also emerge as major players for a few episodes. The ones that matter most are: **ALEX** (Tania Raymonde), the daughter of Rousseau, who had been abducted as a baby and raised as Ben's daughter; and **RICHARD ALPERT** (Néstor Carbonell), a seemingly ageless immortal whose time on the Island predates all of the Others. The end of the season also sees the surprise arrival of **NAOMI DORRIT** (Marsha Thomason), who drops in by parachute and claims to have been sent by Desmond's true love **PENELOPE WIDMORE** (Sonya Walger)—but who is actually part of a team of experts anchored offshore, all hired by Penny's scheming, malevolent father **CHARLES WIDMORE** (Alan Dale).

Though some fans would continue to insist for the rest of the series that Lindelof and Cuse were too stingy with explanations of how everything having to do with the Island "worked," from a narrative perspective by the end of Season Three they established most of what any viewer would need to know to understand the basic mechanics of the plot.

See, there is this Island—not visible on any maps—charged with a power that has made it very valuable to different groups of settlers across centuries. The people we know as the Others lived here for a long time before the arrival of the Dharma Initiative, whose experiments and expansion plans were so disruptive that the Others (known to Dharma as "the Hostiles") eventually killed most of them off. Since then, the 815ers and a handful of other people have shown up on the Island, usually by accident but rarely by coincidence. These newcomers—often unbeknownst to them—sometimes have ties to the Island's history.

That's really the gist of *Lost*. The other questions—what is "the Monster" and why did Oceanic 815 crash there?—matter to the audience, understandably, and they do drive a lot of the plot in Seasons Four, Five, and Six. But by the end of Season Three, the hard work of setup has been done—perhaps later than Lindelof and Cuse would have liked.

Perhaps more importantly, the brilliance of so much of *Lost*'s third season built up a lot of trust among the viewers. The writers knew what they were doing. Even seemingly trivial episodes like "Tricia Tanaka Is Dead"—mocked at the time as "Hurley Finds a Groovy Van"—are later revealed to be plot-relevant, connecting unexpectedly and hauntingly to the tragic story of how the Others "purged" the Dharma Initiative. This is the key to making—and watching—serialized television. The writers can introduce all kinds of seemingly random stuff that baffle and even irritate viewers. But in the end, storytelling is like shoplifting: Until you leave the store, you haven't done anything wrong. —*NM*

INTO THE DOLDRUMS

"A TALE OF TWO CITIES"

–

SEASON 3, EPISODE 1
ORIGINAL AIRDATE 10/4/06

The first half of *Lost* Season Three is the "Abandon all hope, ye who enter here" section of the show's run, when the series' buzz had started to turn rancid, and younger, hotter series* had come on the scene to steal the show's thunder. In the generally accepted narrative of the show, this is the dark period the series had to get through to hit the heights it would hit as soon as the second half of Season Three.

---

* Like *Heroes*, which debuted in the fall of 2006.

That narrative of the show's run isn't *wrong*, necessarily. The very worst episode of the show ("Stranger in a Strange Land," Season 3, Episode 9)—one so bad that it inspired showrunners Carlton Cuse and Damon Lindelof to request a hard-and-fast wrap-up plan from ABC, so they wouldn't keep churning out increasingly bad flashbacks—resides here. And the cliffhanger at the end of episode six—meant to carry viewers into a long break between episodes—dangles limply; even if a bingeing viewer can blitz right by it.

Yet I think that narrative also obscures what is a flawed but ultimately strong half-season of television, and "A Tale of Two Cities," the second and final episode of the series to feature a script credit from co-creator J. J. Abrams, is a good example of this section of the series' strengths and faults. In many ways, it feels like a new iteration on some of the ideas that powered Season Two, while it also strives to chart its own course. And when it comes to the characters we've known since Season One, the show feels a bit long in the tooth.

Let's tackle the strengths and weaknesses of this episode (and this section of the show) one by one:

Strength: The show has embraced a more diffuse storytelling style. "A Tale of Two Cities" doesn't check in with the other 815 survivors, opting, instead, to spend all its time with Jack, Kate, and Sawyer after the three are taken prisoner by the Others. There, they get to see the inner workings of the Others' operation, and viewers get to learn the real name of the mysterious Henry Gale who so dominated the second half of Season Two. (It's Ben. Benjamin Linus, to be precise.) Because the series doesn't need to jump back to the beach constantly, the stories can tighten the screws on the characters at their center in a way they can't when every member of the increasingly unwieldy ensemble needs a quick check-in.

At the time, many saw this diffusion as a weakness in the show's storytelling, but in the binge-watch era, its strength as a way to expand the world of the show without becoming completely unsustainable is more apparent. Jack, Kate, Sawyer, and new character Juliet all get full arcs in this episode, which wouldn't have been possible if the episode were also checking in with everyone else.

Weakness: The flashbacks for Season One characters are completely out of gas. At their best, the flashbacks offered new and surprising information about the characters on the Island, but even at their worst in Season

One, the flashbacks allowed the show to flex its storytelling muscles by expanding into other genres. Yet the longer the show runs, the less impressive and the more repetitive this trick becomes, especially as the Island continues to swallow up new storytelling concepts in and of itself. (The Others seem to live in a suburban cul-de-sac straight out of a prime-time soap, for instance.)

In "A Tale of Two Cities," we're checking in with Jack yet again, but now, his megalomania and need to control every aspect of his life have been hammered into our heads so often that it simply becomes exhausting to check in with him at his lowest ebb over and over and over again. There are worse Jack flashbacks to come, but this episode's flashback, in which Jack accuses his father of sleeping with his ex-wife, is still quite a lowlight.

Strength: The Others are a compelling spin on the "us vs. them" dynamic at the show's core. "A Tale of Two Cities" doesn't give us much in the way of immediate information on the Others, but we do get the sense that they were built out of the ashes of the Dharma Initiative and are, therefore, some kind of sick psychological experiment gone horribly wrong. Jack, Kate, and Sawyer are all subjected to what amount to tests of their intelligence and willpower, and the mere presence of Juliet (Elizabeth Mitchell) suggests that if given enough time, the Others would be able to turn just about anybody to their side, including a very nice doctor lady.

Juliet is by far the most promising element of "Tale." Mitchell's performance very nearly matches Michael Emerson's Ben for strange inscrutability, and she plays equally well off Matthew Fox's Jack. What's key, however, is that Juliet never seems like she's as committed to the cause as Ben is. She's here to do a job, and once the job is done, maybe she'll head out (if she even can). On a show that is still relatively starved for good woman characters, Juliet instantly becomes one of the best.

Weakness: But haven't we done this already? It doesn't take a great deal of imagination to see how similar the setup for Season Three—three characters are kidnapped by the show's new faction, while everybody else is back on the beach—is to the setup for Season Two. And with the Tailies, the show at least had the immediately compelling hook of "two different groups of people deal with the long tail of tragedy." The Others don't have this just yet. They are, instead, the oppressors of those we've come to know so well, and even if they have book clubs and nice little suburban communities, it's hard to sympathize with them in quite the same way as the Tailies. It will take the show quite some time to solve this problem, but it's able to skirt around it in this episode by making Juliet a compelling figure.

Strength: The show is leaning into our over-familiarity with it. Do you feel like you've seen everything *Lost* has to offer? The show worries that you have, too, and Season Three is positively full of episodes that seem suffused with dread at the prospect of having to keep making this show—and to keep its audience invested in solving its mysteries. Sawyer's quest to get a machine to dispense a simple fish biscuit reads almost as the fans' quixotic attempt to figure out what's going on from limited information, finally putting the puzzle together and being gifted an underwhelming prize.

Again, at the time these episodes aired, many viewed this darkly pessimistic take on the show as a kind of self-defeating prophecy. In a binge-watch—and especially with the bulk of Season Three ahead of a viewer—it becomes easier to see these stories for what they are: darkly comic looks at a series that is spinning its wheels, waiting for someone to tell it that it's safe to end.

Weakness: But wait. Is this show *ever* going to stop introducing new mysteries? To best explain this point requires mildly spoiling the season's fourth episode, "Every Man for Himself." *Lost* has always been obsessed with con artists and scams, and that episode plays out as a lengthy con Ben plays on Sawyer for purposes that remain inscrutable even with the complete hindsight of where the show is going. The episode ends with a major "reveal": Jack, Kate, and Sawyer are being held on a different island off the coast of the main Island. To which most viewers said—OK? So?

It is in the nature of the mystery box show that every mystery solved must spawn at least one more mystery and ideally two or three. But it is also in the nature of the mystery box show that as these mysteries proliferate in number, viewers will start to become exhausted from the sheer volume. Once *Lost* receives an end date, it can start resolving some of its mysteries, but at this point in its run, the mysteries run so rampant that the show occasionally seems to throw up its hands and say, "There's another island, OK? It's smaller."

"A Tale of Two Cities" isn't the show at its best or worst. As season premieres go, it's pretty good, and it's worth having the episode if only to introduce Juliet and a new storytelling vehicle. But it does underscore the most damning thing about *Lost* at this point in its run: It just seems tired. How it shakes off that malaise is the story of Season Three. —*ESJ*

"THE GLASS BALLERINA"

—

SEASON 3, EPISODE 2
ORIGINAL AIRDATE 10/11/06

On the Island: Sun, Jin, and Sayid, suspecting their fellow castaways have been taken by the Others, attempt to set an ambush to strike back. The ambush mostly fails, but Sun does accidentally shoot a woman, seemingly fatally. Sawyer and Kate are pressed into service in a quarry. Ben reveals to Jack that the Red Sox won the World Series.

In the flashbacks: When Sun's father learns of her affair, he tasks Jin with killing Sun's lover Jae Lee—though Jin does not know Sun has been unfaithful. Jin cannot bring himself to do it, but Jae Lee dies anyway.

If the first six episodes of Season Three have a bad reputation, the reasons for that ignominy are noticeable in "The Glass Ballerina." In a vacuum, this is a perfectly enjoyable hour of *Lost*. Viewed in the overall scope of the show so far, it makes more sense why contemporary viewers were growing impatient with the series' storytelling.

The single biggest fault of this stretch of episodes is that it constantly sets the characters up to fail. Though Sun is able to shoot Colleen, a random Other played by the wonderful Paula Malcomson, the ambush she, Jin, and Sayid set up cannot be a rousing success because the Others need to be antagonists for far longer than the first few episodes of the season. Similarly, Jack, Kate, and Sawyer cannot escape their captivity just yet because that would make the Others look totally ineffectual and weaken their placement as the season's overarching villains.

These episodes also are right around when the show is at its most painfully male-gaze-y. The shots of Sawyer appreciating Kate in her slinky dress while she breaks rocks in a quarry (seems impractical on multiple levels!) can only prompt eye rolls, and his passionate kiss with her seems driven less by the characters' undying desire for each other and more by the writers mashing the two together to make them kiss.

To the show's credit, it seems aware that it's sailing in circles. The saving grace of "The Glass Ballerina" is the flashback storyline, which offers a darker take on Sun. In her off-Island life, she was similarly trapped by circumstance. Her marriage to Jin was meant as a way to escape the circumstances of her birth, but she only became further enmeshed with her tyrannical father. These flashbacks have a cynicism at their core that gives the episode some heft when the on-Island plot risks running out of story to tell.

And even in the most listless of Season Three episodes, viewers can count on Ben Linus to pop up and offer a delightful scene or two. In the conclusion of this episode, Ben reveals to Jack that life off the Island continues apace. The masterstroke comes from Jack trying to call Ben's bluff when he says the Red Sox won the 2004 World Series, their first since 1918. But as viewers at the time surely would have known, the Red Sox really *had* won that World Series in the most unlikely fashion possible. For once, life was so strange that *Lost* had no choice but to copy it. —ESJ

"FURTHER INSTRUCTIONS"
—

SEASON 3, EPISODE 3
ORIGINAL AIRDATE 10/18/06

On the Island: The aftermath of the Hatch explosion is explored, as Locke enters a sweat lodge hoping to have visions that will lead him to the missing Mr. Eko. Meanwhile, Hurley returns to camp, and Desmond survived the Hatch explosion but seemingly with some manner of precognitive abilities.

In the flashbacks: Locke's time in a Northern California commune is disrupted by a young drifter who befriends him—and turns out to be an undercover cop.

One of *Lost*'s boldest choices as it opened Season Three was to split the resolutions of its three Season Two cliffhangers across three episodes, meaning that whole episodes would go by without appearances by several major characters. If the first two episodes devoted themselves to what happens on the Others' side of the Island, this one finally returns to the beach camp and the many characters still there, particularly John Locke.

A major character going on a vision quest to answer some big questions is a trope that pops up with some frequency in genre television. For instance, *The X-Files* not only did a very similar version of Locke's story in this episode with Mulder, but that series also did that story to open its third season. This sort of episode really hinges on how well a series can create freaky dreamscapes that nevertheless give the audience something to ponder. And *Lost* knows freaky dreamscapes.

"Further Instructions" perhaps doesn't go far enough into dreamland, however. Because this episode needs to get viewers caught up on everything happening at the beach camp—and introduce the brand-new characters Nikki (Kiele Sanchez) and Paulo (Rodrigo Santoro), positioned as if they've just Always Been There—it cannot spend very long in Locke's vision. Instead, it takes up the first third of the episode, mostly confining itself to a spirit Boone taking Locke through the Sydney Airport in hopes of getting the man to realize Mr. Eko is in danger from a polar bear. It's good enough, but it's also over far too quickly.

Granted, suddenly spending the third episode of a season that already feels like it's running in place in an endless dream sequence might have been just the thing to get some portion of the audience to tune out for good. The solution "Further Instructions" lands on, however, doesn't really justify the dream sequence at all. Locke probably could have figured out that a polar bear had captured Mr. Eko without all the *Sturm und Drang*, and the ultimate plot resolution—Locke resolving to rescue Jack, Kate, and Sawyer—is one that is easy to see coming. And the less said about the utterly forgettable flashbacks, which only underline once again that Locke is a dupe, the better.

That said, it sure seems like Desmond can see the future now. So that's interesting! —*ESJ*

"EVERY MAN
FOR HIMSELF"
—

SEASON 3, EPISODE 4
ORIGINAL AIRDATE 10/25/06

On the Island: The Others trick Sawyer into thinking he has a pacemaker that will kill him if his heart races too quickly, successfully subduing him for a time. They then reveal to him that he, Kate, and Jack are on a completely different island, off the coast of the Island. Meanwhile, Jack tries to help Juliet save the injured Colleen—and gets a look at some X-rays of a spinal tumor in an unidentified patient.

In the flashbacks: While in prison, Sawyer rats out a fellow inmate to the warden, in exchange for a reduced sentence and a cut of the loot authorities recover. He sends his cut to the daughter he's just learned he has.

The Jack/Kate/Sawyer love triangle! Heavy sigh!

Without much else to drive the story in the first few episodes of Season Three, *Lost* has gone all in on the love triangle, to diminishing returns. "Every Man for Himself" is the episode in which Kate admits to loving Sawyer—granted, under duress, because Colleen's husband Danny is beating the tar out of Sawyer—but the moment feels like the faintest of exhalations. Right when this triangle should be crescendoing, with all three members held in captivity by master manipulators, all of the air is going out of the tires.

Lost can certainly come up with a great love story when it wants to, as we've seen with Sun and Jin, and Rose and Bernard. But this love triangle works best when the characters all have a lot of momentum and room to collide with each other recklessly. Now that all three of them are trapped—with Sawyer and Kate literally in cages—that momentum is nowhere to be found. When you begin to think about any two members of this triangle actually having a *relationship*, it becomes trickier to imagine.

Lost also isn't quite sure what to do with Sawyer at this point. It tried making him a more straightforward antihero in Season Two, but that read didn't really stick. Anytime it tries to set him up as a master con artist, somebody pulls one over on him that you'd really expect him to see through. Plus, now that actual master con Ben Linus is so central to the show, it's a lot harder to invest all that heavily in Sawyer's criminal skills.

Lost is in a rut where *too many* of its characters fall for cons that you'd really expect them to see through. How can Sawyer possibly believe a pacemaker has been installed that will cause his heart to explode if it exceeds a certain rate? Yes, the Others are a lot more technologically advanced than the castaways thought they were, but they don't seem capable of performing that level of surgery. "Every Man for Himself" just makes Sawyer seem a little unintelligent in the name of what's ultimately a lackluster twist. *Oooooh!* There's *another island*! Whatever. —*ESJ*

"THE COST OF LIVING"

–

SEASON 3, EPISODE 5
ORIGINAL AIRDATE 11/1/06

On the Island: Locke leads an expedition to a Dharma surveillance station, which ends in tragedy when the Smoke Monster kills Mr. Eko, who has been seeing visions of his brother. On the other island, Ben asks Jack to operate on his spinal tumor, while Juliet surreptitiously asks Jack to kill Ben while operating on him.

In the flashbacks: Eko's time as a priest is explored, as he essentially takes over Yemi's life. He comes to believe he owes Yemi "one church."

Mr. Eko's death is the first death on *Lost* that feels purely motivated by circumstances external to the show's storytelling. Yes, some of the deaths on *Lost* to this point have been motivated by a need to write an actor out of the show—especially Ana Lucia's—but those deaths have driven the storytelling in interesting ways. It's hard to say the same for Eko's death at the hands of the Smoke Monster, which mostly serves to make viewers fear ol' Smoky for slightly more tangible reasons.

Adewale Akinnuoye-Agbaje, who played Eko, found *Lost*'s filming locations in Hawaii to be too far away from his native England, leaving him feeling isolated. After he requested to be released from his contract, showrunners Damon Lindelof and Carlton Cuse convinced him to stick around for a few episodes in Season Three, to wrap up his storyline more satisfactorily. It's also easy to wonder if they were motivated by a desire to not kill off all three main Tailies in a handful of Season Two episodes. Eko's death getting pushed to Season Three somewhat alleviated that concern.

It's too bad. Eko is a terrific character, with one of the series' best backstories, and his foundational relationship with brother Yemi is the sort of story that *Lost*, a show lousy with bad-parent issues, could have used more of. Similarly, he is only the second Black man with a major role on the show, after Harold Perrineau as Michael, and the show wrote both off within the space of six episodes. (We're not counting Walt, who is, after all, a kid.) While *Lost* would add other characters of color going forward, it added no other major Black characters from this point.

That said, in a vacuum, "The Cost of Living" is one of the stronger episodes of this dreary stretch. Eko's flashbacks are always compelling, the sudden sight of a man in an eyepatch on a monitor in the Dharma station is a good jump scare, and the Smoke Monster's murder of Eko is one of the show's better visual effects sequences to this point. If Juliet's attempt to manipulate Jack into killing Ben by showing him a video in which she flashes cue cards at him makes no sense on a logistical level (how did she make this video without Ben knowing and/or how does she expect Jack to believe she made it without Ben knowing?), it's still a great sequence of visual storytelling. And, hey, now we know that the tumor Jack looked at in the previous episode belongs to Ben, which is at least *a* revelation.

Alas, "The Cost of Living" is overwhelmed by offscreen circumstances. *Lost* gave Eko a great arc, and the stories of many other characters end in death. "The Cost of Living" just doesn't make terribly clear why Eko's arc had to end that way. His death resolves nothing in his story and provides no further momentum for the overall plot. Obviously, death feels meaningless in life all the time—but it's rarely so meaning-less on *Lost*. —*ESJ*

"I DO"

—

SEASON 3, EPISODE 6
ORIGINAL AIRDATE 11/8/06

On the Island: Jack agrees to operate on Ben's tumor—after seeing on one of the Others' many monitors Kate and Sawyer cuddling after sleeping together. Yet when the time for the surgery comes, he nicks Ben's kidney with his scalpel, then calls Kate on a radio, telling her and Sawyer to make a run for it.

In the flashbacks: Kate's brief marriage to police officer Kevin ends when she starts to get itchy to go on the run again—even though the man pursuing her promised to lay off if she'd just stay put.

"I Do" found itself with the unfortunate task of standing in as a midseason finale at a point when Season Three had barely gotten started. ABC's decision to air *Lost*'s third season in two chunks *did* minimize the amount of time the show was off the air, but it also turned those first six episodes into an island unto themselves, which did them no favor. *Lost* builds momentum slowly, and nowhere is that truer than in the start of Season Three.

"I Do" *is* propulsive in its own way. The conclusion—Kate insisting she can't leave Jack behind with the Others, even as he tells her she must—makes for a good cliffhanger, and the episode wraps up a handful of plotlines in a mostly satisfactory fashion. Kate and Sawyer finally having sex (in a cage, no less) takes a little pressure off the love triangle storyline, and the burial of Eko on the other side of the Island offers a quiet coda to the beach camp storyline. Also, genre TV superstar Nathan Fillion turns up as Kate's ex-husband in the flashbacks. It's hard to get mad at that.

Where "I Do" turns sour is in how it handles Kate, as so often happens on this show. The episode ostensibly centers on her, yet she is almost entirely a reactive character throughout. Can she be a good little housewife? Will she choose Jack or Sawyer? Will she run when Jack tells her to? Even when Marshal Mars tells her he'll stop pursuing her if she just stays with Kevin, it's framed as him clicking his tongue and shaking his head at Kate's inability to just settle down and be some guy's wife, instead of constantly going on the run.

"I Do" arrives smack in the middle of *Lost*'s attempt to reframe Kate's whole storyline as being about her fear of commitment, but that reframing always seemed like a bad misreading of what made the character so compelling in the first place. Does she have commitment issues? Maybe! But a person who tries to kick her way through every wall because she's running away from something usually has something very big to run away from. *Lost* gave Kate that very big something, in the form of the crime she committed back in the States, then seemingly lost track of it across Season Two. Now, she exists mostly to pick a handsome man to sleep with. The show hasn't quite failed her, but it feels like it's running out of stories it wants to tell about her. —*ESJ*

DOCTOR, DOCTOR

"NOT IN PORTLAND"

—

SEASON 3, EPISODE 7
ORIGINAL AIRDATE 2/7/07

Lost is the kind of show where on any given week the backstories can take place anywhere in the world—and so the episode's cold opens are often fiendishly clever in their misdirection. Think of "Man of Science, Man of Faith" and "A Tale of Two Cities," both of which start in spaces that look pleasant and normal—non-Island-y, in other words—before the frame expands and we see that we've been on the Island the whole time. *Lost*'s writers loved to put the audience in Charlie's shoes, asking, "Guys, where *are* we?"

"Not in Portland" flips that shtick. We open on Juliet, sitting on a beach and crying. She enters some kind of official-looking facility with flickering hallway lights, where she walks past Ethan, the Other who embedded himself with the Oceanic 815 survivors. "Not in Portland" is preceded by six episodes mostly set among the Others at the Dharma Initiative's Hydra station. Viewers are clearly meant to believe that we're still grinding away on Hydra, with Juliet.★

But no! This is actually Miami, where the episode's flashbacks take place. This is the first *Lost* episode explicitly dedicated to a character who—at this point in the story at least—sides with the "villains." And while the episode as a whole doesn't clarify whether Juliet is really "good" or "bad," it does establish her as one of *Lost*'s most sympathetic characters: a smart, compassionate woman who has a sardonic sense of humor about all the times in her life that she's been lied to and manipulated. Like Desmond in Season Two, Juliet joins the story late and immediately becomes someone fans care about more than some of the original 815ers.

In Season Three's first six episodes, Juliet is a bit of a mystery woman, sometimes coming across as a potential ally (or potentially more) to Jack, while other times appearing more beholden to the Others. Sure, before the midseason hiatus Juliet asks Jack to kill Ben Linus during surgery. But who's to say that this request isn't some kind of trick?

The Juliet we meet in Miami is very different from the steely, scheming woman we first see on the Island. Before she became an Other, Juliet was taking care of her sick sister Rachel (Robin Weigert) while doing advanced, off-the-books research on fertility treatments. She was more emotionally fragile then, after years of seeing her work and her life controlled by her ex-husband and boss, Edmund (Željko Ivanek). But then her research captures the attention of the secretive company Mittelos Bioscience.† She tells the Mittelos recruiter, Richard Alpert, that the only

---

★ On the official *Lost* podcast episode that accompanied the airing of "Not in Portland," Carlton Cuse both echoed and gently spoofed fans' frustrations with how Season Three began, saying to Damon Lindelof, "Are we *done* with that frickin' island? Are we *done* with the Hydra station? Are we *done* with Alcatraz?"

† "Mittelos" being an anagram for "Lost Time" (just as Ethan's full name, Ethan Rom, is an anagram for "Other Man").

way she can get clear of Edmund is if he were to get hit by a bus. And then guess what? Edmund gets hit by a bus.

When *Lost* returned from its Season Three hiatus with "Not in Portland," the episode proved there was still a lot of life in this show. The episode matters to the mythology, both for introducing Richard—originally meant to be a one-off character, until Lindelof and Cuse became enamored with Néstor Carbonell's portrayal—and for firmly establishing something only hinted at before: that the Island plays havoc with women's reproductive systems.

But it also matters because *Lost* is a very dude-heavy show, with a lot of episodes focusing on a moody doctor with a brusque demeanor, a hero complex, and daddy issues. And then here comes Juliet, also a doctor and also very complicated, but with a different energy.*

The Island scenes in "Not in Portland" follow up on the midseason cliffhanger, in which Jack once again defies all the conventions of medical ethics by nicking Ben's kidney and demanding that the Others let Kate and Sawyer escape before he sutures it back up. What follows is a tricky power struggle. Who's in charge here? Jack, who could let Ben die? Juliet, who flatly gives the order to get Kate and Sawyer back, dead or alive? Ben's right-hand man Tom Friendly (M. C. Gainey), who has a lot of sway over the Others? Or Ben himself, who is still semi-conscious on the operating table?

The action is even more intense outside the OR, as the escaped Kate and Sawyer scramble to find a way off Hydra island, with the help of Ben's adopted daughter Alex. In pursuit? One of the meanest of the Others, Danny Pickett (Michael Bowen), an arrogant bully who doesn't need to be told twice that it's OK to kill the 815ers if he gets a clean shot. While dodging Danny, Kate and Sawyer find time to help Alex free her boyfriend Karl (Blake Bashoff) from the freaky "Room 23," where he's being tormented with loud music and flashing images and messages. (Pertinent sample: "God loves you as he loved Jacob.")

The point of all this—besides delivering an exceptionally entertaining and exciting hour of television, of course—is to emphasize just what

---

* The *Lost* writer Elizabeth Sarnoff said in the "World of the Others" Season Three DVD featurette that it was also important to establish early in Season Three that Ben Linus has lots of underlings and not all of them are happy with his leadership.

this crazy Island does to its inhabitants. Among other things, it seems to free them from any inhibitions when it comes to hurting or even killing other people. While freeing Karl, Kate calmly advocates shooting one of his captors in the knee. When Danny gets the drop on our heroes as they finally reach their escape boat, Juliet swoops in and shoots him dead without a second thought.* Then she forbids Alex from leaving Hydra, knowing Ben wouldn't want her to go. All the brutality in the first six episodes of the season are a bit exhausting, but they do start to pay off in this episode, as everyone's abominable behavior—on both sides—raises questions about how different life on the Island might be if everyone could be just a *little* less uptight.

Instead, it's a never-ending maelstrom of violence. At the center of it all in this episode is Juliet, a character viewers had just met a few episodes earlier but are already fully invested in. She's a character who in her former life used to smile a lot and try to take care of everyone . . . until the Others dragged her to the Island, and turned her cold as hell. —*NM*

"FLASHES BEFORE YOUR EYES"

—

SEASON 3, EPISODE 8
ORIGINAL AIRDATE 2/14/07

On the Island: Desmond's seeming ability to see the future is explored, complete with a dire prophecy for Charlie: No matter what anybody does, Charlie is going to die.

In the flashbacks: A lengthy flashback that nearly takes up the entire episode sends Desmond back to the dissolution of his relationship with Penny

---

* Elizabeth Mitchell, in the "World of the Others" featurette, said she thinks Juliet's motivations are simple: "The most important person in her life has no idea where she is. So she'll do anything to get off the Island."

after the explosion of the Hatch seemingly sends his consciousness back in time. He tries to stop himself from breaking up with Penny, only to realize that the universe has a certain way it needs events to proceed.

"Flashes Before Your Eyes" is one of the very best episodes of *Lost*, and it's an episode that bodes well for the rest of Season Three. It shows the series loosening up, stretching its muscles, and getting ready to enter a long run across the back half of the season.

To this point, the series has experimented slightly with how it presents flashbacks—notably in Season Two's "Maternity Leave" and "Three Minutes"—but "Flashes Before Your Eyes" is the first episode to treat the flashback as the meat for almost an entire episode. What's more, outside of Desmond and Charlie (who pops up both on-Island and in the off-Island flashback as a busker singing Oasis's "Wonderwall"), the episode barely features any of the characters. The doomed romance of Desmond and Penny, so central to the wonderful Season Two finale, returns here with even greater pathos.

Sneakily, the episode also replants the show in thematic territory it loves to explore but via a different angle. From its earliest episodes, *Lost* has been fascinated by questions of fate and free will. Did the Island *want* these people to come to it? Or do they still have a say over their actions? "Flashes" takes this approach and expands it to include all of time. If you can suddenly see the past, can you change that past? And if you can't, does that mean you were always destined to live out events in a certain way? That the series weds this idea to a story of two people who probably belong together but just can't figure things out gives the episode an emotional heft that dovetails with the show's thematic ambitions. "Flashes" is a really, really good episode of television.

That "Flashes" arrives when it does in the show's run is part of what makes it such a jolt to the system. Though *Lost* is in a period where it's groping in the dark just a bit, "Flashes" is the kind of episode only a TV show very confident in its ability to tell the stories it wants to tell could make. It's as though the show suddenly found a light switch in "Not in Portland," then used this episode to start to take stock of the room it was in.

We're not out of the woods yet—the next episode is near universally hailed as the very worst one—but we can at least see the tree line. —*ESJ*

THE BEGINNING
OF THE END

"STRANGER IN A STRANGE LAND"

—

SEASON 3, EPISODE 9
ORIGINAL AIRDATE 2/21/07

"Stranger in a Strange Land" has the unfortunate reputation of being the single worst episode of *Lost*. Even co-creator Damon Lindelof has singled it out as a stinker, and it routinely lands at the bottom of both critics' lists and fan polls.

Here is the part where I would love to tell you that this episode's reputation is unearned, that it is, in fact, a secretly solid episode of television, like, say, Season Two's "Dave." Alas, no. The reputation of this one is well-earned. Yes, it's *Lost*, and even bad *Lost* is better than a lot of television. But it's clearly a *Lost* running on fumes.

Intriguingly, "Stranger" comes after "Not in Portland" and "Flashes Before Your Eyes," which offered one of the better one-two punches of episodes that the series ever had. The episodes that follow "Stranger" are similarly scattered with gems. In general, the second half of Season Three is perhaps the show's strongest stretch, which makes "Stranger" stand out even more.

Yet the qualities that make "Stranger" so bad are what lead to the second half of the season—and the last three seasons of the show—making such dramatic shifts in storytelling rhythms, pacing, and quality. "Stranger" is the end of a certain kind of *Lost*, and it marks the beginning of a new version of the show, even if that might not become clear for several episodes. Sometimes, you need to reach the nadir to figure out what it takes to start climbing again.

The central problem with "Stranger" stems from its flashbacks to when Jack got his tattoos. For one thing, we don't really need an answer to the question "Where did Jack get his tattoos, and what do the Chinese characters in them mean?"[*] The answer, clearly, is "Well, a tattoo artist gave them to him," and that's, indeed, the answer to the question, even as *Lost* attempts to fill the moment when tattoo needle meets skin with dread portent.

If this moment revealed something new about Jack, we might be more forgiving of its superfluousness as a mystery. Instead, however, it serves as the latest in a long line of examples of Jack Shephard being a sad, desperate man who had lost control of his life. This time, however, Jack's (literal) bad trip involves a weird twist of Orientalism and a truly unfortunate performance by guest actress Bai Ling[†] as Achara, the woman who becomes Jack's lover and tattoo artist.

In and of itself, Jack being the universe's punching bag can work. It has been able to keep even other mediocre Jack-centric episodes afloat. The show gets some leeway in depicting how bad Jack's life was pre-Island— the savior complex that motivates him there is driven by all of those terrible experiences. It also introduces a ton of tension to the idea that he's so devoted to getting *off* the Island[‡]—what does he really have to return to?

"Stranger," however, offers a narrative cul-de-sac for Jack to wander into. We learn nothing much about him from his time in Thailand, his tattoos add nothing to either the Island mythology or his character arc, and the whole thing comes with a healthy dollop of "Wow, Asian countries sure are mysterious and menacing!" Eventually, Jack leaves Thailand, and there's little reason for him to have been there.

Again, the show has survived bad flashbacks before, but what makes "Stranger" so tough to bear is that the on-Island action similarly feels stuck in a rut. Though Sawyer and Kate have escaped the Others' offshore mini-island, the episode mostly concerns itself with how they're

---

[*] Perhaps marking the period the show was made in, when audiences weren't particularly exposed to non-English-language shows and a series like *Lost* could feel free to just make things up, the translation of those characters offered in this episode is not what they mean at all. Which is, y'know, not great!

[†] At that point in time an up-and-coming star and, as such, a get for the show.

[‡] Or says he is. Remember: He wanted to bail on the beach and go to the caves way back in Season One.

going to rejoin the other characters, a thing we know they must do for the show to keep going. Again, *Lost* has made "How are the characters going to do the thing we know they will?" interesting many times in the past, but in this case, they mostly discuss whether to take a boat or walk, then enter the ten thousandth argument about whether Kate will choose Jack or Sawyer to take as her lover.

Similarly, the Others decide to pack up and return "home," to their little suburban neighborhood in the middle of the Island. They decide to take Jack with them. Ben continues to recover from surgery. Juliet continues to feint toward joining Jack's side more completely but maintains just enough plausible deniability to give the writers room to turn her into a villain should they so choose.

In TV writing, an "up-and-back" is a story where the characters go on some sort of adventure, then return to exactly where they started. To be clear, most TV writing consists of up-and-backs because television loves a status quo and will do anything to return to it. At its best, however, TV writing disguises minimal plot momentum due to something significant changing in the characters or the setting.

For a *Lost* example, the show opens the Hatch, only to destroy it many episodes later, returning the characters to the status quo from Season One, more or less. In so doing, however, the series builds a space where the characters could examine their own relationships to the Island and where lots of Island mythology can be unpacked. The Hatch isn't the show's best storytelling hour, but it certainly gives the show far more than the Others' mini-island does.

The worst up-and-backs, however, expend a lot of energy on convincing you important things are happening when, really, nothing is happening at all. The end of "Stranger," which features a montage of the characters going back to the places they started out from, having barely changed at all, leans heavily on Michael Giacchino's score to make it seem like Big Things Are Happening, but we who are watching know nothing is happening at all. It's such a hilarious disconnect between text and subtext that it might be tempting to throw in the towel on the show at this point.

All TV shows have bad episodes. Indeed, the very best shows to ever have existed often have some of the rottenest episodes of all—see "Christopher," *The Sopranos*—because if you're taking big shots, you will sometimes miss horribly. What's most telling about a series isn't how bad its worst episodes are, however. It's how the show recovers from them. "Stranger in a Strange Land" is a bad episode of television, and the many, many angry reviews that landed in 2007 weren't wrong to throw up their hands in frustration.

Yet what marks *Lost* as the kind of show we're writing a book about twenty years later is the fact that its showrunners took this exact episode to ABC and said, "Hey, we need to start thinking about how to wrap this show up," and in so doing, they changed TV history.* Now, with twenty years of hindsight, I can safely assure you the show has nowhere to go but up. —*ESJ*

"TRICIA TANAKA IS DEAD"
—
SEASON 3, EPISODE 10
ORIGINAL AIRDATE 2/28/07

On the Island: The string of bad events that have befallen the castaways leads Hurley to hope they could just get a tiny win. He decides that win could take the form of an ancient, run-down Dharma van he finds in the jungle, which he, Sawyer, Jin, and Charlie decide to fix up. That they are able to buoys all of their spirits.

In the flashbacks: Guess who else has father issues? It's Hurley! His father, who left when Hurley was a kid, returns after his son wins the lottery, and things don't go particularly well.

"Tricia Tanaka Is Dead" is another terrific episode of *Lost* but in a very different mode from "Not in Portland" and "Flashes Before Your Eyes." As Season Three has explored some darker and darker territory, the gentle stories of beach camp life, of the survivors trying to make the best of a bad situation, have largely filtered out of the series. "Tricia Tanaka Is

---

* More on this as we reach the season's end!

Dead" isn't the very last time the show will tell that type of story, but it does feel a little like a farewell to lower-stakes storytelling for the series.

"Tricia Tanaka Is Dead" is also one of those episodes lots of fans grouse about. It is, after all, about Hurley and his friends fixing up a van at a time when Jack is still being held captive and when they don't know if the Others will be coming to destroy them. Shouldn't they be out trying to explore the many mysteries of the Island? Shouldn't they be seeking answers to the big questions that plague them? If you are of the opinion that these characters should largely be there to service the plot, then, yeah, this episode probably drives you bonkers.

Yet what made *Lost* so great was its desire to try to be all TV shows to all people at once. That could give the series a shaggy dog quality that didn't always work, but it also meant that the series could go from a dense sci-fi story like "Flashes" to something gentler and more comedic like this. *Lost* is a character-driven show in the sense that whatever character is at the center of each week's episode determines what kind of story the show will tell. And with Hurley, it simply wouldn't make that much *sense* to tell a dark story about Island mythology.

There are things to quibble with. The flashbacks' implication that Hurley's disordered eating can be traced directly to one encounter with his dad is preposterous, and of all characters, Hurley probably didn't also need to have a heaping helping of father issues.

But try not to be moved when Hurley, Charlie riding shotgun, gets the Dharma van's engine to turn over, narrowly avoiding splattering themselves against some rocks. Try not to be just a little enthralled at the use of Three Dog Night's "Shambala." Try not to feel the weight of Hurley insisting that there *is* no curse. Regardless of what you think of "Tricia Tanaka Is Dead," *Lost* might be the only show in TV history that could have made this episode at all. And that makes it all the more special. —*ESJ*

"ENTER 77"
—
SEASON 3, EPISODE 11
ORIGINAL AIRDATE 3/7/07

On the Island: Sayid, Locke, Rousseau, and Kate come to a farmhouse with a satellite dish on its roof, where they meet Mikhail, a man wearing an eyepatch who claims to be the last living member of the Dharma Initiative. He's an Other, of course, and after a series of clashes, the group extracts valuable information from him. But before Sayid can call the outside world with the satellite dish, Locke unintentionally blows the farmhouse up.

In the flashbacks: Sayid's past catches up to him while he's working as a chef in Paris. A woman he meets claims he tortured her in Iraq. Eventually, he begs her forgiveness, and she gives it.

"Enter 77" is meat-and-potatoes *Lost*, but it's very good meat-and-potatoes *Lost*. Though it checks in on the beach camp a few times—mostly for a ping-pong match between Sawyer and Hurley—it's far more occupied with the tense showdown between the castaways we already know and the mysterious Mikhail Bakunin, whose motivations aren't immediately clear. But this is *Lost*. *Of course* he's an enemy.

Buried perhaps a little too deeply in Season Three is an examination of the ways that revenge and violence ripple outward from their source, something that directly drives both the Island story and the flashbacks in "Enter 77." The Others took Claire, then Walt, from the castaways, and since then, the two sides have been locked in an escalating game of tit for tat, one that threatens to turn deadly yet again multiple times in this hour.

Lest that sound too heady, "Enter 77" also features some fights, Locke playing computer chess, a possibly magical cat, and even more weird remnants of the Dharma Initiative, an organization that seemingly prided itself on making everything as complicated as possible. If you want to contact the outside world, you have to defeat a computer at chess? Sure!

Yet by centering this episode on Sayid, *Lost* considers if there are ways to break the cycles in which we become trapped. The woman he hurt in Iraq has her husband revisit that hurt on Sayid, but she eventually accepts his apology. So, when Mikhail begs for death in the jungle, Sayid stays his hand. Yes, being able to interrogate Mikhail might gain the castaways valuable intel, but the series also frequently uses Sayid to present the idea that we are *not* defined by our worst actions and that we can find ways to transcend them and break cycles of violence.

The last several episodes of *Lost* have been more good than bad, but episodes like "Flashes Before Your Eyes" and "Tricia Tanaka Is Dead" felt ever so slightly un-*Lost*-like. "Enter 77" isn't as good as either of those episodes, but it is a straight-ahead episode of *Lost* that captures some of that Season One vibe. This show is very much back on track. —*ESJ*

"PAR AVION"
—
SEASON 3, EPISODE 12
ORIGINAL AIRDATE 3/14/07

On the Island: Claire spies a group of seagulls and thinks she might be able to attach a rescue message to one of them. Desmond keeps foiling her plans. Elsewhere, Locke and company reach a strange set of pylons in the jungle. When they push Mikhail through, blood trickles from his ears, and he seemingly dies. They find their way past the barrier and into the Others' camp—where they see Jack playing football with Tom Friendly.

In the flashbacks: After a horrible car accident puts her mother in a coma, Claire is surprised to find the man paying the hospital bills is her father— none other than Christian Shephard.

Of the still-living castaways from the Season One cast, viewers know the least about the past of Claire Littleton. Only one episode prior to this one (Season One's "Raised by Another") covers her time off the Island, since her Season Two episode ("Maternity Leave") had an on-Island flashback. From her earliest scenes, Claire's existence within the show has been tied inexorably to her son, Aaron. Yes, the characters are all thinly sketched types in the early going of Season One, but the show eventually deepens most of them, and it kills off the ones it isn't sure what to do with. Except for Claire. She was pregnant, and then she was a mom, and that's about it.

"Par Avion" aims to rectify that mistake. Its flashbacks delve into Claire's troubled relationship with her mom, and they reveal that she was a bit of a goth before she became the sunbeam of a woman we know and love. They also confirm that Christian Shephard is her dad, making her Jack's half-sister, something fans of the show had been speculating about for some time. They're frequently moving in a way many Season Three flashbacks haven't been, simply because Claire is still a character we don't know much about.

And the on-Island story has . . . very little to do with those flashbacks.

To be fair to "Par Avion," we're in a stretch of the series where the brewing showdown with the Others demands more and more plot focus, so events at the beach camp often get pushed to the side. And Locke and company's trek through the heart of the jungle to the Others' barracks is filled with great moments, especially the surprisingly gross fate of Mikhail, who seemingly has his brain evaporated by the Others' "barrier." (Locke's irritation when everybody blames him for killing Mikhail—when he had no way of knowing the Others possessed a "sonic weapon fence"—is very funny.) And the concluding image of Jack playing football at the barracks is a great way to welcome the character back into the storyline. (Jack hasn't been around since "Stranger in a Strange Land." Did you notice?)

Yet even at the beach camp, Claire's clever plan to capture a bird and tie a message to its foot gets shunted aside in favor of Desmond's ongoing attempts to save Charlie's life. Even in what might be her single best episode to this point, Claire continues to be most defined by her boyfriend and her baby. Maybe we shouldn't have expected more. —ESJ

THE DEFENESTRATION OF JOHN LOCKE

"THE MAN FROM TALLAHASSEE"

—

SEASON 3, EPISODE 13
ORIGINAL AIRDATE 3/21/07

Terry O'Quinn won an Emmy for his performance in "The Man from Tallahassee," the Locke episode that effectively ends the character's off-Island flashback story—and with a literal bang, too, as we finally get to see the moment when Locke became paralyzed, after getting pushed out of an eight-story window by his father. Both halves of this episode are excellent.

On one level, this is the same as every Locke story, in that it's about a poor schmuck who keeps getting his ass handed to him by life off the Island, while on the Island he feels a sense of power and connection and righteousness that he wishes his fellow castaways respected more. But on another level, "The Man from Tallahassee" is about how there really is no difference between off-Island Locke and the one who struts around paradise, talking about faith. No matter where he ends up, Locke is a born sucker.

Throughout *Lost*, O'Quinn strikes a very careful balance with Locke, playing him as a sap, a seeker, and a capable man of action, all at once. Different sides of Locke dominate at different times, but none is ever completely absent (except in the later seasons, for reasons too spoiler-y to get into now★).

★ O'Quinn was a trouper throughout the run of *Lost*, but he has said at times that he wasn't thrilled about what ultimately happens to Locke in later seasons. This

On the Island, Locke has joined Kate and Sayid on a mission to rescue Jack, which ultimately ends with Kate getting captured and Sayid—who spends an awful lot of *Lost* in shackles—getting chained to a swing set by the Others. And Locke? He sneaks in to see Ben, who is still recuperating from his surgery in a comfy Dharma house with a fridge full of Dharma food. Locke holds Ben at gunpoint and grills him for info about the Others' whole setup, and how they can come and go from the Island. Ben then tries to regain the upper hand by telling Locke just how much the Others know about all the 815ers—and by telling his people to go fetch "the Man from Tallahassee," who will be waiting for Locke in the "magic box" that Ben says can bring people whatever they most desire.

Given the explosive havoc Locke unleashed at the Flame station in "Enter 77," there's little mystery surrounding what he plans to do when he arrives at Otherton with Kate and Sayid on their rescue mission. Locke's not especially passionate about saving Jack. He's more interested in destroying the submarine that Mikhail told them about, to continue his own mission cutting off the Island's contact with the outside world.

What's interesting is the reason Locke gives for his radicalism. He calls Ben a "pharisee" who doesn't deserve what the Island has to offer. He also mocks Ben for being stuck in a wheelchair and healing slowly, using Ben's condition as proof that he, Locke—a paralyzed man who walks around freely on the Island—is the true chosen one.

And on the Island, even as he's blowing up the sub and pontificating about spiritual communion, he pauses to apologize to Alex, somewhat sheepishly, for manipulating her into helping him, after she walks into Ben's quarters during Locke's siege. One of the major recurring themes of *Lost* is what it takes to be a good leader/father/guru, and Locke's one of the most fascinating cases over the first few seasons, because he tries so hard to get by on a not-always-compatible mix of fanatical confidence and democratic benevolence. Mostly, he defines himself by what he's not: not his father Cooper, not Jack, and definitely not Ben.

episode illustrates why he might've become frustrated. Here, he has so many notes he gets to play, both in the flashback and on the Island, making Locke a much more rounded character than he even is on the page. And later? That dimensionality disappears.

153

Michael Emerson always did his best work on the show in his scenes with O'Quinn. The two actors delivered their lines to each other with a mix of smugness and self-doubt, shifting from scene to scene—and often with a fine comic snap. (Example: When Locke asks if "man from Tallahassee" is a code, Ben hilariously replies, "No, John, unfortunately we don't have a code for 'There is a man in my closet with a gun to my daughter's head' . . . although we obviously should.") The Locke/Ben dynamic is richer than the Locke/Jack, really; because the "man of faith"/"man of science" roles for Locke and Jack are a little too broad to produce more than a frustrating stalemate. Ben and Locke are so alike, though, in so many ways: both connected to the mystical properties of the Island, and both overcompensating for crummy childhoods. The difference is that Locke's an idealist and Ben's a cynic, which is why it's so fun to watch him control Locke just by dangling the two things he *thinks* he most wants: to expose Ben as a phony, and to learn the secrets of the Island.

In the flashback scenes of "The Man from Tallahassee," meanwhile, Locke has a somewhat cocky edge even when he's in the process of being duped by his dad yet again. The pre-wheelchair Locke meets a man named Peter Talbot (played by Patrick J. Adams, soon to be famous as one of the stars of the legal melodrama *Suits*), whose mother is about to marry Locke's father Anthony Cooper. Locke pays a visit to his father to persuade him not to ruin another family with his swindling ways. The result of his efforts? Peter turns up dead, and Cooper pushes Locke out of a very high window.

"The Man from Tallahassee" is the rare Season Three episode that uses the flashbacks to answer one of the audience's lingering questions. There was a lot of frustration from fans with the flashbacks at this point in the series, as a direct result of how compelling the Island storylines had become. In the weeks just prior to this episode, we'd met Mikhail and seen the Sonic Weapon Fence; and here Ben promises to Locke that he can "show you things I know you want to see very badly." It's almost like Ben's talking directly to *Lost* fans. After two-plus years of mostly teases, *Lost* started piling up the mythology in the back half of Season Three (with so much more still to come).

This is also one of the rare episodes in the entire run of *Lost* that directly—as opposed to just thematically—connects the past and the present, via a mind-blowing final scene that reveals the title character.★ As if the shot of Locke being pushed out of a window weren't enough of a "holy crap" moment, the final revelation of what Ben has brought to the Island in his "magic box" for Locke—the actual Anthony freakin' Cooper!—is a devastating stunner. Not only does Cooper's surprise appearance suggest something awesome and ominous about the power of the Island, but it also throws an unexpected roadblock in Locke's path to glory. He had a plan. Those plans have now changed.

On a week-to-week basis, the first few seasons of *Lost* deliver a lot of "this may be the way out . . . nope, it's locked" mini-arcs; here one of the main purposes of the on-Island plot is to take away an escape route, by eliminating the sub. But it's still a very exciting hour, from the intense rescue action to the almost playful Locke/Ben banter—and then the ending elevates what the whole episode has been about. Locke knows what he wants, Locke is on the verge of getting what he wants, and then Ben throws him—and us—a curveball by saying, "Or you could go for what's behind door number three . . . It's your dad!" —*NM*

★   This is a standout episode for Michael Giacchino, whose score at times is half Bernard Herrmann and half John Williams, effectively capturing both the suspense and the sense of derring-do at play here.

SICK, TWISTED, AND AMAZING

"EXPOSÉ"

—

SEASON 3, EPISODE 14
ORIGINAL AIRDATE 3/28/07

Perhaps only the *Lost* finale is as controversial an episode of the show as "Exposé," the closest thing the show has to a love-it-or-hate-it episode until the series finale. The episode exists solely to sweep a storytelling mistake under the rug, it has almost no bearing on the show's larger mysteries, it seems at time to be poking fun at the series it belongs to, and it ends on one of the nastiest twists in the show's entire run.

Also: It *rules*. Count me firmly in the "love it" camp.

"Exposé" only exists because of an oft-uttered question about the first two seasons of the show: Was the audience ever going to get to know the many random castaways who wandered around the background of shots? The show had added a handful of recurring characters from this general pool of people,* but never any new series regulars. On a show that needed to pull off the magic trick of seeming like everything was planned from the start (even if it wasn't), abruptly adding new characters who'd been there all along might have felt like a cheat.

Still, after the show had killed off two of the three main Tailies in Season Two and was about to kill off the third, it behooved the series to add new characters in *some* way. Enter Nikki and Paulo, two castaways who had supposedly been there from the very beginning, even though the audience was just meeting them now.

As played by Kiele Sanchez and Rodrigo Santoro, they spent the first half of Season Three wandering around and butting in on conversations

---

* Most memorably the eventually dynamited Leslie Arzt.

with the main characters, who seemed to treat them as either confusing glitches in the matrix or folks who had always been there. Why are you asking if they've always been there? Of course they have! "Exposé" has Sawyer take the "Who are these people?" approach and Hurley take the "Of course we know these guys!" approach. These conversations arise after they believe Nikki to be dead. Even the castaways we know and love aren't sure why Nikki and Paulo are here.

It didn't have to be this way. *Lost* kept introducing new characters, and it had a surprisingly strong track record at coming up with characters who stuck, especially compared to similar shows of its level of popularity and acclaim. Even characters like Ana Lucia, who weren't fan favorites and exited the show relatively quickly, left some sort of mark upon the series or had their fans. Even more common were characters like Juliet, who immediately carved out a space for themselves among a crowded ensemble.

What's notable about these characters is that the writers followed the natural inclinations of both the actors and the audience. Elizabeth Mitchell keeps turning in quietly compelling work? Give her more quietly compelling stuff to play. Though Juliet joins the cast as a brand-new regular, the audience discovers her alongside the characters, which lets the audience feel subtly like it has chosen to add her to a story it already knows, rather than having been made to care about her.

Not so with Nikki and Paulo. From their earliest appearances in Season Three, it feels jarring to have new characters suddenly hanging out on the beach we know and love, acting not just as if they've always been there but also as if they've been a part of the entire story so far. It might be one thing if enough of the original castaways had died to necessitate pulling from a "B-team" of passengers we just hadn't seen before, and if Nikki and Paulo stepped into that role to serve their own ends. But the show instead shoved Nikki and Paulo into an already-crowded ensemble, and it was not helped by Sanchez's and Santoro's performances, which are slightly more arch and detached than the norm on the show at that point, much more in line with the performances of the by-then–departed Ian Somerhalder and Maggie Grace (both of whom guest star in this episode's flashbacks).

When the series was at the peak of its goodwill from the audience (probably somewhere in early Season Two), it probably could have gotten away with adding two new characters in this fashion. But the audience had viciously turned on *Lost* by this point in Season Three, and it was obvious that the show simply needed to cut bait and move on. By the time the writers had committed to "Exposé," it had become clear that Nikki and Paulo were not working as characters, and it was clear the audience had rejected them. Therefore, the series chose to give them a deeply memorable exit.

"Exposé" plays as a strange hybrid of an old "Crime Doesn't Pay!" comic book combined with a bunch of classic *Lost* moments scattered out across its running time like so many puzzle pieces. When it begins, it's already in meta-land, as Nikki is revealed to have been an actress playing a crime-fighting stripper whose character was killed off the show she had been starring on.* Already, the episode is telling you the normal rules of the show don't apply. Nikki is dating the show's producer, which turns out to be part of an elaborate long con† by her and Paulo (the producer's chef) to kill him and steal a bunch of diamonds. They hop a flight back to the US from Australia and crash on a mysterious island. Hijinks ensue.

Most of "Exposé" is an excuse to replay moments from *Lost* with Nikki and Paulo present, highlighting not the stuff we were told to pay attention to but the characters' hilariously inept venality. We are led to believe that the two discovered not just the crashed drug-smuggling plane but also a Dharma station long before any of the other castaways, but they chose not to say anything about either because what they cared most about was the diamonds. The subtext is clear: If you think the main characters are incurious and bad at solving the Island's mysteries, it could have been *so much worse*.

Many of the episode's other moments play out as a simultaneous satire of the show's first two-and-a-half seasons and an exploration of what the characters could have been doing with their time on a mysterious uncharted island if they weren't constantly going to war with various other factions. We get to meet Dr. Arzt's spider collection of

---

* It is not worth digging into too much here, but she is killed after she exposes Billy Dee Williams as the show-within-a-show's Big Bad, and I so wish *Lost* had made Billy Dee Williams a recurring villain somehow.

† OF COURSE IT DOES.

plot significance. We get to see Nikki and Paulo tag along on missions of great importance to the other characters that turn out to mostly be chances for them to try finding their diamonds. We even see Paulo spy on Ben and Juliet talking about how to take Jack, Kate, and Sawyer *and* revealing that Michael will be key to this plan. Does he care? Of course not. He's got his diamonds to find.

In the end, those plot-significant spiders paralyze Nikki and Paulo, but before either of them can explain the paralyzing powers of the spiders' venom to the other castaways, who believe them to be dead, they've been buried alive. A failed storytelling experiment at least goes out in a memorable, gut-churning twist.

There is a part of me that bucks against the ways that "Exposé" plays into some misogynist tropes. Nikki turns out to be a bit of a browbeater, constantly haranguing Paulo about finding the diamonds, while he's just a sweet guy who wants to keep his girlfriend happy. Yet when you consider the episode via the lens of the noir genre, in which Nikki fits somewhat uneasily as a femme fatale, much of what "Exposé" does clicks into place. These two think they're in one kind of story, but they're actually in a very different one, where a literal magic Island can mete out karmic justice. And if you think you're in a noir, the last place you want to be is anywhere that can mete out karmic justice.

At any rate, lots of fans hated "Exposé," but in the 2020s, it almost plays as a strange nostalgia piece. Yes, it fails to advance the story's plot at all, but it's a nasty little poison pill of an episode that has no reason to exist other than to toss some dark, acidic twists out there for you to groan and laugh at. It's a reminder of a time when TV seasons were so long that they *had* to do a couple of episodes like this each season, and those episodes were usually memorable. After all, if you've seen "Exposé," love it or hate it, you surely remember it. That is its own testament to the episode's power. —*ESJ*

"LEFT BEHIND"

—

SEASON 3, EPISODE 15
ORIGINAL AIRDATE 4/4/07

On the Island: The Others prepare to leave, and Locke goes with them. They leave behind Kate and Juliet, who wake up handcuffed to each other in the jungle. They make their way back to the Others' barracks, evading the Smoke Monster all the while, then find Jack and Sayid. As they set off for the beach camp, Jack says Juliet is coming along—to Kate and Sayid's concern.

In the flashbacks: Kate, on the run from the law, attempts to contact her mother, despite heavy police surveillance, with the help of Cassidy, Sawyer's former lover and the mother of his child.

"Left Behind" could lean into so many of *Lost*'s worst tendencies when it comes to telling stories about women. Indeed, at one point, Kate and Juliet get into a fight in the middle of a jungle rainstorm. Later, they get covered in mud. Shades of *Dynasty* catfights abound!

Yet "Left Behind" remains thoroughly aboveboard throughout, possibly thanks to the work of episode director Karen Gaviola, one of just three women to ever direct an episode of *Lost*. (She also helmed Season Two's "The Whole Truth," making her the only woman to direct more than one episode of *Lost*.) Every time the action between Kate and Juliet might turn tawdry, Gaviola instead makes it visceral.

That fight in the rain isn't shot in a way that will titillate but, instead, in a way that makes clear how brutal and terrifying it might be to suddenly be raining blows down on a woman you're handcuffed to. When Kate dislocates Juliet's shoulder, you *feel* it, and the second the Smoke Monster turns up, the episode forgets anything a lesser show might have tried to make sexy about this core premise.

Gaviola's direction isn't the only thing working in "Left Behind's" favor. Damon Lindelof and Elizabeth Sarnoff's script offers the rare Kate episode where the flashback and on-Island action seem to be in conversation with each other. In both, Kate must team up with a woman she might not otherwise trust, and in both, she continues to hold the other woman at arm's length, even when she might be better off letting go and trusting another person for once. Also, the implication that Kate's "you deserve better, girl" pep talk to Cassidy is why Sawyer—whom Kate had never met at this point—ended up in jail is one of the better examples of the series creating little entanglements among the castaways before they ever reached the Island.

Kate's inability to commit to any relationship is a theme *Lost* returns to again and again, but it's at its most interesting when the show explores the ways her fear of commitment impacts her relationships with other women. Then, the series can dig more into her complicated relationship with the mother who betrayed her, choosing her husband (who abused Kate) over her own daughter. It's a knotty relationship, and you get why Kate might not *ever* trust Juliet, no matter the circumstances.

Kate episodes get a bad rap from *Lost* fans, mostly deservedly. "Left Behind" is a reminder that she's a richer character than the show often lets her be—especially when you get her away from the love triangle that had come to define her. —*ESJ*

"ONE OF US"

—

SEASON 3, EPISODE 16
ORIGINAL AIRDATE 4/11/07

On the Island: Juliet joins the castaways at the beach camp just in time, for Claire is suddenly ill. Though few other than Jack trust her, Juliet is able to find an Others' medication stash, and she successfully treats Claire, grudgingly earning some trust. However, as the flashbacks reveal . . .

On the Island (several years ago): Juliet arrives on the Island and is quickly made aware that pregnancies do not end well there. She becomes Goodwin's lover, and she ultimately is left by Ben to infiltrate the beach camp—where he will cause Claire to become sick that so Juliet can cure her.

At a certain point with the Others, don't you just want them all to stop sextuple crossing each other?

"One of Us" is another strong episode in a strong section of the series, one where *Lost* seems to be building some serious momentum as it approaches the final third of Season Three. It is also the episode that makes abundantly clear just how much more exasperating the Others would be if Juliet and Ben were played by anyone other than Elizabeth Mitchell and Michael Emerson.

By this point, Juliet especially has been (deep breath) an Other who was actually on Jack's side, but at Ben's behest, but who allied with Jack against Ben and was abandoned by the Others to join the beach camp, except she was also doing *that* at Ben's behest. It's dizzying!

The danger in any story that is this enamored of confidence games is that the audience will stop caring what's true because there will have been so many double crosses and reverses that it eventually becomes exhausting to track who's playing who to what end. This danger is particularly acute in television, where there's no set endpoint for viewers to look toward to help make sense of the mess.

TV, then, requires actors who have really good poker faces, and Mitchell and Emerson have some of the best. "One of Us" especially gives Mitchell a chance to put hers to the test. That final reversal—Juliet curing Claire was all part of Ben and her plan to win the castaways' trust—would likely have made viewers utterly give up on the character if a less capable actor were playing her. Mitchell, however, continues to skate across the rapidly thinning ice as though nothing is wrong.

Perhaps this episode works because the flashbacks give us our first real glimpse into how the Others operate. Juliet's arrival on the Island and her slow, grudging acclimation to having been, essentially, kidnapped make for compelling drama, and her connection to her sister back on the mainland marks her as another of just a handful of *Lost* characters who aren't defined by parental junk. When Juliet sees her sister for the first time in three years on one of the Others' fuzzy monitors, Mitchell plays the hell out of it. The emotions carry you through the more complicated twists and turns.

All of this is to say: "One of Us" really shouldn't work, but it does. Somehow, *Lost*'s confidence game has yet to fall apart. —*ESJ*

"CATCH-22"

—

SEASON 3, EPISODE 17
ORIGINAL AIRDATE 4/18/07

On the Island: Desmond receives a jumbled series of visions once again involving Charlie's death—but also potential rescue. He gathers a small group to try to better understand his visions, and they see a helicopter crash into the ocean but also what might be a person jumping out of it. Once again, he saves Charlie's life before the group encounters a parachutist stuck in a tree.

In the flashbacks: The show explores Desmond's time as a monk and his ultimate flame out. On his way out of the monastery, however, he meets Penny.

Lost has a mode of flashback you might call the "So it turns out that . . ." flashback. For example, Season Three's "Further Instructions" contains a flashback in which it turns out that Locke once worked on a hippie commune/secret pot farm. It's a flashback that doesn't really add to the character or the show's mythos in any way but does let the series enter a new location for a few scenes that week, which isn't always a bad thing.

"Catch-22" might be the ultimate flashback in this style. Did we really need to see Desmond's time as a monk, especially since he so quickly flunked being one? Probably not! But "Catch-22" needs to give us a more traditional Desmond flashback—as opposed to the revelatory "Flashes Before Your Eyes"—so we get one where his time as a monk, flailing away at the eternal, is contrasted with his genuine prophetic gifts on the Island. Sure!

"Catch-22" is the weakest chapter of a particularly strong stretch of *Lost*, but it has plenty of good qualities that keep it a cut above average.

The episode's virtues include the opening sequence, which smartly turns an overused TV storytelling device inside out. In it, Desmond leads his little expedition through the jungle, only for Charlie to trigger one of Rousseau's traps and die of an arrow to the throat. At first, it might seem like an in medias res opening, where an episode starts with a hugely dramatic moment, then goes back in time to see how the characters got to that point. Instead, however, we're watching *Desmond* experience an in medias res opening—or, rather, a vision. He knows how the episode is going to end, and he has to stop that from happening, which he successfully does.

The third season has also been very smart at deploying smaller groups of characters to tell stories with, then mixing and matching tried-and-true character pairings within them. Desmond, for instance, recruits Charlie and Hurley for his expedition, and by now, we know very well how those two play off each other. However, adding both Desmond and Jin to their dynamic increases the fun. Even as the action on the Island gets more serious, *Lost* is figuring out ways to keep things lively.

So, yes, the flashbacks feel staler than usual, especially when you consider that they're for Desmond, the character with the highest flashback batting average. That's hard to hold against an episode with so many other good qualities and another great cliffhanger ending at a point when the show has basically perfected the form. Who's that parachutist? You're going to have to tune in again to find out. —*ESJ*

"D.O.C."
—
SEASON 3, EPISODE 18
ORIGINAL AIRDATE 4/25/07

On the Island: Juliet takes Sun to the Others' medical facility to determine if her baby was conceived prior to her arrival on the Island. If the child was conceived on the Island, then Sun's life is in danger. If it wasn't, then the father is not Jin. Meanwhile, an unexpectedly alive Mikhail helps Desmond's expedition treat the gravely wounded parachutist.

In the flashbacks: An old woman who claims to know Jin's mother was a sex worker blackmails Sun, knowing Jin's parentage would be seen as shameful in Sun's upper-class world.

Once again, as *Lost*'s momentum starts to pick up, the show turns to Sun and Jin to take just enough of a breather to prepare for the final plunge. There are a lot of good Sun and Jin episodes; this is one of the best, thanks to a delicate, lovely performance from Yunjin Kim.

Sun finds herself trapped in a situation where she's damned either way, and Kim plays the nuances of her position perfectly. Her tears when she learns that her baby was conceived on the Island perfectly modulate joy and terror—joy from her learning Jin is the father of her child, not a circumstance of her affair; and terror in knowing that conceiving and giving birth on the Island surely cannot end well.

Bringing Juliet in as a foil for Sun also proves to be a terrific move. Both women have a great degree of latitude within the very narrow range of options their social orders have presented to them, which is to say they can make just about any move they like, so long as it's a lateral one.

Many of the flashbacks have suggested Sun is quite capable of duplicity and deception, but her open-hearted warmth on-Island make this easy to forget. Freed from the expectations of being her father's daughter, Sun can finally be the woman she wants. Where Juliet had a relatively high level of freedom off-Island (at least as much as any woman can hope to have), she's found her range of options on-Island greatly reduced, which has sent her into the same spaces of trying to manipulate events to her own advantage—the position Sun occupied off-Island.

"D.O.C.," of course, says none of this overtly, but the scenes between Sun and Juliet have a tenderness and warmth to them that the show needs as the main story grows ever darker. The audience surely has a sneaking suspicion by now that Juliet will end up playing for "the good guys" in the long run. If the show pulls that card, then it will need to get there by allowing the character to change and grow, through moments like Juliet just getting to do some facsimile of the job that brought her so much joy off-Island without Ben Linus breathing down her neck.

And, of course, balanced against all of this is the fact that someone *did* get to the Island who hadn't been there before—even if she's fighting for her life. Who is this parachutist Desmond and his team might save? Well, she sure seems shocked to find survivors of Oceanic 815. Wherever she came from, authorities found the remains of that plane—and everybody on it was dead. —*ESJ*

"THE BRIG"

—

SEASON 3, EPISODE 19
ORIGINAL AIRDATE 5/2/07

On the Island/In the flashbacks: In another episode with on-Island flash-
backs, the series explores Locke's time with the Others since he left with
them in "Left Behind." Ben brings Locke's horrible father to the Island
and bids Locke to kill the man, but he can't do it. You know who might be
able to, though? Sawyer, whose life was also ruined by Locke's dad.

"The Brig" is another tremendous episode of *Lost*, one of the best the
show made. It's a dark and grimy episode, and it takes seriously the idea
that the castaways might all be dead. When Locke's dad, Anthony
Cooper, tries to convince both his son and Sawyer that they're dead and
in Hell, well, do you really blame him?

Have we just been watching these characters navigate a particularly
horrible afterlife? It seems unlikely, but "The Brig" might give you pause.
As an audience member watching now, who knows there are three seasons to go after this one, you'd surely know that it's unlikely *Lost* would
drop an answer this big halfway through its run, yet the last two episodes make a real run at "They were dead all along" as the ultimate
answer to all that's happened. If the real Oceanic 815 was recovered, then
who are all of these people? And if Locke's dad doesn't remember how
he got to the Island beyond a car crash, well . . . maybe he's dead, too?

The scenes set in the Black Rock—where Locke has tied up his
father—play with the grim intensity of a particularly nasty stage play.
Both their limited physical space and their limited cast (only Locke, his
father, Sawyer, and Rousseau factor into this story) ramp up the claus-
trophobia in a way that *Lost*, with all its sweeping vistas, rarely comes
close to pulling off.

The Locke flashbacks also go a long way toward filling in some of the
season's storytelling gaps. Many of Ben's actions snap into place once you

understand Ben's spent the season playing a series of games meant to (a) get Jack to treat his spinal tumor and (b) keep Locke from so impressing the Others that he threatens Ben's position. The strange, obfuscatory qualities of the Others continue to *exist*, but the audience can see through them a little better now.

At their most opaque, the Others felt not like human beings but like enemies in a video game; after the last few episodes, and especially after "The Brig," they make more sense as a community of people so steeped in odd ritual and relentless paranoia that they're unable to trust anybody anymore. The Others were not *born* that way; they've been shaped by the man leading them. Were John Locke to lead them, they might find a new way forward, or so Richard Alpert seems to hope.

Finally, "The Brig" rights the course for Sawyer, a character who has felt adrift for two seasons now. Sawyer has killed before, and he's done terrible things. Yet he's also one of the show's most popular characters, which means that he can never be in *too* much danger. "The Brig" pushes him into a situation where we want to see him commit murder—because Locke's dad is a terrible person and because we want Locke to be able to return to the Others, which he can only do with the body in hand—but also shows the terrible intimacy of that murder, so he can be repulsed by what he's become. Sawyer's antiheroic qualities redound against him, and he ends up vomiting in the woods. It feels, for the first time in a while, like *Lost* has a handle on him as a character. —*ESJ*

NOTHING UP HIS SLEEVE

"THE MAN BEHIND THE CURTAIN"
—
SEASON 3, EPISODE 20
ORIGINAL AIRDATE 5/9/07

Ben Linus was never a joiner.

After his mother Emily (Carrie Preston★) died, Ben's father Roger (Jon Gries) dragged him to the Island to join the Dharma Initiative, where the two men were treated as outsiders, more suited to manual labor than to joining the organization's grand social and scientific experiments. So, a surly Ben started exploring on his own, and got to know the Island natives that Dharma dubbed "Hostiles." Later, he helped these Hostiles exterminate the Dharma bums—and eventually became their leader.

But does he ever actually believe anything they believe? Is he just using them as a way to wield power? Or is some larger force using him?

"The Man Behind the Curtain" is an all-time great *Lost* episode—thrilling, surprising, alarming, and loaded with lore. It nods to the series' *Wizard of Oz* obsession, toys with the fans' anxiety that the big mysteries of the Island will turn out to be another "long con," and—perhaps most importantly—addresses the question of who's in charge here and whether they deserve to be. After years of teases, the show finally starts giving the faithful much of what we'd been waiting for. That this episode aired the same week as ABC's announcement that *Lost* would end after Season Six only added to fans' sense of the series moving ahead with real purpose.

★   Michael Emerson's real-life wife! This is either a very sweet bit of trivia or a some-what creepy one.

The present-day story begins with Locke arriving in the Others' traveling camp, having followed Ben's order to bring back the corpse of Anthony Cooper and now demanding that Ben explain the Island's whole deal. Ben responds that the real boss—the man with all the answers—is someone named Jacob, whose name had popped up here and there in earlier *Lost* episodes but who at this point had yet to be formally introduced or even described. But Locke's not buying it, saying to Ben, in a direct reference to *The Wizard of Oz*, "You are the man behind the curtain." In the 1939 movie *The Wizard of Oz*, an ordinary man, hiding behind a curtain, uses stage magic to pretend to be an all-powerful wizard. So here is the Big Question: Does Ben know anything about the power he commands as the Island's forward-facing representative, or does he just know how to fool people into believing he does?

There are two crucial "oh wow" moments in the Locke/Ben storyline. First, Ben leads Locke to what looks like a serial-killer cabin, inside an ominous-looking circle of ash. There, he gestures to an empty chair, where he says Jacob is sitting. But just when Locke calls Ben "crazy" and is about to leave, the cabin starts rocking, and Locke—and Locke alone—hears a voice whispering, "Help me." But what/who exactly is Locke hearing? And why doesn't Ben hear the same thing? (Because the producers knew fans would scrutinize this scene via their DVRs, they made sure to fill the screen with bits of imagery that suggested a human person is in that cabin without showing him in a recognizable way.)

We'll get back to the second big moment, because it ties into what this episode reveals in its flashbacks, which cover the adventures of Young Ben Linus (Sterling Beaumon). The flashbacks are cleverly structured, with every scene taking place on the same date—Ben's birthday—in different years. It's an origin story no one expected, showing Ben as a kid growing up alongside Dharma. But it's a story fans needed. Previously, the Dharma Initiative and its relationship to the Others had been revealed in dribs and drabs, via the occasional orientation video or a stray piece of writing in the rusted-out remains of what Dharma built. But here we're immersed in Dharma-iana: the jumpsuits, the vans, the Apollo bars, and the world-saving optimism. We even get a new orientation film, explaining the existence of "the Hostiles" and how the Dharma compound is protected by the "Sonic Weapon Fence" that we saw in "Par Avion." For fans who'd been gobbling up every tiny clue to the history of the Island, here suddenly is a banquet.

The bulk of "The Man Behind the Curtain" is about where Ben came from, but it's telling that in the present day Ben reveals almost none of it to Locke. He does confess that he's been lying to everybody (except Richard, who met him as a kid) about being born on the Island, and he does show Locke the mass grave full of Dharmans that he and the Others gassed to death. But only the viewers learn about Annie, the little girl Ben had a crush on when he first came to the Island; and only we know that Ben grew up with a jerk of a father and that he spent most of his youth nurturing an animosity toward Dharma before he destroyed them. In other words, the tragedy of Ben Linus remains his secret, even though Ben does show Locke two key pieces: the mysterious home of an invisible man, and the site of a mass execution. The former Ben barely understands. The latter he understands all too well—as he proves when he shoots Locke and leaves him for dead in that pit of corpses.

Which brings us back to that Big Question: Who is "the man behind the curtain"? Is it Ben, who at the least appears to be in control of what happens on the Island, if he doesn't know why? Or maybe Richard, who helped put Ben in that position? Or whatever the hell was in that cabin—an entity that appears to be confined against its will?

"The Man Behind the Curtain" exemplifies *Lost* doing its best job of repurposing the preexisting and giving it new meaning. Just consider the Dharma van where Ben has his last conversation with his father, "Roger Workman." Introduced in "Tricia Tanaka Is Dead" as just something else weird and inexplicable on the Island, the van here becomes a poignant symbol of Ben's lousy childhood, and his ultimate betrayal of the people who raised him. This wasn't one of the big mysteries that people were waiting impatiently for the show to solve, and yet the writers came up with a satisfying explanation anyway, and one that no one would have guessed back when Hurley was trying so hard to get the van up and running again.

In a way, Ben himself is an example of *Lost* finding an unexpected use for something it already had on hand. Because Michael Emerson was so much fun to watch, the creative team kept expanding the role of "Henry Gale," until he became the leader of the Others (a character they'd reportedly only roughly conceived to that point, and certainly hadn't cast).* Similar to the late-arriving Desmond, Ben quickly became not just a fan favorite, but someone capable of carrying the larger themes of the show in more complicated, sophisticated ways. The "man of science"/"man of faith" dynamic of Jack and Locke can get a little reductive, but Locke's gullibility versus Ben's cynicism has a lot more to offer, especially given Locke's sense of disdain and moral superiority toward Ben. There's a cockiness to the way Locke deals with Ben, as though he sees right through him. And maybe he does! Perhaps not coincidentally, "Emily" is also the name of Locke's mother—sort of like how Superman and Batman both have moms named Martha. (Plus, judging by Locke and Ben's similar backstories, having a lousy childhood is a prerequisite for Island leadership.)

But this is where it pays off for Ben to frame so much of what he knows about the Island as esoteric woo-woo. He tells Locke that learning the truth is "not as simple as opening a dusty old book"—which is pretty convenient, because that means Ben can interpret the concepts of "Jacob" and "The Island" in whatever way will make him seem sage and plugged in.† Every day for Ben is new. He improvises, he scrambles, he lies . . . and somehow, he turns situations to his advantage. Locke's fundamental sense of decency makes it easy for a guy like Ben to subvert his will.

The soul of "The Man Behind the Curtain" is part Ben, part Locke. It spins a convincing yarn, but it also believes. This episode sees the significance of everything, from Dharma vans to spooky cabins in the woods. Nothing is exactly as it seems, or exactly as it's touted. There's always something else to peel back. —NM

---

*   Carlton Cuse, on the DVD commentary: "It's kind of hard now to imagine how we motored along for, you know, a season and a half without an antagonist on the show."

†   A case in point can be found in one of the deleted scenes for this episode, where Ben defends stealing Alex from Rousseau by describing her to Locke as a crazy woman who killed her research team and then disappeared into the jungle—which is not really the whole truth, but certainly sounds true-ish.

REQUIEM FOR A ROCK STAR

"GREATEST HITS"

—

SEASON 3, EPISODE 21
ORIGINAL AIRDATE 5/16/07

You do not have to stretch very far to argue that Charlie Pace is the reason *Lost* became a hit.

When the series debuted in 2004, Dominic Monaghan was all over the series' promotional materials, with good reason. Monaghan was fresh off Peter Jackson's massively successful *Lord of the Rings* trilogy, where he played the lovable hobbit Merry, and the movies' cultural footprint was then sizable. Yes, the first-season cast of *Lost* is full of actors viewers knew from other series and movies,★ but the thing Monaghan was best known for when the show debuted also happened to be the biggest thing in pop culture. It's impossible to know how many people watched *Lost* just because Merry the hobbit was in it, but it's surely a number larger than zero. And even if you had no idea what a hobbit *was*, ABC got so much mileage out of the clip of Monaghan saying, "Guys . . . where are we?" in the pilot that you still might have been prompted to watch because of him.

Yet across the run of the first three seasons, the series struggled to know what to do with Charlie, despite Monaghan's winning, impish performance. In the pilot, Charlie certainly seems like the third lead behind Jack and Kate, with the flashbacks to the plane crash paying special attention to his mad dash into the bathroom to snort heroin and the on-Island action making sure to keep him vaguely central to the action.

★   Matthew Fox had been in *Party of Five*; Naveen Andrews had been in *The English Patient*; Harold Perrineau had been in *Oz* and the *Matrix* sequels; and so on.

As Season One went on, however, the show struggled to think of what to do with the character. It returned to the addiction well a few too many times, and it turned his relationship with Claire into one of its romantic mainstays. But for much of his time on the show, Charlie was a character defined more by what Monaghan brought to him than what the show offered him to do.

Yet Monaghan's status as (still) one of the better-known actors in the cast and a fan favorite made it seem likely the show would never kill Charlie off, despite how much sense that choice might have made for the story. Thus, the storyline the writers came up with for Charlie in Season Three became a bit of a masterstroke. They simply pulled this metatextual conversation about whether Charlie could be killed off directly into the show's text. Desmond starts having visions of Charlie's death. Initially, he prevents said death, but the deeper the show gets into Season Three, the more the series suggests that Charlie *has* to die for the rescue of the castaways to be possible. It finally makes that plot point overt in "Greatest Hits," where Desmond says that Claire and Aaron getting off the Island depends on Charlie dying.

And yet you know how TV works! You know how much the fans love Charlie and/or Dominic Monaghan! You assume the series will figure out a loophole!

"Greatest Hits" is quietly a series finale for the first half of *Lost*. It doesn't seem like it is when you first watch it, but it serves as a reminder of how good the show could be in its "classic" mode. By this point, the writers were aware they were building toward the series' end, and they knew that the third-season finale would be the first big step toward that end. Therefore, "Greatest Hits" had to put a capstone on something more than the life of Charlie Pace.★ It also had to wrap up the show as it had been.

By this point, *Lost* had reenergized a lot of its most critical fans. The second half of Season Three is perhaps the best sustained stretch of episodes in the show's entire run, telling one coherent story that plays out with plenty of twists and turns. Mysteries are resolved, answers are

---

★ Who *doesn't* die in the episode, despite the show doing its level best to convince you he will. Even when Charlie seems pretty clearly doomed, *Lost* finds ways to keep you guessing.

offered, and still more questions are asked. It's the show operating at its very best. Except for one thing.

That one thing is the show's use of flashbacks, which have long since lost their potency and power to surprise. A handful of Season Three episodes feature strong flashbacks, but they typically involve characters whose backstories are still mysterious* or they completely change how the flashbacks operate.† After the show reveals how Locke ended up in his wheelchair,‡ it has run out of mysteries it can resolve in flashback, or ways to make them feel novel.

If you know anything about the Season Three finale, "Through the Looking Glass," you'll know the show found a solution to its problem. But one of the best things about "Greatest Hits" is how it *also* finds a way to inject new life into the flashbacks for Charlie, a character whose past already seems pretty well strip-mined. By using the flashbacks not to tell a continuous story but to highlight five specific memories that Charlie has from his life that he wants to hang on to in case he's about to die, the show takes something closer to a pointillist approach to the past. At their best, the flashbacks deepened characters or offered commentary on the on-Island action. "Greatest Hits" instead aims for something more poignant that nevertheless deepens Charlie's character and offers commentary on the on-Island action. If this man is about to die trying to help his friends get off the Island, then here are a handful of moments when he was glad to have been alive, both on- and off-Island.

If you'll permit a moment of editorializing, I was one of the *Lost* viewers who had long since lost patience with Charlie, and if you had told me that the show would spend most of Season Three flirting with killing the character, I might have said, "Oh, do it already!" Yet by the time "Greatest Hits" rolled around, I found myself hoping the show would continue to find improbable ways to keep Charlie alive. The episode ends with him completing an impossible underwater swim and gasping for breath when he comes back up for air, and I thrill every time.

Thus, "Greatest Hits" stands in for one other quality that made *Lost* so good where other shows that followed in its footsteps could never quite

---

* The Ben-centric "The Man Behind the Curtain."
† The Desmond-centric "Flashes Before Your Eyes."
‡ In "The Man from Tallahassee."

compete: It was incredibly good at steering into the skid and turning its weaknesses into strengths. If a sizable portion of its fanbase wanted to see Charlie killed off and an even larger portion wanted to see him survive, well, the show's writers would simply make that Charlie's storyline for a season, waggling a finger in the Charlie haters' faces while saying, "Are you *sure* you want us to do this? Are you *sure?*" By the time "Greatest Hits" aired, I was no longer sure, even as I knew that the show had made a strong argument that he *had* to die. By giving me what I thought I wanted in the worst way possible, *Lost* had somehow gotten me on board with all the Charlie fans who would have been devastated if he had died back in Season Two.

It's easy for TV shows with high body counts like *Lost* to make death feel more than a little cheap. When characters become cannon fodder, it becomes easy to detach from *everyone* on the show, not just the characters who are killed off. "Greatest Hits" serves as a reminder that even fictional deaths have to feel like they belong to people who had full, rich lives that we can never know everything about because we are only seeing pieces of the whole. Charlie Pace isn't real, and I didn't actually know him. But "Greatest Hits" makes me feel like I did, and it prepares me to mourn his inevitable loss, no matter when it arrives. It's a triumph of TV craft, a celebration of how to take a whole bunch of problems a show might be having and then bundle them together into the same solution. —*ESJ*

A HAIL MARY
THAT WORKED

"THROUGH THE
LOOKING GLASS"
–
SEASON 3, EPISODES 22 & 23
ORIGINAL AIRDATE 5/23/07

It is a little reductive to say "Through the Looking Glass" was the finale that saved *Lost*. After all, the show had already been renewed for its final three seasons a few weeks before its broadcast in late May 2007. The show was going to finish out its story regardless.

It's difficult to overstate how groundbreaking this deal was. In TV's past, the network would have forced *Lost* to run itself into the ground. The deal to save *Lost* was a major turning point in TV's evolution toward the idea that serialized shows should have definitive endpoints that are planned for in advance, and ABC's willingness to explore the idea when the show was still a top twenty hit was unusually forward-thinking.

Yet even though the *business* side of saving *Lost* had been hammered out, the series still had to win over a bunch of its biggest skeptics. Creatively, it had yet to make the case that it deserved to be saved. The second half of Season Three had won back some fans, but many watched the series with arms crossed over their chests, a scowl on their faces. They wanted the show to prove itself to them, and "Through the Looking Glass" was *Lost*'s big gambit to win those viewers back.

It's a bit of a miracle that it worked. I can't think of another time in TV history when a show called its shot with this much on the line and then hit the home run.

Consider this: Two of the most iconic moments in all of *Lost*—"Not Penny's Boat" and "We have to go back!"—occur within the same half hour of this episode and perfectly hit the target the show needs to hit. If the finale had just one of those moments, it probably still would have been seen as a success, but with both, it became one of the most acclaimed episodes of the series *and* one that so skillfully shifted the show's paradigm that even its biggest skeptics had to applaud.

So, let's consider those moments in isolation and see how they work together to benefit the episode, the season, and the show.

NOT PENNY'S BOAT: If there's a moment from the series that begged to be turned into a meme, it was Charlie holding his hand up against the window of a flooded room, the words NOT PENNY'S BOAT scrawled on it. You could imagine any number of other things written on that hand. Wouldn't that be fun to mock up and post online?

It would, and plenty of folks have done so. But "Not Penny's Boat" endures because it neatly knits together a bunch of things the show does really well—emotional character beats, big plot reveals, resolutions to long-running story threads, and introductions of new mysteries.

We've been waiting most of the season for Charlie to die after Desmond said his death was inevitable, and the show has done an amazing job of keeping us guessing as to whether it would actually stay true to its word of killing the character. When it does, it maximizes the emotion to the hilt. For one thing, it involves Charlie and Desmond, the two characters tied up in this storyline. For another, it places them in a situation where they need to communicate but cannot, as they're sealed on either side of a thick bulkhead door, Desmond watching the room slowly fill with water. And when Charlie writes NOT PENNY'S BOAT on his hand and presses it against the glass, it's an emotional moment for Desmond on *multiple* levels, as he realizes that he's no closer to reuniting with his lost love. Henry Ian Cusick perfectly plays the moment where Desmond's fingers trail along the glass over Charlie's hand. He's wracked with guilt and horror and sadness and relief all at once.

On a raw plot level, however, the scene also introduces a brand-new mystery to the story: If that's not Penny's boat that's floating just offshore, then whose boat is it? Can we trust them? Why are they coming to the Island anyway?

That reveal heightens the on-Island action, which mostly wraps up the war between the castaways and the Others in a way that ratchets up a new kind of tension: Naomi, the woman who arrived from the freighter, says she's there to rescue them. But is she? When Jack places his call to the freighter, is he actually dooming everyone on the Island like Ben and Locke say? Sure, Ben lies all the time, but Locke? And all the while, we know that the people Jack is about to call have nothing to do with Penny, a character we know and trust. It's perfect.

"We have to go back!": Up to this point, the superstructure of *Lost* has been one of slowly widening its scope on-Island. Yes, the flashbacks add an element of playing around with how time functions in the story, but by and large, we're watching the castaways slowly get to know the Island a bit better. There have been occasional scenes in the present set off-Island,★ but for the most part, when we're in the show's present, we're stuck in this one location.

Throughout "Through the Looking Glass," however, the latest round of miserabilist Jack flashbacks start to feel like they might be something different. For one thing, his beard is so thick. For another, he's overwhelmed by an obituary in the newspaper—but it's not for his ex-wife, who's very much alive. Finally, at one point, he becomes very obsessed with examining flight trajectories. Somewhere in there, you start to suspect that maybe the show isn't showing us the past. It's showing us the *future*. Then when a car pulls up to where a drunken Jack stands just outside of LAX and Kate gets out, you know. These characters do get off the Island, and it destroys their lives. They have to go back. It's an *amazing* reveal.

Shifting the flashbacks to flash-forwards is a smart move and an incredibly risky one. The show needs to start going off-Island for more of its storytelling. There are only so many variations on "There is a new group of people on the Island for the survivors to battle with" the show can pull off. It also needs to move beyond the increasingly confining straitjacket that is the flashbacks, which have run out of new things to say about almost all of the characters. And there's a whole growing mythology around the people who want to find the Island who aren't on it, often for nefarious reasons. That mythology has been building on the edges of the show, but wouldn't it be better to see it for ourselves?

The risk, of course, is that you turn off viewers who've gotten used to a version of the show that they like very much that *doesn't* involve

★ The final scene of Season Two, where two polar-region-located researchers working for Penny discover the Island's location, is an obvious example.

storylines taking characters off the Island. TV loves a status quo, and even if the show's first flash-forward promises that Jack wants to go back to the Island, the very idea they would get off to begin with absolutely destroys what still existed of *Lost*'s status quo. It's easy to imagine plenty of viewers hopping off the train at this point if the execution weren't pitch-perfect.

Yet the execution is pitch-perfect. Every little moment from the season—even ones that seemingly had little purpose, like Hurley fixing a broken-down van—adds up to a finale that feels both thrillingly conclusive and wildly open-ended for what might come next. At the end of "Through the Looking Glass," *Lost* once again feels like a show that can do anything it wants and somehow pull it off. —*ESJ*

FURTHER READING: FAILURES OF IMAGINATION: *LOST* AND NON-WHITE CHARACTERS

(Unlike most of the essays in this book, if you have never seen Lost and want to remain unspoiled, then you should perhaps skip this essay.)

In May 2008, after Michael Dawson had been written off of *Lost* for the second time, Harold Perrineau opened up about his frustrations with the show's handling of his character. Speaking to *TV Guide*'s Shawna Malcom, the actor underscored how badly he thought the show had served the relationship between Michael and Walt. Perrineau argued that the show's treatment of the character perpetuated a pernicious stereotype about absentee Black fathers.

"I wanted Michael and Walt to have a happy ending. I was hoping Michael would get it together and actually want to be a father to his kid and try to figure out a way to get back [home]," Perrineau told Malcom. "This is [the producers'] story. If I were writing it, I would write it differently."

The 2008 interview with Perrineau has become a sort of Rosetta stone for understanding the betrayal many *Lost* fans of color feel around how the show came to tell stories about non-white characters. Since *Lost* ended, several people of color involved in making the series have spoken openly about both the show's lackluster storytelling around non-white characters and the often racist experiences they had behind the scenes of the show, most notably in Maureen Ryan's 2023 book *Burn It Down*. While *Lost* was on the air, however, Perrineau's *TV Guide* interview was essentially one of the few times an actor involved in such a huge hit show criticized it even mildly.★

While the issues behind the scenes on *Lost* have now been well-documented, I was interested in the question of how those storytelling choices filtered out to the show's fandom. For the most part when the show aired, discussion was centered around white voices. When you look at contemporaneous discussion of Perrineau's comments, you see a fanbase seems irritated by the idea of someone questioning a storytelling decision the series made. The few fansites and blogs that dominated discussion of the show in May 2008 and that still exist—including some from major critics—largely wrote off Perrineau's frustration with the series as sour grapes at being killed off.

Now, however, as we† are more aware of racially insensitive and even racist storytelling on TV, the conversation around shows like *Lost*, which were seen as diverse at the time of their airing, has shifted. I talked to over a dozen non-white fans of the series for this essay, and the majority expressed some version of the same narrative. When the show debuted with one of the most diverse ensemble casts broadcast TV had seen to that point, these fans had at least mild hopes that it would tell stories about characters of color with more nuance than they'd seen at the time, a very low bar to clear in 2004. And then, the longer the show ran, the more the series' potential was squandered in this regard, the non-white characters largely being sidelined in favor of a series of heroic white guys and occasionally Kate.‡

Michael's death in Season Four's "There's No Place Like Home, Part 3," then, was a major moment that crystallized the split between the series' initial potential and its eventual execution. But it was a culmination

---

★ Perrineau is even more forthright in his criticisms in *Burn It Down*, including documenting his frustrations throughout the show's second season, as he attempted to get the producers to give more story to Michael in the wake of Walt's disappearance.

† By which I mean, let's face it, "white people." The issues discussed in this essay and elsewhere in this book *were* talked about during the show's run, but the voices raising those issues were rarely centered. To pretend these conversations are a recent invention is to flatter the present and ignore the ways in which TV discussion has traditionally been—and largely still is—driven by white voices, including mine.

‡ The show's treatment of women? Also troubling. See page 119.

of a trend that had been building for a while, not a sudden, out-of-nowhere betrayal. Similarly, a lot of these fans cited the events of Season Six's "The Candidate" in which three characters of color (Sayid, Jin, and Sun) die to save the lives of the white characters, with just a handful of episodes remaining until the show's finale—as a moment of supreme irritation with the show's treatment of its non-white characters.

Melody Simpson is the co-editor of the anthology *Writing in Color*. She came into *Lost* deeply skeptical of its ability to tell stories about Black characters, given the majority-white creative team. Still, she liked the show's storytelling style and loved many of the characters, and she found lots of friends in the incipient fandom. Yet all her cynicism about how the show might treat non-white characters proved to be well-founded.

"From the jump, I knew what was going to go down. I knew we were going to be pushed to the side, and boy, were we," Simpson said. "The problem is there was no depth in these characters and their layers. When you have one Black writer or one Asian-American writer, there's no way you're going to get that depth."

Andrea Zevallos watched the series live from its earliest episodes, and at the time, she felt glad to have any people of color on TV at all. When she revisited the series during the Covid-19 lockdowns, after studying media studies and screenwriting, she found her feelings around the series shifting.

"A lot of stories in their flashbacks were stereotypical and rarely to turn the stereotype on its head. It was, like, 'Here's a stereotype,' and that was it," Zevallos said. "I think expecting perfect representation is not the best way to approach [any TV show], but I was disappointed to revisit it and see how one-dimensional a lot of those stories felt compared to the white characters, who had multiple flashbacks and depths and were able to grow and change."

Think of it this way: *Lost* started with fourteen characters, and of those fourteen characters, the series' endgame largely boiled down to Jack, Locke, Kate, Sawyer, and Hurley. Of those five characters, only Hurley was a character of color. He and Sayid were among the few characters of color to ever be drawn into the main Island narrative, and even then, they would find themselves in the series' main plot only sporadically, when their roles of "happy-go-lucky nerd" and "tortured former torturer" specifically intersected with that main narrative. Other characters of color found themselves cordoned off into their own storylines, which rarely had any bearing on the larger storylines.

For instance, several fans I talked to pointed to the love story of Sun and Jin as being well-done—and breaking new ground for American television showing *anything* with subtitles. Yet they also pointed out how that love story was such that both characters mostly existed in a narrative cul-de-sac, where they might pop up to play a supporting role in one of the larger storylines but rarely drove that storyline forward on their own. Contrast this with, say, the Jack/Kate/Sawyer love triangle, which existed in tandem with the Island's mysteries and occasionally even drove the investigation of those mysteries forward, as in the infamous early Season Three episodes when the Others lock them all up in cages. Or perhaps even more significantly, contrast it with the Desmond and Penny romance, which connected with essentially every major story beat through the show's third, fourth, and fifth seasons.

Again, the Sun and Jin love story is one of the best stories in *Lost*. It's also a story that leaves both characters largely out of the spotlight for long stretches of the show's run and often separates them entirely, giving them even less story weight as individuals. That *Lost* could tell a whole bunch of different kinds of stories within its larger framework is part of what makes it such a good TV series, but it is worth noticing just how frequently those smaller stories were used to focus on the non-white characters.

Travis Bruggeman started watching the show with a lot of hope for the stories it might tell, and as a biracial person, he was excited to see Rose and Bernard, whom he describes as incredibly similar to his parents. Yet he also found himself wondering why the show seemed so uninterested in a character like Rose, one of the very first people to have a line of dia-logue in the entire show, to the degree that she would disappear for long periods of time. By the end of the show's run, Bruggeman had essentially stopped being a fan, finding the show's sidelining of his favorite characters—especially Sun, Jin, and Sayid—driven less by organic story-telling choices and more by how the show's fandom reacted to characters who weren't core to the show's mystery box stories.

"There would be weekly recaps and analysis of everything, and if a particular character's story wasn't building out the main mystery box, then this cottage industry of reviewers and recappers were a little hostile to the situation," Bruggeman said. "Since the mystery box almost never involved people of color, the stories of those people were never as important to the fandom."

Not every *Lost* fan I talked to has entirely turned on the show, and some even highlighted the show's ultimate treatment of Hurley as a bright spot within an otherwise lousy record. But even as I write these sentences, I feel myself indulging in a frequent tendency among white critics, to nod toward a show's most problematic aspects, then pluck out a few small highlights and say, "See? It wasn't *all* bad."

But to say "It wasn't all bad" is to let the show off the hook. It is possible to love *Lost* and accept that when it came to telling stories that would allow nuance to its non-white characters, it almost always fumbled the ball. White fans can, I promise, hold these nuances in our minds when revisiting the show or even thinking of it fondly. *Lost*, like all American television, was made in a country built atop long histories of systemic racism, misogyny, and queerphobia. And like all American television, it reflects those values all too often. To pretend otherwise is to turn a blind eye to far too many terrible things.

To pretend *Lost*'s failures were an inevitable offshoot of the time in which it was made is a blinkered perspective as well. Simpson points to one of *Lost*'s contemporaries to show how even TV at the time was telling these stories with more nuance. When *Grey's Anatomy* debuted in 2005, yes, its main characters were almost all white, but it had a large, diverse ensemble, and because the series was created by Shonda Rhimes, a Black woman, the stories of those characters were treated with more nuance than television usually afforded them at the time—and still affords them with now.

"It's one thing to have diverse characters on your show," Simpson says. "It's another thing to actually care about them and give them stories that aren't the same five stories we've all seen before." —*ESJ*

SEASON FOUR

FLASHING
FORWARD

Isn't it funny how something as simple as switching from flashbacks to flash-forwards could change the whole rhythm of watching *Lost*? By the middle of Season Three, fans were becoming less excited about getting "a Locke episode" or "a Jack episode." We knew more or less all we needed to know about every castaway. But in Season Four, the purpose behind each episode's little interludes became more focused again. We stopped learning about who these people used to be and started finding out who they were going to become.

Really, the whole feel of *Lost* changes beginning with Season Four. There are fewer episodes that are just about moving the pieces around a bit on the big board or about shading in minor details from the character's histories. From here on, the story starts barreling forward.

There are downsides to this. For all their lulls, Seasons One through Three do have a heft to them, such that when you reach their finales, you feel like you've been on a journey. Seasons Four through Six each zip by quickly; and there aren't a lot of ins for new viewers. *Lost*'s writers expected anyone who made it this far to be dedicated.

Yet aside from a few special episodes the rest of the way, Lindelof and Cuse never ditch the storytelling structure that makes *Lost* distinctive. This was always going to be a show where what happens on the Island has echoes in the outside world—in the past and into the future.

With Season Four, this allowed the writers to have some fun coming up with new kinds of stories to tell about the group they dubbed "the Oceanic

Six." The timeline in these episodes can be a bit confusing, but essentially, on the Island, the entire season is about what happens after Jack signals to the freighter offshore that the 815ers are ready to be rescued. What follows is a mad scramble, as the ideologically divided survivors—scattered across various locations—try to prepare for extraction, while dealing with a pack of new arrivals from the boat, who actually don't seem all that interested in saving them, because they have their own agendas.

The newcomers include

FRANK LAPIDUS (Jeff Fahey), a gifted and multi-talented pilot who is largely unaware of the larger issues at play and is primarily interested in keeping people safe.

DANIEL FARADAY (Jeremy Davies), a brilliant physicist with a tender heart and a fragile psyche.

CHARLOTTE LEWIS (Rebecca Mader), an anthropologist (and a love interest for Daniel) who has an unconscious connection to the Island.

MILES STRAUME (Ken Leung), a grumpy and greedy psychic who has his own secret ties to the Island and has his own secret agenda.

MARTIN KEAMY (Kevin Durand), a ruthless mercenary who is completely mission-oriented and has no stake in what any of the freighter's passengers are up to.

While telling the story of this ramshackle rescue operation—which actually doesn't take up too much on-Island time, even though it occupies fourteen episodes—this *Lost* season follows up on the shocking flashforward in the Season Three finale by showing what Jack and Kate and the other evacuees were up to in the outside world before a desperate Jack howled, "We have to go back!" It turns out that the Oceanic Six—Jack, Kate, Hurley, Sayid, Sun, and baby Aaron—do not have a happy homecoming. Wracked with guilt over those they left behind, and peppered with questions they can't answer honestly about what happened to them, they go from being minor celebrities to the subjects of skepticism and conspiracy theories. And this is before they cross paths with all those mysterious power players who have an interest in the Island and are watching the O6 closely.

Behind the scenes, Season Four was affected by a writers' strike in Hollywood, which cut the original episode order down from sixteen to thirteen (which ended up becoming fourteen after a two-part, two-hour finale was expanded into a two-part, three-hour finale). It's hard to say what Lindelof and Cuse would've done with the extra time, but in this season's breathless rush to the Oceanic Six exodus, there are definitely fewer quieter character moments on the Island—and a lot less mythology. (Season Five would make up for the latter lapse in a major way.) The decision to set an end date for *Lost* juiced up the storytelling, proving ABC's good decision.★

But the executives probably also congratulated themselves once they saw how Season Four's ratings started slipping. The show was still, by any reasonable measure, hugely popular; but it had begun to settle down into the level of a cult hit (which was about as good as anyone at ABC could've hoped for back in Season One).

It's possible to interpret *Lost*—lightly, mind you—as an expression of what its creators were going through during any given season. Any long-form artistic project can't help but be influenced by what is happening in the artists' lives during the making of it, even if the work itself was carefully planned out in advance. (And *Lost*, no matter what Lindelof and Cuse may have said at the time, was not as fully mapped out as fans hoped.) So, for example, in the first six episodes of Season Three, when the writers felt trapped by ABC's unwillingness to let them start moving toward the finish line, the main storyline involved Jack, Kate, and Sawyer in detention—and feeling miserable.

When it came to the mysteries of the Island, by Season Four Lindelof and Cuse had become a lot like Ben Linus, capable of tapping into the magic and wonder of this place to produce a spectacular effect, even if they didn't fully understand how and why it worked. They knew how to put buttons on episodes that would make audiences gasp and then scramble to their laptops to post theories on the internet.

There's a bit of a stalling tactic going on with this season, no matter how exciting the results. (And they are quite exciting.) These fourteen episodes essentially circle back around to a point in both timelines where fans already know they're headed: the Oceanic Six leaving, and the Oceanic Six making plans to return.

★   NBC's *Heroes*, the critics' darling of the 2007–08 network TV season—the show that many believed had learned from what *Lost* was doing wrong—ended its first season with a howler of a finale, followed by an even worse Season Two. That, coupled with the conceptual coup of *Lost*'s Season Three finale, proved how hard it is to do what *Lost* does.

But there are a few surprises in Season Four, including the appearance in the flash-forwards of two key people who are not part of the Oceanic Six: Ben and Locke. How and why they got off the Island has a lot—*a lot*—to do with the Island's mythology and the way *Lost* eventually ends. With all the pieces more or less where they need them to be at the end of Season Four, Lindelof and Cuse are ready to tackle Season Five: *Lost*'s wildest and most wildly entertaining season. —*NM*

"THE BEGINNING OF THE END"

—

SEASON 4, EPISODE 1
ORIGINAL AIRDATE 1/31/08

On the Island: The castaways divide into factions, with some waiting with Jack for the "rescuers" on the freighter to arrive and some following Locke to the barracks to prepare to defend against the invaders.

In the flash-forwards: Hurley struggles with the notoriety of being one of "the Oceanic Six" who returned from the Island, and he gets himself re-committed to a mental institution.

After the Season Three finale re-bent *Lost*'s narrative arc, Season Four's premiere revealed just how much of a fresh spark the new "flash-forward" gambit could offer. By the end of Season Three, the flashbacks were getting thinner and weaker. But the show's sudden flash-forwards gave a lot more for fans to dig into, beginning with some basic questions: Who left the Island and how? What happened to them after they returned? And what exactly led a bearded, drunken Jack to believe that leaving the Island had been a huge blunder?

These questions invigorate "The Beginning of the End," which introduces the concept of the Oceanic Six but does not tell us exactly who they are. We know about Jack and Kate, for sure; and the Season Four premiere focuses on Hurley, which is a bold and refreshing choice, given how often *Lost* anchors its biggest episodes to Jack and Locke. By making Hurley the lead here, the writers show the consequences of a Jack/Locke philosophical divide that—as the series plays out—will escalate into an increasingly violent and destructive battle.

In "The Beginning of the End," Hurley is haunted by what happened on the Island prior to his escape, and by whatever part he played in it. When Jack comes to visit him at the Santa Rosa Mental Health Institution—not so much to see if he's OK but to make sure he won't say anything damaging to the press—Hurley apologizes for siding with Locke and plants the seed of the idea that they all need to return to the Island, to fix their mistakes.

What mistakes? That remains to be seen. But back on the Island, Hurley offers his usual everyman perspective, as confusion mounts over whether the freighter folk can be trusted. Once Desmond reveals that Charlie is dead and that Penny didn't send any rescue party, Hurley makes the choice he later refers to at Santa Rosa, following Locke to the barracks rather than sticking with Jack at the beach. (Jack doesn't help his case when he steals Locke's gun and tries to kill Locke with it, only to find that the weapon is unloaded. Not exactly Good Guy behavior.)

As some of the confirmed Oceanic Six unexpectedly move further away from leaving the Island, it becomes clear that "What happened after Jack left?" isn't the only question Season Four has to answer. How these six castaways got back together and got off the Island is a mystery in itself. And how did it all hurt Hurley? That's the kind of question that gets fans invested on a deeper level. —*NM*

THE FANTASTIC FOUR

"CONFIRMED DEAD"

—

SEASON 4, EPISODE 2
ORIGINAL AIRDATE 2/7/08

Another new season of *Lost*, another new group of characters popping up on the Island. By now, this continued expansion could feel wearisome, even as we understand *Lost* has a fairly high body count.* Yet there's an even better reason for *Lost*'s continued expansion beyond needing more and more cannon fodder: With each new season, the show telescopes outward just a little bit more, and every new character helps with that expansion of scope.

Season Two's addition of the Tailies expanded both the size of the Island and its number of inhabitants, thanks to the way it bolstered the threat the Others posed. Similarly, introducing Desmond Hume brought a whole host of other parties with interest in the Island, from the Dharma Initiative to Charles Widmore. Season Three, meanwhile, made the Others into characters themselves, adding a healthy dollop of Island history and lore.

Season Four knits together the Island world and the "real" world. We know that at least some of the characters will be getting off the Island at some point in the near future, so we need everything off-Island to start feeling more central to the narrative. We also know that there are many interested parties on the mainland who want to exploit the Island for their own ends. What we need is a group of characters who can bridge both worlds.

Enter the freighter folk.

---

*   Though not nearly as big of one as shows that followed in its footsteps, like *The Walking Dead* and *Game of Thrones*.

"Confirmed Dead" is a terrific episode of *Lost*, continuing the break-neck pace the series has been on for several episodes by introducing not one new character but four *and* giving them all representative flashbacks. The episode starts with an undersea salvage crew discovering the "wreckage" of Oceanic 815, then lets us know just a bit about what the rest of the world has been up to since the crash, the sort of thing *Lost* just did not do to this extent in its first three seasons. The storytelling only gets more brazen in its shattering of the old rules from there.

Gone are the days when a new character got a full episode to fill in their whole deal. Now, we get to learn that Miles Straume (Ken Leung) can talk to ghosts (probably) and that Daniel Faraday (Jeremy Davies) is a brilliant physicist with a burden so heavy he can't stop weeping. We learn that Charlotte Lewis* (Rebecca Mader) dug up a Dharma polar bear in the desert, and that Frank Lapidus (Jeff Fahey) knows the sea-floor wreckage of Oceanic 815 is a fake because they show footage of the dead pilot's corpse on TV (?!) and he notices the man is not wearing his wedding ring. Lapidus knows that the *real* pilot *always* wore his ring.

Also, Matthew Abaddon (Lance Reddick), who was properly introduced in the previous episode, gains added layers of mystery here by hiring Naomi (Marsha Thomason) to head up the freighter team, then promising her there are no 815 survivors on the Island. She, of course, will immediately be killed by one of those survivors, shortly after landing on the Island, which only makes things more difficult for Jack and Kate when they attempt to ask Daniel and Miles to please get them off the Island, *no, for real.*

There are plenty of moments in "Confirmed Dead" that hit beats *Lost* has hit two or three times too many at this point. Does Ben really need to be threatened with death by another character, only to squirm his way out of things, yet again? Maybe not. But the episode takes a fantastic turn when Ben reveals that he knows Charlotte's name and everything about her—Ben knows *everything* about the freighter folk somehow?—and then goes on to name everybody else the audience has just been introduced to.

On a show like *Lost*, viewers will forgive a whole litany of sins if it feels like the plot has some sort of forward momentum. "Confirmed

---

* Her name is Charlotte Staples Lewis, making her C. S. Lewis, ha ha.

Dead" offers an example of this principle in action in basically every scene. By truncating all the freighter folk's flashbacks to single scenes, we get a potent sense of who they are as characters, even as the show leaves them plenty of room to grow. On the Island, their presence upends the tentative status quo struck at the end of Season Three, as the four end up scattered between Locke's group and Jack's group. Lives are threatened, desperate plans are launched, and now, there's a helicopter. How convenient for getting off the Island!

Furthermore, the new characters hasten *Lost*'s embrace of outright genre storytelling. Yes, the series has always included plenty of fantastical elements, but the four new characters all seem drawn from different genre archetypes. The theoretical physicist who understands more than he lets on, the haunted man who talks to ghosts, the professor studying the hidden secrets of human history, the ace pilot who can fly into and out of any danger—these are all archetypes we know from decades of genre fiction. Yet they're archetypes the show had not yet employed, which may be why they integrate into the story so easily where previous groups of characters have struggled to gain a foothold among the unwieldy ensemble.*

It's often difficult to find a quick and easy comparison point for *Lost* when trying to pin down which other stories it's most like. It feels a little like a mystery show (think *Twin Peaks*) but almost as much like a Stephen King novel (especially *The Stand*). "Confirmed Dead" and Season Four more generally reveal that the show's closest comparison point is "all of the above." If there's a genre-fiction trope the show hasn't deployed yet, it will find a way to blend it into its enormous, fantastical stew. If you tuned in for the early episodes about Island survival, tough. This is what the show is now. Take it or leave it.

That swaggering confidence leaves the overall impression that the show is operating at a peak level, rushing from strength to strength. Even when an individual scene or character motivation is dodgy, the series can push it over the finish line, thanks to its seeming belief that it can do anything it puts its mind to.

The sheer joy that is the start of Season Four couldn't have come at a better time for the show—or its medium. After the doldrums of early

---

* See also: the Tailies, Paulo and Nikki, and so on.

Season Three, it's thrilling to see *Lost* so thoroughly reinvigorated. More, the first eight episodes of Season Four aired at a time when almost nothing else was on TV, thanks to the 2007–08 Writers Guild of America strike, which made them feel even more exciting.

Lost was never a show content to rest on its laurels. It wanted to keep trying new things and expanding its storytelling sphere. Most shows—even shows that might ultimately prove more consistent than *Lost*—fall apart when they bite off more than they can chew, but *Lost* needs to take enormous bites to thrive. It'll worry about chewing later. For now, there's more pulpy storytelling to eat. —ESJ

PULP FICTION

"THE ECONOMIST"

—

SEASON 4, EPISODE 3
ORIGINAL AIRDATE 2/14/08

What genre is *Lost*? Science fiction? Adventure? Drama?

The answer is: Yes. All of those. Also, on some weeks: a domestic comedy, a medical melodrama, a history play, a romance, a horror show, or an ancient myth. And in "The Economist," an international spy thriller.

It's a special gift for Sayid (and Naveen Andrews) to get an episode like "The Economist," where he could use his suavity and military training to become "Sayid the Avenger: Skilled Assassin and All-Around Sexpot." Every one of the Oceanic 815 survivors—or at least the ones who became major characters on the show—could be called "tragic." They all have unresolved issues with their parents or siblings (or both), and nearly all of them have experienced some kind of traumatic death or injury . . . or just general misery. But one could argue that Sayid Jarrah—the man who became a torturer against his will and was then

193

separated from the love of his life—is the most tragic of all. He needed a showcase like this episode, to take his turn as an action hero (albeit a very complicated one).

When first we see Sayid off the Island in this episode, he is duffing his way across an exclusive golf course, waiting for his target: an affable Frenchman who starts to panic when he realizes that Sayid is one of "the Oceanic Six." And rightfully so, since Sayid immediately plugs him with a pistol.* Later, Sayid travels to Berlin and cozies up with Elsa (Thekla Reuten), a seemingly trusting young woman whom Sayid woos and beds in order to get closer to her employer, "an economist" whom Sayid means to murder because he's "on the list." Instead, he has to gun down Elsa, who it turns out was using *him* to uncover *his* employer. At the end of the episode, bleeding from a bullet lodged in his chest, Sayid stumbles into a kennel to have the bullet extracted by his handler, whom we all know better as . . .

Well, let's back up. On the Island, Sayid is also at the center of the episode's action. Determined to get to the freighter sooner rather than later, Sayid makes a deal with their pilot, Frank, to catch a ride on his helicopter in exchange for retrieving the anthropologist Charlotte from the clutches of Locke and his reluctant disciples. Sayid, Kate, and Miles travel back to the Others' barracks† . . . where they're ambushed by Locke's crew thanks to a good piece of decoying by Hurley.‡

Meanwhile, back at the helicopter, while Jack waits for Juliette to return from the beach with Desmond—so that Jack can ask why the freighter's initial emissary Naomi was carrying a picture of the wry Scot around—fidgety physicist Daniel Faraday performs an experiment with the help of his shipmate, setting up a beacon and asking her to send a small guided missile toward it. The missile arrives roughly half an hour after it's supposed to.

"The Economist" has a lot of layers. First, we start to feel the ramifications of the original castaways' split. With Kate imprisoned by her former lover Sawyer at the barracks and Hurley deceiving his friends in

* Apparently, he doesn't like it when people try to play through!
† As the *Lost* engineers once again make good use of the big Island playset they built for Season Three.
‡ Hurley, when Miles calls him "tubby" the first time they meet: "Oh. Awesome. The ship sent us another Sawyer."

order to prove his loyalty to Locke (a role Hurley hates to play, especially after he sees how undemocratic Locke is going to be), the title of this episode becomes almost like a metaphor, describing our heroes pulling out their figurative charts and graphs to do a little cost–benefit analysis. They'll make deals with any devils around, if that's what it takes to get what they want.

Nowhere is that more apparent than in the big final reveal of Sayid's off-Island employer: none other than Benjamin Linus, who in the episode's final scene lays a long line of jive about why Sayid needs to get back to killing as soon as possible, working down a list of potential victims whom Ben insists really need to die. (Ben, like his invisible boss Jacob, does so love to make a list.)

One other major point to ponder in "The Economist" is the result of Daniel's experiment.★ *Lost* theorists frequently speculated in the early seasons that maybe time moves slower on the Island; and this strange game of rockets-and-beacons seems to be a confirmation of that. Though only eighty nautical miles offshore, the boat is apparently located thirty-one minutes in the future.

Time may be moving differently off the Island too—again, at least in a metaphorical sense. How patient does Sayid have to be in order to get the information he needs from Elsa? By the time he kills her, they're already talking about "love" and making plans for their future. Their relationship has a whole arc that takes place during the three scenes we see of them: the one where they meet and flirt, the one where they go on a date, and the one where they try to kill each other. For Sayid and for the rest of the Oceanic 815 survivors, if there's something you want— that you *really* want—then you must be willing to live lifetimes while you wait. —NM

★   The experiment shakes Faraday up so much that he makes extra sure to tell Frank that when he flies off the Island to stay on the proper bearing.

"EGGTOWN"

—

SEASON 4, EPISODE 4
ORIGINAL AIRDATE 2/21/08

On the Island: Jack and Juliet get frustrated by the freighter folk's inability to communicate with their people back on the ship, while at the barracks Kate collaborates with Miles and they both earn Locke's ire.

In the flash-forwards: Kate stands trial for what she did before her Island adventures and is granted leniency thanks to Jack's testimony and her mother's forgiveness.

In terms of *Lost*'s overall story arc and mythology, "Eggtown" is mostly memorable for one scene: the climactic reveal of Claire's baby Aaron as one of the Oceanic Six, introduced to the world as Kate's child, delivered while the survivors were sheltering on a charted, non-mysterious island. As presented, the moment is weighted with import, with the implication that Kate's decision to claim Aaron as her own—and Jack's unwillingness to visit his nephew—is incredibly meaningful, for reasons that will become clear later in the series. Ultimately, that importance feels way oversold. But we'll get to that later.

In this episode, Kate's bond with Aaron ends up mattering just a smidgen, in that it illustrates both her own post-Island maturity and the way that the torturously twisted alliances forced by the Island's overlords have made concepts like "family" feel much more fluid than they are in the ordinary world. But the meat of the latter theme won't be fully cooked until the reality-bending shenanigans of Season Six.

"Eggtown" itself is more about how Kate in every timeline and location excites and irritates the men in her life. In the flash-forward, Jack lies his stubble off in the courtroom, protecting Kate by positioning her as the main hero of the O6, who helped keep the small handful of 815 survivors' optimism up until they found an island (not *the* Island) where they could shelter and regroup. He also labels her as someone he greatly admires but does not love. Later, privately, he admits to her that he does love her—which is when she springs her strange complaint about how he won't drop by to see Aaron. Meanwhile, on the Island, Kate helps Miles get an audience with Ben so that Miles can offer to save Ben's life in exchange for $3.2 million. Sawyer is upset at Kate's defiance of Locke, mainly because it screws up his not-so-secret hope that they'll finally get to be a couple at the barracks.

All of these soapy romantic twists and turns presume that the Jack/Kate/Sawyer love triangle is still vital to what *Lost* is about, and not—as it had really become by this point—kind of exhausting. As the show roared into its back half, it was much more exciting to see the staple characters' reactions to newcomers like the spacey Daniel and the opportunistic Miles—both of whom had vital information to deliver to the audience, having to do with why the lives and futures of the Island inhabitants mattered. These characters were already feeling like the future of the franchise, while Kate increasingly seemed like a remnant of the past. —*NM*

A LOVE STORY

"THE CONSTANT"

—

SEASON 4, EPISODE 5
ORIGINAL AIRDATE 2/28/08

What can one possibly say about "The Constant" twenty years after *Lost* debuted?

It is by far the most celebrated episode of the show, routinely topping lists of the best *Lost* episodes. It was nominated for Emmys for its cinematography and original score. It has become a shorthand for a certain *kind* of TV romance, where the lovers are separated by gulfs of space and time that seem impossible to cross, even as they find ways to cross them. When the website The Ringer made a list of the 100 best TV episodes of the twenty-first century so far in 2018, "The Constant" topped it, and almost no one quibbled. Even if you don't love *Lost*, you probably love "The Constant."

On paper, "The Constant" sounds incredibly complicated, the sort of thing you can't believe works. It involves a Desmond who has become completely unstuck in time, thanks to flying through the electromagnetic interference around the Island. His consciousness keeps flashing between 1996 and Christmas Eve 2004, trying to make sense of what's happening to him. As the episode continues, he tries to use the flashes to his advantage, to figure out a way to re-stick himself in time by consulting with the past version of Daniel Faraday. He starts to get nosebleeds, and as the episode continues, they get worse and worse. His brain won't be able to handle flashing through time much longer. He must either find a way to solve his predicament, or die.

The solution involves the power of true love. Of course.

Lost is a show filled to bursting with terrific love stories.* Even more impressive, they're all different *kinds* of love stories. Sun and Jin are in a failing marriage until crashing on the Island reminds them of why they fell in love in the first place. Charlie and Claire had a classic meet-cute romcom deal, with the faded rock star also having to step up and be a surrogate father. Sawyer, Jack, and Kate have a good, old-fashioned love triangle, the kind TV has long thrived upon. Rose and Bernard have a good marriage and have the comfort level of two people who've been through everything and keep finding their way back to each other. Not every love story on the show works,† but the vast majority of them do,‡ something that's surprising not just for sci-fi TV but for TV in general.

And even then, with all of that said—Desmond and Penny tower above them all.

Damon Lindelof's television career is marked by his ability to tell great love stories,§ and Desmond and Penny exemplify a reason he's so good at the form. Lindelof understands intuitively that a great romance requires

---

★   Terrific *heterosexual* love stories, about which more in a second.

†   Sorry, but Sayid and Shannon never did anything for me.

‡   *Well* . . . the Jack/Kate/Sawyer love triangle is *very* long in the tooth at this point, but the hints that Jack and Juliet might be better together keep it from collapsing entirely. It will come back to life in a big way in Season Five.

§   See also: Kevin and Nora in *The Leftovers*, another TV love story for the ages.

proximity, characters who are constantly bumping up against each other in ways that fuel their ever-growing attraction. But a great *love story* requires separation. If you are truly in love with someone, then being ripped apart from them is a fate worse than death.★ You will move Heaven and Earth to be together again. You will rewrite the cosmos. You will find a way to defeat time itself to ensure that you have a chance to be together again.

Even by *Lost*'s extremely earnest standards, Desmond and Penny's love story is incredibly earnest. It's one reason the show can get away with how swooning and over-the-top it is. What's more, it's not a terribly complicated story at all. The two fall in love, break up, then realize how much they love each other basically when Desmond becomes the captive of a magical Island that is (probably) somewhere in the South Pacific. Penny has spent the series thus far hoping to find Desmond; Desmond just wants to get off the Island and back to his lady. It's so simple that it shouldn't be able to spawn multiple seasons worth of stories. Yet it does.

Originally, the Island was going to be all that separated Desmond and Penny. She would conduct her own search, and Desmond would send up little signal flares here and there. You can see the remnants of this in "Live Together, Die Alone," the Season Two finale, which introduces the main beats of the Desmond/Penny romance pre-Island. In early Season Three, however, Adewale Akinnuoye-Agbaje left the series instead of continuing on as Mr. Eko. The show's plan had been to give Eko visions of the future that would become intertwined with Charlie's fate. When Akinnuoye-Agbaje left, the "someone knows Charlie's about to die" storyline had to go to somebody, and by simple fact of Desmond having been in the same incident as Mr. Eko, it made sense for him to gain the visions.†

There is a part of me that would dearly love to see the Eko version of that story, if only because Eko is one of those *Lost* characters I never got enough of. But wedding the already-existent "Desmond wants to get back to Penny" arc to a "Desmond keeps skipping through time, where he

---

★   Indeed, in a lot of great love stories, the thing separating the lovers *is* death. See also: Orpheus and Eurydice.

†   Damon Lindelof revealed this at a talk on October 19, 2011, available on the You-Tube channel of Alice Lin.

encounters earlier versions of Penny" arc proved sensationally effective. It provided a dimension wherein Desmond and Penny weren't just separated by space but also by *time*. With Desmond effectively entering his own flashbacks most times an episode centered on him, his relationship with Penny could be threatened not just by his boneheaded decisions in the past but the boneheaded decisions from the future he *brought* to the past.

The show first explored this idea in Season Three's also terrific "Flashes Before Your Eyes," but "The Constant" takes everything that episode did and sharpens it to a fine point. Where "Flashes" spends much more time in the past than present, "The Constant" keeps the ratio fairly even, and where "Flashes" makes the Desmond/Penny romance an important part of its story, "The Constant" makes it everything, to the degree that the title itself refers to Penny. She's Desmond's constant, someone who is present for the most important moments of his life and who can ground him in time when the need arises.

The final phone call between the two goes on the short list of the most iconic *Lost* scenes of all time. Desmond, who might have only one shot at saving his own life, places a desperate phone call to Penny on December 24, 2004. He told her in 1996 to expect that call and *when* to expect it,★ but the two had just endured a rough breakup. He has no reason to expect Penny to answer the phone and save his life. The choice of Christmas Eve as the date for this call provides just the right level of heightened sentimentality for the scene. On a practical level, Desmond doesn't have to give Penny an exact date to remember. He can just say "Christmas Eve 2004." And on a "this scene will get stuck in your heart until you die" level, the sight of Penny swearing she loves Desmond, even as their call is about to drop, is only enhanced by the vision of the Christmas tree Desmond should be able to enjoy beside his love, but for the vast gulfs of space and time that separated them.

It is here that I will note, as a queer woman, that *Lost* is a deeply, deeply straight show.† Its vision of romance, while swooning, melodramatic,

---

★ To the still linear Penny, these events happen eight years apart. To the nonlinear Desmond, the gap between them is about fifteen minutes. If that.

† It has, by my count, one canonically queer character who recurs with any frequency: M. C. Gainey's Mr. Friendly, a mainstay of the Others. Leave it to *Lost* to make its one semi-major gay character a bear with a deep appreciation for stagecraft.

and deeply moving, is a vision of romance that centers masculine men who head into the unknown to conquer their demons before returning the feminine women who stay behind at home to build a life for them for everything that comes after. I do not issue this as a complaint, though I do wish *Lost* had found room in its vast arsenal of romance for a queer couple or two, especially given the series' feints toward diversity elsewhere. Instead, I aim to suggest that Desmond and Penny's Christmas Eve phone call is perhaps when male-driven heterosexuality peaked as a storytelling mechanism, and everyone should have started looking elsewhere for romantic side plots. I don't know if I've seen a scene of a man and woman declaring their love for each other as good as the one in "The Constant" since it aired, and I wonder if I ever will.

So, is "The Constant" the best episode of *Lost*? It is certainly, for my money, the episode you can most easily strip out of the show to display its strengths to a newcomer, and it is the episode I return to with the most frequency. That I leave every viewing deeply satisfied speaks to its power. Whether it's your favorite episode of the show or not is a matter of personal taste, but every time I rewatch the series, I'm reminded anew that "The Constant" offers a fitting comparison to the whole of *Lost*— just a little too complicated for its own good, unbelievably romantic, and somehow perfect. —*ESJ*

"THE OTHER WOMAN"

—

SEASON 4, EPISODE 6
ORIGINAL AIRDATE 3/6/08

On the Island: Daniel and Charlotte sneak off to Dharma's "The Tempest" station to neutralize the store of poison gas that Ben deployed on the Island over a decade ago.

In the flashbacks: Juliet's affair with Goodwin ends up getting him killed, as a smitten Ben maneuvers to get him out of the way so that he can have Juliet to himself.

"The Other Woman" has one of *Lost*'s most cleverly punny titles. Juliet is "the other woman" in the melodrama sense, coming between Goodwin and his wife Harper . . . who also happens to be Juliet's therapist. (Cue a dramatic sting on the soundtrack.) She's also an Other. Much of this episode slyly deals with what exactly that identity has meant to her mental and spiritual health. As Juliet wryly says to Jack when he's surprised to hear that she had a therapist on the Island: "It's very stressful being an Other, Jack."

The main source of that stress is that dastardly old Ben Linus, who keeps manipulating Juliet even after she's fled his camp and joined Jack. Ben sends word through Harper (a cruel choice for a messenger) that Juliet needs to kill Daniel and Charlotte. Ben lies about the scientists' intentions and says they intend to unleash his poison gas supply and kill everyone. And because Ben has been in Juliet's ear for so many years— telling this lonely and overwhelmed woman wondrous things that are usually at least plausible if not actually true—she almost does what Ben asks. But then Daniel, Charlotte, and Jack prove to be pretty convincing, too; and in the end they're much easier to trust. That's one advantage Juliet has, being an outsider even within her own Island faction. She can function as a free agent.

With Juliet having betrayed him, Ben redoubles his efforts to turn a sworn enemy into an unlikely ally. Playing on Locke's fanatical need to protect the Island, Ben spins a story—again mostly but not entirely true— about Charles Widmore and his minions coming to exploit and destroy this place they both love. The stinger image in this episode is of Ben walking freely around the barracks' campus, having convinced Locke they have the same goals. Prisoner and captor, turned master and pupil. A bond is forged. —*NM*

A ROMANCE

"JI YEON"
—
SEASON 4, EPISODE 7
ORIGINAL AIRDATE 3/13/08

I love the idea* that every great TV show can be boiled down to a single word. The idea runs deeper than simply a theme. That word serves as a Rosetta stone one can use to dissect every element of the series because those elements either explore the ramifications of that word or cast it in relief. What's more, every viewer's answer for what that word is will be different, showing what one values.

For example: I would say *The Sopranos* is about "family," *Game of Thrones* is about "power," and *Breaking Bad* is about "change." If those sample words seem a little obvious, well, that's somewhat the point. Yes, *Game of Thrones* is self-evidently about power, but once you start exploring the ways in which that idea runs through every single aspect of the show, you discover its omnipresence.

Our ideas of what the word for any given show is can change, too. For many, many years, I would have told you that *Lost* is about "redemption" or maybe "purpose." But now, after having rewatched the show again nearly twenty years after it debuted, I've started to think the show is about "belonging," about the idea that everybody wants to find somewhere that feels like home to them.

Or *someone* who feels like home to them.

A healthy vein of domesticity runs throughout *Lost*. It's the natural offshoot of the show's fondness for love stories. Once the separated lovers are reunited, then they can move in together in domestic bliss, at least until the Island comes calling for them. What makes the show's exploration of this theme via Sun-Hwa Kwon and Jin-Soo Kwon so

---

* First introduced to me by the blog of screenwriter Alex Epstein.

compelling is that Sun and Jin are only able to find that belonging *on* the Island.

Of the Season One castaways, Sun and Jin might have the single best track record for episodes about them. For one thing, their status as a married couple means that they can typically share flashbacks, which means their stories can be spread out in more directions than a character who must handle their flashback burden on their own. If both Sun and Jin have their secrets,* then any given flashback can delve into one's darker side while the other will still be there to play off them. Also, the two's marriage was strained and on the verge of divorce off-Island, while on-Island, they've rediscovered what made them fall in love. That divergence adds a layer of irony to any interaction they have in the past. We know Sun and Jin belong together, but in their pasts, they don't just yet.

I argued in the review of "The Constant" that great love stories are about separation and great romances about proximity, and for the first three seasons of the show, Sun and Jin are forced to be together all the time and exemplify the trope our friends in the romance novel world call a "second chance romance." Yet by the time the show gets to Season Four, the two are sufficiently reconnected—they're expecting a baby together, for goodness' sake—that the show needs to pivot from a romance to a love story, which necessarily means that one is going to get off the Island (Sun) and the other is going to be stuck there (Jin). Then the show will take its sweet time reuniting them.†

"Ji Yeon," named for the couple's daughter, who will be born off the Island, sets up this dynamic. The structure is different from anything else the show tried to this point, with Jin's story taking place as flashback before the Island and Sun's taking place as flash-forward after she left the Island as one of the O6. Even when you know that the series is trying to play timeline games with its off-Island cutaways, the storyline is still effective because it so thoroughly reimagines the Sun/Jin dynamic, subtly switching the genre of story that they've been in all along. Suddenly,

---

* If you have gotten this far in this book and not realized that I would poke light fun at the slightly sexist assumptions within the show making Jin's secret "he's a mob guy" and Sun's secret "she's having an affair," you don't know me at all!

† This episode ends at Jin's tombstone, but c'mon. You have to know that *this* show isn't going to permanently separate two halves of a great love story.

they're in a time-travel story (sort of), but without the time machine that might reunite them.

The series started playing with the structure of its flashbacks in Season Three, but here in Season Four, it's *really* begun to toy with them. Across the first eight episodes of the season,* only the sixth—the Juliet-centric "The Other Woman"—has a traditional flashback structure, and it pales in comparison to the episodes on either side of it. Clearly, everybody involved in the series felt emboldened to mix up its storytelling and to broaden the show's canvas considerably.

In some ways, having Sun leave the Island without Jin could feel cheap. The second the two of them get happy, the show tears them apart? At a certain point, that choice could start to feel like the show's only move. Similarly, the scene where Juliet finally spills the beans on Sun's affair to Jin (one of the show's longest-standing secrets) feels like tension introduced for the sake of tension. It can feel at times as though *Lost* isn't sure how to tell stories about the mostly functional couple Sun and Jin have become and is casting about for ways to drive a wedge between them. They opt for one of their favorite tricks: to split them apart.

Yet these choices *don't* feel cheap. Some of that is on the actors, who play both the revelation of Sun's infidelity and the ultimate resolution of the dual flashback/flash-forward puzzle with the appropriate feeling and gravity. Some of that is on an incredibly strange but nevertheless necessary scene where Bernard† takes Jin fishing to give him some advice on marriage, one of those great *Lost* scenes that shouldn't work but delivers perfectly. And some of it is just on how much we long to see Sun and Jin get some sort of happy ending after all this ridiculous drama. Of all the people who landed on the Island in Season One, Sun and Jin seem like they would best be able to simply go back to some approximation of the lives they had before the Island, the experience having made them, somehow, a stronger couple.

But I would argue the core of the episode's success returns to "belonging," one that powers so much of *Lost*. What we want for Sun and Jin is

---

* So chosen because episode eight, "Meet Kevin Johnson," was the last whose script was completed before the 2007–08 writers' strike. The strike shortened the season and split it into two chunks of eight and six episodes.

† The only other married man on the Island!

for them to find a place where they can live with their daughter in peace, but the show keeps making clear that the only place the couple can truly be together is on the Island. Once they're able to leave and return to their normal lives, who's to say they wouldn't fall back into the patterns that nearly destroyed their marriage in the first place?

Within the world of *Lost*, many different characters end up calling the Island something like home, from the Others living in their weird suburban enclave to Rousseau hiding out in the jungle and quietly seething about the loss of her daughter. The tension that so defines the series has always been between the castaways' desire to return home and the sense that the Island might be a place where they can finally achieve inner peace by way of confronting their darkest selves. Belonging is a state of mind, but it's a lot easier to find when you're in a mystical paradise that gives you a blank slate upon which to write the person you'd like to be.

Yet only Sun and Jin make the Island feel like it could be a place like any other, a place one might make their home, a place one might belong. Could they raise Ji Yeon here? It seems a stretch, yet other babies have grown up on the Island. Why not theirs? *Lost*'s characters mostly long to return to a life of quiet domesticity, their adventuring done.* Sun and Jin underscore that when you have the right person, the idea of home is as movable as the Island they stand on. Belonging isn't a thing one achieves; belonging is a thing one comes to understand or does not. Sun and Jin have, so even when they are separated, they're together. —*ESJ*

---

* The exceptions are characters like Ben and Locke, who know there's no going back for them.

ACCIDENTALLY LIKE A MARTYR

"MEET KEVIN JOHNSON"
—
SEASON 4, EPISODE 8
ORIGINAL AIRDATE 3/20/08

We haven't seen Michael Dawson for some time, until "Meet Kevin Johnson." We last saw Michael leaving the Island with his son Walt, after making a deal with Ben Linus that ended with the deaths of Ana Lucia and Libby and the capture of Jack, Kate, and Sawyer. We didn't know if he'd actually escaped. If he *had* escaped, we didn't know what he'd been up to during the months when our heroes had been running all over the Island, dodging the Others. Those were questions worth asking. And the answers "Meet Kevin Johnson" provide . . . ?

Well, the perspective on those answers has changed over time. Back in 2008, the episode was divisive primarily because of its place in Season Four's production order and release schedule. This was the last episode scripted before the four-month writers' strike; and while Lindelof and Cuse were involved on the production side at first, they eventually ceased their showrunning duties in support of the strike. The news that Lindelof and Cuse didn't see "Meet Kevin Johnson" through to completion— coupled with the news that they had urged ABC *not* to air it right before *Lost* went on a one-month hiatus—led some fans to see the episode as inherently flawed.

Nowadays, the concerns with "Meet Kevin Johnson" have more to do with the way it pays off Michael's story—and, as we touch on elsewhere in this book, with Harold Perrineau's frustration at having to play the heel, over and over. Fans also took issue with Michael's wonky off-Island timeline in this episode, which doesn't quite line up with what we see in episodes like "Confirmed Dead," which attempt to explain Widmore's elaborate "staging of the 815 wreckage" hoax.

It's too bad that the extra-textual stuff weighs so heavy on "Meet Kevin Johnson," because this is such a pivotal Season Four episode—and, on its own merits, an exciting one.

We begin at the Dharma barracks, where a motley band of friends, enemies, and frenemies alike—including Ben, Locke, Hurley, Miles, Alex, and Rousseau—try to figure out their next steps, as the freighter folk begin to invade. There are two big reveals in the opening of this episode; give credit to the writers for understanding that most *Lost* viewers had already figured out both of them. When Ben demands that Miles tell the assembled group at the barracks that the freighter crew didn't come to the Island to rescue anybody, Hurley speaks for all the savvy fans, saying they'd already figured that out "forever ago." Ben also warns everyone that as soon as the Freighties capture him, they have orders to exterminate everyone else on the Island. And then with no fanfare at all, Ben confirms what the *Lost* audience had seen in the previous episode—and had guessed long before—that his "man on the boat" is our old chum Michael, now a miserable soul, cut off from his son Walt because he confessed to killing Ana Lucia and Libby in order to get them off the Island.

In what amounts to an episode-long flashback★ (framed by some other Island business, which we'll get back to shortly), we see Michael soon after his return to the mainland, desperate and suicidal. Walt won't see him, because he knows what his dad did to get them off the Island, betraying friends and killing strangers. The situation gets so dire that Michael trades the Korean watch Jin gave him for a gun. And then, to make matters worse, he sees a news story about how the (fake) wreckage of Oceanic 815 had been found, making it increasingly unlikely that he'll ever be able to be honest about who he really is and what happened to him.

Then Michael runs into Tom, aka "Mr. Friendly," aka the chummy gay Other. Tom explains that some Others can come and go from the Island (suggesting a hierarchy that Ben also hinted at back in "The Man from Tallahassee"). Tom then invites Michael up to his off-Island love

★   Michael's previous flashback, in "Three Minutes," was also a "catching audiences up on what has happened to Michael since the last time we saw him" flashback.

nest at the Hotel Earle and explains to Michael that he's not going to be able to kill himself because "the Island won't let you." Instead, he offers Michael the chance to earn redemption for his past misdeeds, by saving his Island pals from the imminent wrath of Charles Widmore and his band of freighter commandos.★

Which pretty much brings us up to date. Michael gets on the boat as a deckhand under the name "Kevin Johnson," and he embarks on a campaign of sabotage that keeps the freighter from completing its mission. Tom has also sent "Kevin" a bomb to blow the boat up, but our man wavers, because he's met the people on the boat, and some of them don't seem so bad. Sure, the brutish mercenary Martin Keamy and his goon squad make life on the ship pretty miserable with their bullying. But Michael has also talked with Miles, Frank, Naomi, and the affable communications officer George Minkowski (Fisher Stevens) and they all seem like decent sorts.

Still, he sets the bomb, and when the timer reaches zero, a message pops up: "Not Yet."

This episode ends with a pair of ripping cliffhangers. After Michael finishes telling Sayid his story, Sayid drags him to the captain and spills Michael's secret. Was that the right thing to do? Given that we know Sayid will also end up working for Ben eventually after the Oceanic Six leave the Island, probably not. Meanwhile, back on the Island, Rousseau is in the middle of leading Alex and her boyfriend Karl to hook up with the rest of the Others, when all three of them are ambushed by a hidden cadre of blow-dart-wielding . . . somebodies. Did Ben send them into a trap? Or is this Widmore's doing?

Earlier, when Michael's bomb failed to go off, he got a call from Ben, who smugly noted the non-combatants on the freighter and said that even in a time of war, he won't kill innocent people.† When Michael reminds Ben about Ana Lucia and Libby, Ben replies that no one told Michael to kill those two fine ladies. That was all Michael's idea.

Or was it? Here we see the return of some of tried-and-true *Lost* themes. First: the question of free will. If Ben presents Michael with an

---

★ There's something perhaps meta-metaphorical here, with *Lost* itself not just letting Harold Perrineau's character die, because they too still need Michael.

† So, how does he explain that Dharma mass grave? Hmmm . . .

impossible choice—to save Walt by betraying his friends, by any means necessary—then isn't Ben responsible for pulling the trigger, at least a little? But also, this episode is very much about the question of who is "good" and who is "not good." Is Ben a villain, or not? Are the Freighties "bad"? As the show asks us to pick sides, it's really asking, "Which set of morally ambiguous characters do you care about more?" —*NM*

"THE SHAPE OF THINGS TO COME"

—

SEASON 4, EPISODE 9
ORIGINAL AIRDATE 4/24/08

On the Island: The Freighties, led by Keamy, begin their full-scale assault on Ben and his people, and in the process Keamy kills Alex, and Ben unleashes the Smoke Monster to exact vengeance for his daughter's death.

In the flash-forwards: Ben, off the Island, pays a visit to Sayid to recruit him to be an assassin and then pays a visit to Widmore to announce his intention to kill Penny.

"He changed the rules."

That line—said by Ben after his adopted daughter Alex is killed, and then referenced again when Ben pledges to retaliate against Charles Widmore's daughter—got the *Lost* fandom buzzing back in the spring of 2008. Much like "The Constant" set the die-hards on a fun but ultimately irrelevant quest to figure out who each *Lost* character's "constant" might be, so the very mention of "rules" sparked thousands of feverish theories. What are these rules? How did killing Alex break them? What has just been set in motion here?

As the series reached its end and filled in some of the backstory involving Ben and Widmore, it became clearer that Ben was mostly referring to the wary détente between all the various Island factions, which had existed for decades before the crash of Oceanic 815 breached the peace—and not, as many assumed, to some kind of cosmological contract.

Still, the choice of words was fitting, for a couple of reasons.

First, it fired up the fanbase's imagination—which was always reason enough for the *Lost* writers to do anything. And it did so in an episode where we see Ben at his mightiest, making full use of both his wits and his willingness to cynically exploit the Island's power. The scene where Ben disappears into a hieroglyphic-strewn safe room and emerges covered in soot, as the Smoke Monster rages? Sublime. The strange mojo he uses to appear suddenly in the Sahara Desert and then begin his off-Island campaign of vengeance? Beguiling. At the time this episode aired, viewers didn't know yet how—or when—Ben got off the Island, and with *Lost*'s usual crosscutting structure, it seemed like he might actually be jumping through time as well as space. That's the stuff that gets *Lost* buffs excited.

But also: *Lost*, like a lot of epic fantasies, is a story about cycles. Generation after generation, clashes between the forces of light and darkness recur, with the same kinds of heroes, the same kinds of villains, the same kinds of outcomes, and the same resets. It's a game, with differing strategies but fundamental—yes—rules. And as with other epic fantasies, the viewers or readers like to know that the version of the story they're watching is significant because it's going to break the pattern. Something new and transformative is about to happen. —NM

"SOMETHING NICE BACK HOME"

—

SEASON 4, EPISODE 10
ORIGINAL AIRDATE 5/1/08

On the Island: While Jack endures an appendectomy on the beach, Miles and Sawyer make their way through the jungle with Claire, who ultimately abandons Aaron and follows the ghost of her father, Christian.

In the flash-forwards: Jack, who is also receiving visits from Christian's ghost, turns to drugs and paranoia as his relationship with Kate begins to sour and the pressure of maintaining the Oceanic Six lie mounts.

"Something Nice Back Home" is the only true "Jack episode" of *Lost*'s fourth season; and it's far from a classic. In retrospect, all the business on the beach with Jack suffering through some meatball surgery feels like stalling for time before the looming season finale. And as fun as Sawyer and Miles are together—and Frank, who stumbles out of the bush to warn the duo that they're in danger—the only real purpose of their scenes in this episode is to establish the moment when Claire and Aaron are separated. (It's a dramatic sequence, though, as the ghost-whisperer Miles sees a spirit in the form of Christian Shephard leading Claire into the wilderness.)

Still, this episode does serve one important function, which is to crystallize the Oceanic Six's post-Island misery and to start connecting the dots between Season Three's finale—when Bearded Jack is so broken that he figures the only way to fix himself is to "go back"—and Season Four's finale, which promises to show us exactly what Jack did during his exit from the Island that has led to him and Hurley both feeling so ashamed.

Season Four's flash-forwards hint and tease that the O6 behaved less than honorably, and that their subsequent notoriety is based on a lie. The very fact that there are only six of them would seem to bear that out. After all, Jack did promise to get everyone off the Island. And he definitely did not—nor does he seem outwardly upset about it (yet).

But can you live happily on a lie? Can you sleep well knowing what it took to buy your freedom? This theme runs through the series from the start—with all the games and cons and double crosses—and it takes root and starts blossoming here as *Lost* progresses toward its conclusion. These questions seem to haunt Widmore and Ben too . . . which is what keeps *Lost* from devolving into a binary clash of good and evil.

But like it or not, Jack is the person this whole story hinges on. He's a confused dude, just like all of us; and over time, he gets further confused by seeing a half dozen or so models for how to behave and what to believe. The person he becomes by the end of *Lost* will determine whether he's really learned anything. —*NM*

"CABIN FEVER"
—
SEASON 4, EPISODE 11
ORIGINAL AIRDATE 5/8/08

On the Island: Locke and his traveling party go looking for Jacob's Cabin and receive a message about how save the Island from Widmore and the Freighties.

In the flashbacks: After losing his mother, a lonely and timid Locke is watched over by Richard Alpert and Matthew Abaddon, who each try to guide him toward his fate.

Which of these belongs to you: a vial of sand, an ancient book of laws, a compass, a Mystery Tales comic book (featuring the story "The Hidden Land"), a baseball glove, or a knife? A word of caution: Don't reach for the object that represents the kind of person you want to be. Reach for the object that represents who you are.

This is the test that Richard gives to a young John Locke in "Cabin Fever"—which not coincidentally resembles a test given to prospective Dalai Lamas. In other words: This is the kind of episode that Locke himself would love to watch. Through his whole time on the Island, he tries to maintain his faith that he's there for a reason—that, at last, he'd found a place where people would recognize that he had something to offer to the universe. "Cabin Fever" confirms to us—if not yet to Locke—that he has been right all along.

"Cabin Fever" is the only old-fashioned castaway flashback in Season Four. (Jin's episode and Michael's episode don't really count, given that neither strictly follows the standard *Lost* flashback format.) We witness the birth of Locke and his not-so-great upbringing: dumped by his teenage mother; pestered by his sister in the home of the family who adopts him; pushed around in high school; and left paralyzed by his father. Yet all along he's being watched. Richard is there when Locke is still a preemie; and he returns when Locke's a young boy to give him the test.

Richard (still having not aged a day since he met Baby Locke) returns yet again when he's a teenager to drop off a pamphlet for a Mittelos Bioscience summer camp, which Locke, denying his destiny yet again, refuses to attend. Finally, the mysterious Matthew Abaddon (first seen briefly in the Season Four premiere, and played by the magnificent Lance Reddick) comes to see Locke when he's rehabbing from his spinal injury and plants the bug in his ear to go on a walkabout in Australia.

So, it turns out that Locke may be the honest-to-goodness One True Savior of the Island, in which case he's spent all his life accidentally avoiding that responsibility. This is a thoughtful piece of character definition by the writers. The model of the reluctant, ignorant, and/or unexpected hero is fairly common in myth (and in fantasy fiction). But the way these archetypes have been combined in Locke is especially compelling. Here's a guy who wants to be a hero, but keeps missing the signs and opportunities, because the model of heroism in his head is all askew.

When Locke finally enters Jacob's Cabin (after the ghost of Horace Goodspeed advises him to return to Ben's mass Dharma grave to find a map), he doesn't find exactly what he's looking for. Instead, he encounters Christian Shephard—or at least an entity posing as Christian Shephard, accompanied still by Claire. This particular ghost gives Locke another chance to prove himself, by telling him he only has time to ask one question, and it had better be the right one. And though Locke had already asked the question he was most interested in—the big one that everyone asks in life at some point: "Do you know why I'm here?"—he finally figures out how to ask what everyone's been wanting him to ask for nearly fifty years. He asks the apparition how he can save the Island. The startling answer? He's going to have to move it. —*NM*

GONE MISSING

"THERE'S NO PLACE LIKE HOME"

—

SEASON 4, EPISODES 12, 13 & 14
ORIGINAL AIRDATES 5/15/08 & 5/29/08

Season Four of *Lost* is a dizzying ride. The central plot of its fourteen episodes—which include all three parts of this finale—encompasses about ten days of time on the Island. Plus, like a roller coaster, the story of the season travels in a loop, one that is full of twists and turns but one that brings you right back to where the last season ended, with an off-Island Jack yelling at Kate that they have to go back to the Island, that leaving was a mistake.

The sense of overwhelming momentum was only enhanced (or exacerbated, depending on your point of view) by the writers' strike. The original season order was for sixteen episodes, and though losing two episodes wouldn't make too many other shows feel all that compressed, the viewer can really feel the compression on *Lost*, particularly in "There's No Place Like Home."

For the most part, the compression helps the finale. Where previous finales might underline the arduousness of whatever task the characters have undertaken, this finale has no time for that. It's all action, all the time. The freighter explodes, the Island literally disappears, Sawyer gives Kate a long kiss before leaping out of a helicopter, the Oceanic Six are rescued—and none of those moments are anywhere close to the cliffhanger, in which the corpse in the coffin at Hoffs-Drawlar Funeral Home is revealed to be John Locke.★

★ The cliffhanger pales a bit in comparison to "We have to go back," though most things would.

When "There's No Place Like Home" is delivering on big character beats, wedded to wild Island lore, it's one of the series' best episodes. The sequence where Ben essentially hands over the keys to the Island to Locke, then enters a frozen passage beneath the Island, where he spins a large wheel and *moves the Island*, is a bravura sequence. For one thing, it centers on the potent actor team-up of Terry O'Quinn and Michael Emerson, as Ben sheds gut-wrenching tears while preparing to leave the Island for what may be the rest of his life. For another, it finds a way to unite every single character on the show. Even though they are stranded across many different locations, they all watch as the sky turns white and things start getting weird.

The finale also gives nearly every major character a big moment or two. Some hit harder than others. Moments like Sun screaming in sorrow after seeing an enormous boat explode with Jin still on it or Desmond and Penny reuniting after so many years apart from each other carry a little more emotional weight than Lapidus being able to pilot a helicopter through the worst conditions imaginable. But Lapidus still gets a great character moment. The episode is generous like that.

The finale is also, it has to be said, kind of a mess—a generous feast of a mess that has a little something for everyone, but still a mess.

Let's start with the bomb on-board the freighter and the fact that its detonation is tied to whether Keamy, the season's main heavy, dies. As a plot device, everything about the bomb is ludicrous, a fact Lindelof and Cuse acknowledge in their DVD commentary for the episode. Where did Keamy get that much C4? How did he have the time to rig it without anybody noticing, not to mention find a way to tie its detonation to his heart continuing to beat?

Grant, perhaps, that Keamy is a demolitions expert. It's not so hard to believe. Even then, the bomb smacks of the show desperately needing a way to further separate certain characters, particularly Sun and Jin, and believing a literal bomb is the best way to enhance the tension of an already-tense episode. The bomb, ultimately, exists *only* for plot reasons, and if its existence were tied to a character we actually had strong feelings about like Charles Widmore, it might gain a little juice. As it stands, it becomes a bit of a cheat, a too-easy shortcut to excitement that makes less sense the more you think about it.

What's perhaps worst about the bomb is that it ushers Michael out of the show once and for all. Harold Perrineau's return to the series in

Season Four was much hyped, but his summary episode ("Meet Kevin Johnson") was the episode perhaps most affected by the writers' strike, and his storyline became incredibly truncated in the season's back half.

All in all, Michael hardly appears in the season, his big showcase episode is uneven, and he dies unceremoniously in an explosion. Yes, his death occurs because he's trying to save his friends from the bomb, but his sacrifice does little to resolve his character arc on a show that tends to reserve big, explode-y deaths for characters whose stories have come to an end. Insult to injury: Walt appears in the episode but in a flashforward. He and his dad never reconnect. There *is* a poignancy to this, but "There's No Place Like Home" underlines at every turn what a missed opportunity the Michael and Walt storyline was.

The breakneck pacing in the Island story also makes clear how much the flash-forwards are marking time. When Ben tells Jack that he has to get everybody who escaped the Island to go back, while both stand over Locke's corpse, it barely moves the story a centimeter from where the last moments of Season Three left it. To be sure, having the flash-forwards offer as much forward momentum as the on-Island story would likely exhaust the audience, but for the first time all season, there's a sense of them running in place just a bit.★

The on-Island action benefits from the pacing, but it also leaves the audience unable to take a breath, racing as it is to make sure the characters are in place for the next big set piece. Those set pieces are so awesome that the connective tissue between them almost never bothers you while you're watching. Yet throughout, the storytelling utilizes devices like the bomb to force characters to do things other than what we'd normally expect them to do.

With two additional hours over which to tell this story, it seems likely that the events of the finale might have had more space to breathe, that even something as abrupt as Michael's death might have felt more earned. We will never know. We have the finale we have, and it's a wild ride that throws you all over the place and maybe makes you a little sick to your stomach.

However, that dizzied feeling is appropriate to Season Four as a whole. There is perhaps no better season to exemplify why *Lost* is such an

---

★   That sense will almost immediately disappear in Season Five, fortunately.

endlessly compelling show. Even when stuff is just sort of happening and you're not sure why, it's directed, written, and performed so beautifully that you end up just going with it. If you find yourself asking, later, while getting ready for bed, "Hey, *why* did Keamy have a bomb?" . . . well, you still had a great time, didn't you? —*ESJ*

FURTHER READING: SPOILER CULTURE AND INFORMED GUESSWORK: WHY SOME *LOST* FANS TRIED TO STAY A STEP AHEAD

As *Lost* moved through its final two seasons, devoted viewers could be largely subdivided into three groups. The largest group—the "normies"—watched each episode as it aired, thought about it for a bit, and then went on with their lives until the next week rolled around. A smaller but more involved tier of fans spent that same week haunting message boards and the comment sections of reviews, unpacking the hidden meaning of every line and image and then using what they found to speculate on what might happen next.

But an even tinier subset of viewers felt no need to speculate—not because they didn't care but because they were active on *other* message boards, where they scrounged for spoilers from people who had inside info about *Lost*, gleaned from leaked script pages and secret set visits.★

Why did they do this? Or perhaps the more important question: For a show as dense with self-reference and mythology as *Lost*, what even *is* a spoiler?

In May of 2007, the journal *Participations* published the article "Speculation on Spoilers: *Lost* Fandom, Narrative Consumption and

---

★ I've never been a spoiler-phobe so I never got angry when I stumbled across one of these insider reports; but I didn't actively seek them out either. I did enjoy playing the guessing games with fellow fans; and I dedicated a section of each of my A.V. Club reviews to something I called "clues, coincidences, and crazy-ass theories."

Rethinking Textuality," by Jonathan Gray and Jason Mittell. The piece contained the results of an anonymous survey the authors had conducted, gathering input from various online *Lost* discussion communities about why fans might actively seek out spoilers—or why they might participate in speculative discussions about the show's future plot developments that could, if proved correct, have the same effect as reading a spoiler.

The responses were fascinating, and belied some of the conventional wisdom that spoiler-philes had to be one of two types: either impatient viewers who just couldn't wait for *Lost* to tell its story at its own pace; or mean-spirited trolls gathering intel to fling incautiously at the normies. Gray and Mittell found instead that a "spoiler" for *Lost* didn't always fit the usual definition of a surprising plot twist discovered in advance. For a lot of spoiler-seeking fans, these tidbits of early knowledge were just pieces of data they used in their ongoing efforts to understand and appreciate the show. The vast majority of these fans still avidly watched each week; and about half of them watched each episode multiple times. Clearly knowing what was going to happen didn't "spoil" the show for them in any conventional sense.

Some spoiler-craving viewers enjoyed being in an online community with a common purpose. Others wanted to mitigate any potential disappointment with *Lost*'s plot twists by giving themselves time to think about them before they aired. Some found the series hard to follow at times, but easier to understand if they already knew where it was going. Others liked to get a head start on analyzing an episode's themes and motifs, without any distracting surprises.

Then there's the matter of "foilers": items that seem like spoilers but that turn out to be misleading, because they never actually appear on the show as expected. Maybe these spoilers were fake all along, planted by the producers as a red herring or by online mischief-makers as a goof. Maybe the details that one of those script-reading, set-visiting insiders shared were too vague, leading fans to jump to the wrong conclusions. Or maybe Lindelof and Cuse just changed their mind.

This last variety of foilers—scenes and storylines that were cut or changed, either in the script phase or after being filmed—was the most compelling to a particular group of fans, who operated under the belief that *Lost* was a fluid text. Thanks to interviews with writers and cast members, these fans were well aware of arcs that were abandoned; and they knew why certain characters weren't used as much as originally intended. In fact, Lostpedia has a whole page for these "abandoned storylines," with quotes from the creative team explaining why they never happened.

Matthew Abaddon becoming a major character in Season Five? Scotched because Lance Reddick was cast as a regular on *Fringe*. The mysterious people shooting at our time-traveling, seafaring castaways in Season Five? That moment never got paid off because the characters who were going to be in the other boat were killed off earlier than the writers had planned. The volcano on the Island that was teased in the Dharma flashbacks? According to a 2017 interview with Lindelof and Cuse in *Entertainment Weekly*, this was going to be a central piece of the series finale but was scrapped in favor of "the glowy cave" when the budget for a volcanic explosion turned out to be too high.

A lot of fans liked to know about the roads not taken because they still considered them to be part of *Lost* as a whole, even if it only ever existed as apocrypha. Without spoilers, they might be missing out on something they personally considered crucial.

In a way, *Lost* encouraged this kind of intense scrutiny. The show was both a straight-ahead adventure story populated by dozens of fascinating characters and a puzzle with scattered pieces, parceling out bits of information that gradually revealed the larger history of these people and the world they'd been dropped in. For the first few seasons especially, every stray mention of the Dharma Initiative or the Others would lead to viewers rewinding, rewatching, and pausing specific scenes, looking closely for anything that could hint at what might be coming. In other words: Some spoilers were embedded within *Lost* itself, in the form of visual clues and portentous name-drops.

Gray and Mittell acknowledge this aspect of spoiler-hunting—where just watching a *Lost* episode and spinning theories with a group of friends based on a close reading could end up "spoiling" parts of the story that have yet to be revealed. In their article, they write, "If we think of *Lost* less like a conventional story and more like a puzzle or game, spoilers seem much more legitimate. In attempting to solve any large-scale puzzle or game, players are encouraged to gather as much information and research as possible, not relying on one limited source."

It's to *Lost*'s credit that despite all the spoiler-sharing and forensic fan analysis, the show largely remained unpredictable. In fact, over time this unpredictability led to some frustration in the fan community, as some grew attached to their own theories—their own *certainty*—about what was going to happen. They had their own version of *Lost*, built from rumors and wild flights of imagination. This *Lost* may have never made it to the screen, but it was a diverting pastime regardless. —*NM*

SEASON FIVE

GOING BACK

There were lots of ways the *Lost* writers could've filled in some of the biggest gaps in the Island's backstory. For years, fans had been clamoring for more information about the Dharma Initiative and Charles Widmore and the Black Rock and Richard Alpert and Danielle Rousseau and the giant statue and Jacob and the Smoke Monster and the polar bears. The easiest storytelling choice—one that Lindelof and Cuse did opt for sometimes—would have been to have a character step into the center of the frame and just talk, saying everything the audience needed to hear.

But *Lost* always tried to be more of a "show, don't tell" kind of drama. That was the purpose of the flashbacks: to let us see with our own eyes how Jack, Kate, Sawyer, Sayid, Hurley, Sun, Jin, Michael, Charlie, and the rest were living before they crashed on the Island. That could've been the choice for Season Five as well. The show could've stayed in the world of the present—on the Island and off—and then flashed back in each episode to fill in more of this weird place's past, just as in Season Three's "The Man Behind the Curtain."

Instead, Lindelof and Cuse chose time travel as a useful—and fun—narrative device. They didn't do it in a meta, "After all, aren't flashbacks a kind of time travel?" sort of way, either. All the hints that *Lost* had dropped over the years about the physics-defying properties of the Island—including Daniel Faraday's observations that time doesn't work quite the same way between a boat offshore and a location inland—bore fruit in a season where the Island and some of its inhabitants literally skipped around in time. Why have someone tell us about what Young Charles Widmore was like when a time-traveling Locke can go meet him in person?

As with everything in *Lost*, there are trade-offs to the decision to go this way. Season Five is, to put it mildly, a mind-scrambler when it comes to straightening out a narrative timeline.

Season Four ended with Ben Linus "moving the Island" by descending into an icy underground chamber and turning an ancient wheel, which makes the place disappear from all detection by the people who were either nearby or closing in. The procedure also teleported Ben off the Island, where he would begin the process of gathering the Oceanic 6 for their big return. Throughout the season, even after everyone's back on the Island, we get more flashes (some back, some forward) to the miserable lives the O6ers led before reuniting and hopping on a new doomed plane: Ajira Airways Flight 316,* piloted by our old friend Frank Lapidus. Figuring out when and where everyone is can be complicated at times, especially when some of the Ajira passengers eventually end up on the Island in 2007, while others . . . ?

Well, that's where things get even trickier. Because of a glitch in Ben's use of what fans called "the frozen donkey wheel," the people who were around in 2004 when he moved the Island find themselves being lurched unpredictably through time, seeing what Island life was like there in various eras, such as the '50s and the '80s. Ultimately, Locke has to head down to the wheel himself to stop the skipping. It's a painful choice for him to make, given how much he loves the Island—and it will prove to be even more painful once he's back in the outside world.

The time travelers ultimately settle into 1974, where they live fairly happily with the Dharma Initiative for three years—while in the present, the O6ers have three unhappy years before they board flight 316 in 2007. The ones on the flight who don't land on the Island in the present day—Jack, Kate, Hurley, and Sayid—end up in 1977.

Got all that? The time frame makes more sense if viewers binge-watch this season, which was something fans were doing more and more in the 2000s, thanks to the popularity of DVD and Blu-ray box sets. It's one of the reasons why the declining ratings weren't a major concern to the

---

* *Lost* fans, of course, spent a lot of time trying to figure out if the flight number had some significance (aside from it containing the number "16"). One theory is that the number of people aboard Oceanic Flight 815 (324) minus the eight people who the Oceanic Six claimed had initially survived the crash (in their lie, two of that eight had died) equals 316. This seems like a bit of a stretch, though.

various entities with a financial stake in *Lost*. There were still lots of possibilities to make money off the show. (Plus, *Lost* aired its 100th episode, "The Variable," in this season; 100 episodes is, typically, the kind of milestone that only hugely profitable series hit.)

The season's episode-to-episode flow is *Lost* at its best, especially when we account for the complicated flashback/flash-forward/time-travel structure. There are no real "placeholder" episodes in Season Five. And where Season Four largely seemed designed to move all the characters to the right place so that the story could eventually proceed, in Season Five everyone's where they need to be nearly all the time, making the stories feel more purposeful and action-packed.

In other words: Season Five is a hoot.

There are new characters aplenty in these seventeen episodes, though only a few of them are vital to the larger story as it moves toward the sixth and final season. (No offense intended to the likes of Patrick Fischler as **PHIL** and Eric Lange as **RADZINSKY**, two memorably cranky Dharma guys.) Though she had appeared before, this was the season where **ELOISE HAWKING** (Fionnula Flanagan) became essential to the mythology, as a former Island resident and the mother of Daniel Faraday. And one of the Flight 316 passengers, **ILANA** (Zuleikha Robinson), is introduced as a bounty hunter before being revealed as a die-hard agent of Jacob.

And oh yeah . . . **JACOB** (Mark Pellegrino) makes his official on-screen debut this season, as does a mysterious figure dubbed **THE MAN IN BLACK** (Titus Welliver), who we will eventually learn has been with us since episode one. But we'll get back to that in Season Six. For now, what matters is that these two appear together in the amazing Season Five finale, which wraps up a great run of episodes while signaling another change in *Lost*'s overall narrative game-plan—from "here's what happened on the Island in the past" to "here's what it all means."

The "what it all means" is where some of the divisions emerge among *Lost* fans in the undeniably controversial Season Six. And some of the seeds of that dissent do appear in Season Five, whenever the hardcore woo-woo kicks in. The biggest example of this involves Young Ben Linus, who gets shot and has to be saved by the Hostiles, who warn that he will be "changed" by the healing. Even though it helps to explain Ben's communion with the Island, the whole "Ben gets infected by the Island's evil side" concept is less dramatically compelling than "Ben just turns evil because his life sucks." The compulsion to give too many Island-questions a supernatural answer takes some of the human free will out of the equation.

Ultimately, this is a show about eternal conflicts, personal change, and finding a sense of belonging; and while the time-travel stuff really works from a narrative and thematic point of view, once this season ends it's hardly a factor anymore. The last season is primarily about that struggle through the ages, between opposing forces.

But what happens in Season Five absolutely matters, even if a lot of it is just about the time-traveling castaways witnessing the Island's history. One element of this season that should be talked about more is how it reveals the overall kludginess of the Island's various magical mechanisms. For all of Ben's talk in the early seasons about how the Island is a "magic box" that can make anything appear, there's an art to working its levers, and the results aren't always precise. Some people get hurt. Some die. Some are just disappointed that things don't work out the way they'd hoped.

Let that be a warning, as we prepare for The End. —*NM*

"BECASE YOU LEFT"

SEASON 5, EPISODE 1
ORIGINAL AIRDATE 1/21/09

On the Island: In the wake of Ben "moving" the Island, the remaining castaways find themselves skipping back and forth through time, meeting significant people and witnessing major events.

Off the Island: Jack's plan to bring the Oceanic Six (plus Ben and the corpse of John Locke) back together is already in trouble, with Hurley and Sayid on the run from the law and Sun considering partnering with Widmore to kill Ben.

Lost always had a knack for arresting season-opening scenes, and Season Five's is probably the second best. (It's hard to top meeting Desmond at the start of Season Two.) Dr. Pierre Chang (aka Mark Wickmund, Edgar Halliwax, Marvin Candle,★ etc.) wakes at 8:15 (!), puts on Willie Nelson's *Shotgun Willie* while heating up a bottle for his baby, then prepares to make an instructional film, sans script, for the Arrow station. His patter gets interrupted by a Dharma workman, who tells him there's trouble at the Orchid, where intense heat has been melting the drilling tools. Chang checks out an X-ray—which partially reveals the wheel Ben used to move the Island at the end of Season Four—and then delivers a stern lecture about how the Orchid rests over a source of energy that could allow them to manipulate time. When the workman jokes about how they're going to go back in time and kill Hitler, Chang warns that there are "rules" (there's that word again) that can't be broken! Then, just when the Island backstory and *Lost* mythology reach critical mass, we get the coolest reveal of all: Daniel Faraday is one of the Dharma workers.

But why? And from when?

Right from the start, Season Five introduces its riskiest storytelling conceit, which will end up being both conceptually brilliant and good, rollicking fun. Before the series ends, viewers will need to know a lot more about the history of the Dharma Initiative, the Hostiles, Charles Widmore, Eloise Hawking, and Richard Alpert (among others). But with half the cast already off the Island—and a couple of years into the future too, having gone through the normal method of living their lives—adding flashbacks into the mix in a conventional way would take away from time spent with the cast members still on the Island. So, why not bring those flashbacks directly to Sawyer, Juliet, Daniel, and company, by having them travel through time and live through them?

The premiere gives viewers a generous sampler of what's to come on the episodes ahead. Off the Island, the O6 are in disarray. Kate is distracted by her own personal drama, as a court order from an as-yet-unknown client demands she prove her maternity of Aaron. Sun is on her way from London to Los Angeles, but she seems more inclined to ally with Charles Widmore than with Ben, whom she holds responsible for Jin's death. Sayid, too, has had enough of Ben and tells Hurley not to sign on to any of his plans. (He doesn't need to tell Hurley twice, since our man would rather be left out of *any* schemes.)

★   Again: The man loved candle imagery.

Meanwhile, on the Island the castaways are experiencing a few of the wildest days (years? decades?) of their lives, as a glitch in the Island-moving mechanism leaves it skipping through time unpredictably. Locke witnesses the plane crash involving Mr. Eko's brother, gets shot by Ethan Rom (from a time in the past before they met), and gets medical attention from a future version of Richard Alpert (who tells John he'll need to leave the Island and sacrifice his life to save the Island). Daniel visits the Swan in the past and talks to Desmond, giving him a mission to complete in the present. It's all wonderfully baffling and bizarre.

Perhaps most importantly, though, "Because You Left" lets us know what a joy it's going to be to share the Islanders' freaky adventures alongside the perpetually cranky and skeptical Sawyer. He says the best line of the episode when his group find themselves outside the Swan during the time when Desmond was stationed inside. Warned by Daniel not to knock on the Hatch and go begging for Dharma food, Sawyer snaps that he's not going back to "huntin' boar"! It's a funny remark, but also a signal to the audience: Things are about to change. —NM

"THE LIE"

—

SEASON 5, EPISODE 2
ORIGINAL AIRDATE 1/21/09

On the Island: Sawyer's group crosses paths again with Locke, who helps save them from a band of hostile strangers in military attire.

Off the Island: Hurley gets overwhelmed by all the demands people are making of him and retreats to his parents' house, while Ben meets up with his old acquaintance/enemy Eloise Hawking and learns that the window to return to the Island will be opening and quickly closing in just a few days.

Back in 2009, "Because You Left" and "The Lie" aired back-to-back on ABC, which made the latter seem like less of a wheel-spinning episode but also blunted some of the former's impact. Everything exciting about the season premiere seemed more distant and dissipated after the slower, moodier episode two. (It doesn't help that the time-traveling fun of the previous episode is limited in episode two to a trip to 1954, where a group we will meet more properly in episode three attacks and kills more of the 815 survivors.*)

Still, "The Lie" serves an emotional function by bringing the O6's story down to a human level, showing how this scattered bunch have been put through the wringer by their experiences on and off the Island. Jack and Ben forge an unlikely bond, born of their similar battle scars. Sun and Kate have a nice conversation about their respective babies, imagining a world where maybe the rising generation will play together rather than fighting each other.

But it's Hurley who's the real heart of this episode, as he wrestles with his own conscience and with all the voices in his ear, from the living and the dead: from Sayid (who tells him to do the opposite of anything Ben says), from Ben (who is urging him to return to the Island), from the ghost of Ana Lucia (who tells him that Libby says "hi").

"The Lie" over-works its title premise, which has Hurley feeling so torn apart by his part in the O6's cover story that he can barely function. Ever since their rescue, the five adults in the Oceanic Six have had to pretend that only eight people originally survived the crash, and that they landed in the sea, not on the Island. All the while, they've known that the friends (and enemies) they left behind were likely in grave danger, and that they couldn't ask for anyone to help them. Unable to cope, Hurley confesses the truth to his mother and then runs to the police and confesses to murders he didn't commit—so that they'll lock him up and he'll be left alone.

But much like "trust," "lying" is a concept that TV writers overemphasize in plotting. That's not to say that ordinary people don't care about when people are lying to them or when their friends are untrustworthy; it's just not something that comes up enough in our daily lives to make much sense as a motivator. Most people behave the way they do because of their own personal needs—money, love, what-have-you—and not in reaction to other people's shadiness.

---

*   Including Neil (aka "Frogurt")!

That said, Hurley is such a sweet man—and Jorge Garcia so good in the role—that he's sympathetic regardless. Whether he's offering Sayid some French fries (telling him that maybe some comfort food will chill him out), wishing he had a cool code name, or nervously tossing a Hot Pocket at Ben, Hurley is, always, our everyman. —*NM*

HOW I LEARNED TO STOP WORRYING

"JUGHEAD"
—
SEASON 5, EPISODE 3
ORIGINAL AIRDATE 1/28/09

"Jughead" is an excellent episode of *Lost* that nevertheless might make those who've been following the series from day one stop and say, "Wait. What?"

Did you love the more grounded tone of the first couple of seasons, or the pervasive sense of mystery and dread that surrounded the Island? All of that has mostly gone out the window in favor of more straightforward science-fiction stories about time travel and mysterious energy pockets. "Jughead" even works in a tiny sprinkling of nuclear-powered fears, with the presence of an H-bomb on the Island, as if trying to further underline the mid-twentieth-century *Amazing Stories* quality of the season.

Similarly, did you love the first-season characters, those charismatic castaways who found themselves confronting the underpinnings of space and time? Well, they're barely present in this episode. Of the original fourteen cast members, only Locke and Sawyer appear, and while both men get plenty to do, the bulk of the episode is built around Desmond (introduced in Season Two) and Faraday (introduced in Season Four). A substantial portion of the episode is even built around meeting Charles

Widmore—similarly not present until the very end of Season Two—as a young man.

Jack? Kate? Hurley? Sun? None of them show up. It's rare for a TV show to so thoroughly turn itself over to characters introduced in later seasons, but *Lost* has introduced so many compelling new characters across its run that you'd be forgiven for reaching the end of the hour and realizing how little the show resembles its first-season self.

For many fans, Season Five is where *Lost* simply goes somewhere they cannot follow. The gradual ramp-up of sci-fi elements was sometimes an issue, but Season Five largely eschews so much of Season One's foundation, such that characters fundamental to the show's early success can become afterthoughts. For many, this ends up being a bridge too far.

Not me! Season Five is my favorite season of *Lost* and perhaps one of my favorite seasons of television ever made. Its presentation of time travel is loopy but also surprisingly sound and grounded in something like how such a storytelling device would "actually" work.* And "Jughead" is a perfect chance to pop open the hood and look at what makes Season Five so good.

The scope of the show has never been grander. That this episode can turn over so much of its story to Desmond and Faraday without most of the original cast ever appearing isn't an example of the weakness of the Season One cast or any such thing. It is, rather, an example of just how skillfully *Lost* has expanded its scope until it can seemingly tell nearly any kind of story.

Broadly speaking, the series spends the episodes that kick off this season alternating between on-Island stories (here, the Faraday story) and off-Island stories (here, the Desmond story). Yet because there are so many characters, if the show wants to check in with Desmond, Penny, and their son Charlie,† then it necessarily doesn't have room for Jack, Kate, and all the rest.

It's a show in love with its own sprawl, and it's hard not to get just a little bit intoxicated right alongside it. We might long to see, say, Sawyer and Kate in a scene together, but huge gulfs of space and time separate them. That the show can hold both of them in the same story, if not always the same episode, is a testament to how ambitious it has become.

---

*   So far as we know. I have yet to time travel. I'll let you know if I do.
†   WHAT ARE YOU DOING TO ME, *LOST*?!

The use of time travel works beautifully in concert with the show's themes of fate and destiny. So many time-travel stories proceed from the idea that if you try to change the past, you will, instead, create the future you were hoping to avert. Yes, plenty of stories avoid this framework, but even at this point, *Lost* is already playing around with the idea that if the castaways travel into the past, then they were *always* there in the past. We have already seen an example of this with Richard's "memories" of Locke, which are just his chronological experience of Locke's travels through the past.

So, if you, John Locke, were always fated to do these things because in some sense, you have *already done them* (at least from Richard's perspective), then that must bolster your belief in destiny and a higher purpose. Yet that knowledge might affect someone like Jack or Sawyer differently. It definitely affects Faraday, who preaches a kind of scientific predestination that sounds downright religious in nature.

Broadly speaking (and without spoiling things too much), the final two seasons of the show argue different sides of the same question: Are we powerless against the forces of the universe, or can we push back against them in some small way? Season Five makes the case that we're kind of trapped—and maybe we should be OK with that.

It answers a bunch of questions without seeming like it does. One of the neat things about *Lost* has always been how it hints at the Island's entire, enormous history, yet we get only the tiniest glimpses. In these early Season Five episodes, the show has come up with an ingenious way to give viewers little tastes of that history without abandoning the characters we already know and love.

Want to know why Charles Widmore is so obsessed with the Island? Well, here he is as a young man, living on the Island, no less! Instead of having him, say, explain himself in a long monologue, the show is going to depict a few of the moments that built his lifelong obsession. Want to see how long the Others have been fighting back against would-be invaders? Well, here they are having fought off the US military and taken one of their hydrogen bombs.*

---

*   Juliet's saving her and her comrades' lives by speaking Latin and revealing herself as an Other offers one of those exciting moments where the characters are a couple of steps ahead of the audience.

More importantly, much of the climax of the series, toward which we are now steadily building, hinges on the idea that there are people who long so badly to control the Island that they would kill and destroy for it. It's not that we don't believe they would do so, but seeing just how long the Island has been at the center of brutal fighting, among people whose stories might fuel a whole other TV series, subtly raises the stakes for the series' endgame.★

Above all else, though, episodes like "Jughead" are just *fun*. In most episodes, *Lost* moves its pieces around on the board as powerful forces behind the scenes† manipulate events to lead to the outcomes they find most palatable. Yet at its best, the show does so in a way that both lets you get a glimpse of the players' true motives and disguises from you just how much of this is moving pieces around on a board. Season Five is perhaps the show's most brazen in terms of piece-moving—but at every turn, it's having so, so, so much fun. And so are we. —*ESJ*

"THE LITTLE PRINCE"
–
SEASON 5, EPISODE 4
ORIGINAL AIRDATE 2/4/09

On the Island: The time-jumps begin to cause nosebleeds and blackouts for the people who have spent a lot of time on the Island, though they also keep bringing the castaways back to important Island moments, including the birth of Aaron and the arrival of Rousseau's crew.

★ One clumsy way the episode raises the stakes: Having Faraday proclaim his abiding love for Charlotte doesn't come out of nowhere, but it does feel like it's becoming a plot point just to give her nosebleeds more urgency. It's very in keeping with how rarely the show can think of things to do with its women characters that don't primarily involve motivating men.

† Who, let's face it, might just be the show's writers, rather than someone like Charles Widmore.

Off the Island: Kate discovers that Ben is responsible for the attorneys questioning her maternity, which inadvertently threatens his efforts to bring the entire Oceanic Six together.

Has Sawyer ever been on a boat or a flying vehicle that hasn't wrecked or been shot at? The constant chaos surrounding Sawyer adds some notes of dark humor and a heck of a lot of excitement to the Island scenes in "The Little Prince," which—as is the case for most of Season Five—is where the episode's real action is.

Even as the time-jumps make the jumpers increasingly physically miserable—giving Locke all the more reason to believe that the Oceanic Six need to return to the Island—the effect of those leaps on the larger story is remarkable. Locke gets taken back to one of his darkest moments—on the night Boone was mortally wounded and Locke pounded in futile anger on the Hatch—and is reminded of how far he's come since then. In an unspecified future time, Sawyer and company steal some boats, get shot at by mysterious strangers in the mist, and then time-jump into the middle of the same storm that wrecked Rousseau's ship. (Rousseau's crew, meanwhile, elsewhere in the seas surrounding the Island, find an unconscious Jin, floating on a chunk of the freighter.) We're about to reach a crisis point with the time travel in the next episode; but before this particular chapter of our heroes' lives comes to a close, the writers keep using the time-skip conceit to deepen the characters, answer some questions, and introduce some new mysteries. (Who *was* shooting at Sawyer's boat?)

And in Los Angeles, in 2007? Well, once again the O6 hit some bumps on their journey back to the Island. Same ol' same ol'. Hurley is still in jail, by choice. Sun and Kate have found each other but are steering clear of everyone else for now while Kate deals with her legal troubles and Sun thinks about the best way to get rid of Ben. Sayid and Jack are together but are also unsure if they can trust Ben, after Ben admits that his attorney Dan Norton (Tom Irwin) has been meddling in the O6's lives, by filing the legal claims against Kate and by working to get Hurley freed. Right now, this group doesn't have a lot of chemistry, especially when compared to Sawyer's time-traveling adventurers.

But "The Little Prince" does make good use of its jagged timelines, if only to forge connections between steps in Kate's journey in on-Island and off-Island flashbacks: showing her in 2007, anxious about losing Aaron, then showing her three years earlier on Penny's boat, prepared to lie for Jack in order to keep Aaron safe; and finally showing her three years ago on the Island, helping Claire bring Aaron into the world. In just a few short scenes, *Lost* lays the foundation for what the boy means to Kate.

And as an added bonus to the Claire-giving-birth scene, we have Sawyer watching from the bushes, and then—when the sky flashes and time skips—Sawyer losing Kate, yet again. Sometimes, the way *Lost* tells its stories works out just fine. —*NM*

"THIS PLACE IS DEATH"
—
SEASON 5, EPISODE 5
ORIGINAL AIRDATE 2/11/09

On the Island: Through multiple time-jumps, Jin witnesses the deterioration of Rousseau's crew and then eventually catches up with the rest of the castaways, now led by Locke, who takes them all to the site of the Frozen Donkey Wheel to stop the skipping.

Off the Island: Sun considers killing Ben, but changes her mind and joins him, Jack, Kate, and Sayid at Eloise's church.

"This Place Is Death" is perhaps the weakest of the Jin/Sun-focused episodes, if only because neither of its two most memorable moments are really centered on either Jin or Sun. The episode is primarily known for two things: Charlotte finally succumbing to the time-sickness, after telling Jin to do whatever he must to prevent Sun from returning to the Island (because . . . well, check the episode's title); and Locke making the difficult decision to turn the wheel and leave the Island (the place that means everything to him).

The latter leads to a tense and magical scene where Locke descends into a well at the future location of the Orchid, then busts his leg when time skips yet again to a pre-well era, snapping his rope. At the bottom of the pit Locke meets the ghost of Christian Shephard, who explains that it was always his fate to turn the wheel—and to sacrifice himself. (Ghost Christian then asks Locke to say hi to his son, prompting a funny reply: "Who's your son?" Nobody tells Locke anything.)

As for Jin and Sun, across time and space they find themselves in a kind of twisted Gift of the Magi situation. First, Jin gets to see firsthand something that *Lost* fans had been very curious about for several seasons: what actually happened to Rousseau and her research team, back in 1988 and '89. She had always said that she was forced to kill her colleagues (including her husband) because the Island had made them dangerously sick. Jin, though, sees that the team was actually tormented by the Smoke Monster, and that a perhaps justifiable paranoia got the better of Danielle, who shot them all. With that moment fresh in his mind, Jin finally finds himself in the same time and place as Sawyer's group, where he watches Charlotte die and heeds her warning that the Island is too dangerous for Sun to return to.

Before Locke is zapped off the Island, Jin hands him his wedding ring and tells Locke to tell Sun that he's dead, so that she won't try to come back (and thus possibly risk the life of their baby, who in Jin's timeline is unborn). Instead, due to circumstances as yet unseen on the show, *Ben* has the ring, which he shows to Sun as proof that Jin's still alive, to manipulate her into joining his traveling party.

As always on this show, physical evidence only takes people so far—because the meaning of the totems is determined by the ones who wield them. —*NM*

"316"

—

SEASON 5, EPISODE 6
ORIGINAL AIRDATE 2/18/09

Off the Island: The Oceanic Six (minus Aaron but plus Ben, Frank Lapidus, the corpse of John Locke, and some mysterious newcomers) board another plane, Ajira Flight 316, and do their best to re-create the conditions of their last flight that crashed on the Island.

On the Island: Some of the passengers on Ajira 316 (Jack, Kate and Hurley) experience turbulence and a flash of light and then find themselves back on the Island, with no sign of the rest of their party.

In a 2008 interview with Damon Lindelof and Carlton Cuse in The A.V. Club, Cuse talked about some of *Lost*'s riskier storytelling choices and said, "We're always going to try to push the envelope with the show, and when you try to push the envelope and fly close to the sound barrier, that plane is going to shatter, and sometimes it's going to break apart. And sometimes it's going to blow on through, and it's going to be exciting when it goes supersonic."

The way Cuse describes making *Lost* sounds a lot like what happens in "316." We know from the start of the episode that the Oceanic Six—well, some of them—are, improbably, going to make it to the Island. But it's still nerve-wracking (in a good way) to watch the plan come together, person by person and turn by turn. Eloise Hawking, in a Dharma station known as the Lamp Post, stands beneath a giant pendulum that maps the probabilities of where (and when?) the Island will be next and tells Jack and company to book Ajira Flight 316 to Guam, and to make it as much like Oceanic 815 as possible, right down to carrying a dead body and dressing it in Christian Shephard's shoes. Miraculously, they get pretty close.

"316" demonstrates a fair amount of sly wit and fan-friendly callbacks too, especially in the airport scene, where Jack sees Sayid led on-board in handcuffs (shades of Kate), and Hurley reads a DC-published comic in Spanish (the Vertigo series *Y: The Last Man*, written by *Lost* contributor Brian K. Vaughan), and the Oceanic survivors react to the announcement of the flight's pilot, Frank Lapidus. We're treated to some wonderful character moments: like Hurley buying up as many tickets as he could so that no one would be unnecessarily hurt in the crash; and a deeply sad, Aaron-less Kate accepting Jack and his mission back into her life with weary resignation; and Jack and Ben having a conversation about Jesus Christ's apostle "Doubting" Thomas, and whether he ever became a believer.

There's always been a touch of *The Last Temptation of Christ* to this show—most notably in the classic Desmond★ episode "Flashes Before Your Eyes"—but here that vibe is especially powerful, as the characters contemplate the sacrifice they're about to make and wonder to themselves whether it's necessary. For the first time this season, these people who left the Island seem connected to each other again. They're about to let themselves get swept back up in the weirdness of the Island, and they're facing the opportunity with a combination of wonder and worry.

And then: The airplane crashes (or does it?) as a familiar flash of light appears, implying our heroes may have been wrested out of their plane to a different point in time, perhaps separate from the actual plane going down. They're still reacting with fear, awe, and amazement when suddenly a spiffy, new-looking Dharma bus drives up and a man in a jumpsuit—Jin!—steps out.

Supersonic? That may be a stretch. But it sure is a rush. —*NM*

★　Desmond makes an appearance in this episode too, arriving at the Lamp Post to tell Eloise that Daniel came to see him at the Swan way back in the past (in "Because You Left") and that Daniel needs Eloise's help. She responds that it's *Desmond* who needs to go back—something he is not yet ready to do.

THE ANSWERS YOU
CAME FOR

"THE LIFE AND DEATH OF
JEREMY BENTHAM"
—
SEASON 5, EPISODE 7
ORIGINAL AIRDATE 2/25/09

Why are there polar bears on the Island?

To this day, when I try to defend *Lost* as a series that resolved almost all its many mysteries, I'm hit with that question as a supposed example of something that *Lost* didn't answer. It's obvious why that's the example people jump to. The polar bear in the show's pilot was one of its initial big, buzzy mysteries, and the series never had someone explain just why those dang polar bears were on the damn Island in the first place!

Except the show *did* answer that question. It just did so in a way a lot of viewers didn't notice. "The Life and Death of Jeremy Bentham" snaps the last puzzle piece of that explanation into place—and it serves as a useful example of how *Lost* resolves its mysteries and why viewers so often miss the answers the show provides.

But first: Why were those polar bears on the Island anyway?

The Dharma Initiative first brought polar bears to the Island as part of its larger experiments on wildlife in the strange environment. They were kept in the cages where Sawyer and Kate were kept in Season Three, where the bears had to solve puzzles to receive their daily fish biscuit. Deep beneath the Island is an enormous wheel that allows the Island to move in space★ when turned. That wheel is in a very cold location, and finding an animal that loves the cold and could be trained (say, to get

★   And eventually time.

239

fish biscuits from an elaborate contraption) would be a good way to turn said wheel. An animal like, say, a polar bear. Why not just have a human do so? Well, pushing the wheel is a one-way ticket off the Island, as we learned when Charlotte discovers a polar bear skeleton buried in Tunisia. Then, in this episode, Locke pushes the wheel and is dropped in the same location in the desert, filling in the last little gap in the polar bear puzzle.*

The thing is: Nobody ever sits down and says any of this within the show itself.† All the puzzle pieces existed within the show, but they were spread out across three seasons of television from the initial reveal of those polar bear cages to the final moment of Locke crash-landing in the desert. What's more, if you didn't remember that, say, Charlotte found the polar bear skeleton in Season Four, you'd be unlikely to conclude "Oh, hey, Locke landed in that same place. I wonder if the polar bears were being used to move the Island?" You'd just think weird shit was happening for its own sake. Or, put another way: You'd be a typical fan of the show who turned on it hardcore in later seasons.

The show's stubbornness about rarely, if ever, offering traditional info-dumps led to its reputation as a series that didn't answer questions. Yet on the fan wiki Lostpedia—the online clearinghouse for *Lost* stuff—the number of genuinely unanswered questions is very, very small. With a couple of small exceptions,‡ they mostly deal with character motivations that are open to interpretation or mysteries so big that the characters could not reasonably learn the answer to them.§

---

* Lots of viewers may have already filled in the Tunisia connection after the Season Four episode "The Shape of Things to Come" because Ben is also dropped in Tunisia when he moves the Island. But "Jeremy Bentham" makes this connection *crystal clear* and explains that "the exit" in Tunisia is being monitored by Widmore for anomalies.
† A greatly abbreviated version of this explanation can be found in the show's DVD-only epilogue "The New Man in Charge." That epilogue also says that polar bears can withstand electromagnetism better than many animals, which is not something you can conclude easily from the show proper.
‡ The two most salient ones: What was up with Walt's powers? Who was firing at the castaways from the other outrigger early in Season Five?
§ The biggest is probably "What is the Island?," a question the show answers but so obliquely that it is left to the individual viewer's interpretation. More on this when we get to the final season.

Lost's answers for questions reveal how it uneasily bridges two TV eras. When it debuted in 2004, most American households were still watching TV the old-fashioned way, tuning in once per week at a designated time, and they were mostly watching the big four broadcast networks (ABC, CBS, Fox, NBC). Yes, the TV-on-DVD box set was at its peak when the show was young, and the DVR was entering more and more homes. But by and large, the way people watched TV hadn't changed since the 1950s. In that world, answering a question like "Why are there polar bears on the Island?" with a series of puzzle pieces that snapped into place across three separate seasons of television was a bit ridiculous. You couldn't count on people to have seen every episode, even if they were discussing the show online.

By the show's end in 2010, DVR use was far more common, DVDs were on the way out, and streaming had become the TV viewing method of choice for many, trends that would only accelerate in the decade that followed. When streaming, where viewers can watch many episodes in a row, it's a lot easier to draw connections in the way *Lost* hopes you will, even if it still requires the viewer to make some logical leaps between plot points. Perversely, however, the streaming era has become almost as dependent on dropping clunky exposition as the old broadcast networks were, simply because for many viewers, what's on Netflix becomes background noise.

Thus, while *Lost*'s "puzzle pieces for observant viewers" method of mystery solving seems to presage the streaming era to come, it is best understood as the last gasp of a dying model. *Lost* got away with answering questions this way because it aired in an era when network TV was guarding itself against intruders from all over. If *Lost* could be a hit by letting observant viewers piece things together on their own—or with thousands of their other observant pals online—ABC wasn't going to sneeze at that.

And even if you weren't inclined to hop online and draw connections between a polar bear skeleton and Locke landing in the desert, the show's dedication to answering its mysteries only insofar as the *characters* care about them always kept it on the right track. For an episode that fills in a surprising number of puzzle pieces among a bunch of different *Lost* mysteries, the overwhelming memory one will have of "Jeremy Bentham" is surely the despair of Locke's murder at the hands of Ben Linus.

Yes, there is a man sitting on the beach who looks and sounds like John Locke, but he remembers Ben killing him. Whatever happened after the murder, the experience marked him profoundly.

Across the run of *Lost* to this point, Locke has been a figure with an almost tyrannical sense of purpose. He, alone, can intuit what the Island wants, and he, alone, can make sure that will is carried out. That quality has made him an antagonist, a necessary evil, a messianic figure, a survivor, and a charismatic enigma at various points, and at times, he's been all five at once. He is perhaps the single most fleshed-out, well-developed character in the show, and Terry O'Quinn is remarkable at playing every little micro-expression that might plausibly flutter across Locke's face.

So, you might not have noticed that "Jeremy Bentham" answers the polar bear question, because it's also answering a character question: "Who is John Locke, deep down?" And its answer isn't particularly flattering: He's a bit of a dupe.

Across the course of the episode, Locke endures loss after loss after loss, first losing the Island when turning the wheel boots him off of it, then failing to convince any of the castaways who left the Island to return. The leg injury he sustains from falling into a well results in him being put in a wheelchair again, and he spends most of the episode being literally ferried around by an agent of Widmore. His purpose has been co-opted by other, more bloodthirsty men.

I mentioned in my write-up on "Walkabout" that Locke works within the show as a kind of analogue for the angriest, most vengeance-driven voices in the United States in the post-9/11 period. Across the run of the show, however, the series has taken great pains to explain how a figure like him can so easily be twisted and manipulated by others. The Island might have given Locke some sort of divine purpose, but he is only a single man and can never wholly understand what the divine says unto him. Perhaps the figure on the beach will reveal that Locke had a grand purpose and fate after all, but at the moment of his death, Locke has been cornered into abject despair, to the degree that Ben murders Locke by strangling him with the noose he planned to use in a death by suicide.

Imagine that moment for a second. Imagine that the circumstances of your life trap you in a dingy hotel room, where, with your last few breaths, you realize that your supposedly higher purpose was mostly to be manipulated by others, that your life is coming to a lonely, sorry end, at the hands of your worst enemy. Imagine the last few thoughts you might have as you realized you had been a dupe all along.

And *then* the episode also tells you why there were polar bears on the Island? What a great show! —*ESJ*

SAWYER IS DADDY

"LAFLEUR"

—

SEASON 5, EPISODE 8
ORIGINAL AIRDATE 3/4/09

James "Sawyer" Ford is the kind of character who could only become as popular as he did in a world where TV networks made upward of twenty episodes per season and doled those episodes out once a week over the course of months. In *Lost*'s pilot, he's one of many characters who might charitably be described as "future Smoke Monster food." Yet across the first half of Season One, Josh Holloway's charisma and ability to deliver a pithy one-liner made him stand out from the show's larger ensemble in ways that, say, Boone and Shannon did not.

And then when he had chemistry with Evangeline Lilly as Kate? Well, that's the stuff TV love triangles are made of. And it's good to be in a TV love triangle. You can stay employed many years and make great money as one leg of such an arrangement.

How *Lost*'s love triangle eventually swallowed up the character of Kate is the subject of a different essay, but it was the best thing to happen to Sawyer. Most love triangles on TV have involved one woman (Kate) trying to choose between two men: the righteously uptight one who's not a lot of fun (sorry, Jack) and the bad boy rogue who's a blast to hang out with (hi, Sawyer!). Which character the woman ends up with varies from property to property,★ and each of the two love-interest options will have partisans among the fans. But speaking as a girl who always made the safe choice when it came to her romantic interests, it's *so much more fun* to want the woman to end up with the rogue.

It doesn't hurt that Sawyer is such a fun rogue to be around. Where Jack constantly seems hung up on his desire to find "purpose" and "meaning," Sawyer's a man of action. He swings into battle, if need be, and he'll join your dangerous mission at the drop of a hat. He's also a bit of a swooning romantic underneath everything else, his prickly exterior a product of a bad upbringing and (because this is *Lost*) some intense daddy issues. He's a bad boy, yes, but maybe not if the right woman could fix him?†

The big gambit of "LaFleur," then, isn't just that *Lost* is going to further complicate its love triangle by permanently adding Juliet to it as a *fourth* participant. It also hopes to successfully convince us in one episode that Sawyer could become a dedicated romantic partner and a member in good standing of the Dharma Initiative over the course of three years. The episode pulls both gambits off with flying colors, and when I try to explain why Season Five is my favorite of the show, it's thanks to episodes like this one, where it feels like the show is operating on a level where its characters and sci-fi plot elements keep feeding into each other in an endless ouroboros.

"LaFleur" is a time-jump episode unlike any other, bringing viewers to the precipice of everything changing, then leaping forward in time to see how things have changed. *Lost* has always played with time; here, too, it organizes its time-jump nonlinearly, opening in 1977, when Sawyer (aka "James LaFleur"), Juliet, Miles, Jin, and Faraday are all living and working with the Dharma Initiative, with Sawyer even serving as head of security. Then we're in 1974, in the moment when Locke moved the Island.‡ Locke was booted off and Sawyer and company tried to go back

---

★   Both *Twilight* and *The Hunger Games* end with the heroine picking the dull boy, but *The Vampire Diaries* ends with her picking the rogue. Buffy Summers (of vampire-slaying fame) chooses herself, and good for her.

†   SWOON.

‡   This happened at the end of episode five, and we're now in episode eight, in case you were wondering just how long viewers had to wait to find out what happened to Sawyer et al. *Lost* had gotten bold at how it parceled out character information and waited to resolve cliffhangers by this point in its run.

to the beach but, instead, got involved in the middle of an altercation between Dharma and the Others. The episode jumps between the two time periods with ever-greater showmanship.

The trick of any good time-jump episode is to seed the events that happen after the time-jump in the things viewers see before the time-jump. The 1977 Sawyer that we see working as Dharma's security head and the roguish 1974 Sawyer just trying to survive in the jungle (who is really damn sick of jumping through time) have to feel like the same guy. Thanks to Holloway's work, both Sawyer and "LaFleur" feel like they're the same person, and it doesn't hurt that Sawyer, a con artist, is already used to playing parts to fool people. But the trick of the episode is how skillfully it makes you think that maybe, deep down, Sawyer was always more like James LaFleur than he realized.

To explore this idea, let's go to where "LaFleur" ends, with the return of Jack, Kate, and Hurley to the Island, where they've been dumped into the 1970s timeline.* In the 1977 timeline, Sawyer attempts to comfort a man whose wife's former husband died in the altercation with the Others that Sawyer interrupted in 1974. Sure, she still has feelings around her dead husband, but also, a lot has changed in three years—just as a lot has changed for Sawyer. This whole plot clearly means to get us thinking about Kate and the possibility of the love triangle kicking into high gear again when she returns.

And yet if you watch "LaFleur" and see the way Sawyer and Juliet greet each other at the end of a long, hard day with professional successes for both, do you *at all* buy that he's still going to be hung up on Kate? Because I sure don't!

Lost's flagship love triangle has been on the verge of becoming a love square since Juliet's arrival in Season Three. But for as much as Juliet might've sparked with Jack, the romantic tension never quite caught—they simply made too much sense as a couple. On TV comedies, a couple that makes perfect sense on paper can work,† but on TV dramas, there's a need for constant rising tension. When Jack fought with Kate, it just felt

---

* The other members of the returning Oceanic Six are deposited in 2007, which means that, among other things, Sun and Jin are now separated by thirty years of time. Noooo!

† Though not always! Many, many, many sitcom pairings fall under the broad header of "opposites attract."

like he was yelling at his sister. When Sawyer fought with Kate, it felt like foreplay.

On most TV shows, that would have resulted in Sawyer and Kate ending up together, and *Lost* seemed to be trending in that direction until "LaFleur," which does something I don't think I've seen another show do. In effect, it takes Sawyer out of the love triangle altogether. Yes, we're supposed to think that Kate is still this great, lost love, but c'mon. She left for three years, and Sawyer found the woman he loves. It's hard to see him standing in the doorway to his kitchen, smiling as he presents a flower to Juliet, and *not* imagine them simultaneously as a couple newly courting and one that has been married forty years.

What "LaFleur" ultimately reveals about Sawyer is that once he's out from under the shadow of people he can't help but define himself against, he's terrific at being a boss, a lover, and a friend. When people he perceives himself as being beneath on the social ladder are around, Sawyer will ride himself down and raise hell. But when he can start over as a guy people respect, with a woman who similarly respects him at his side, he'll be the most charming guy around.

TV is famous as a medium that allows characters to "change," but I've always found this to be a misnomer. The best shows simply chip away at characters until we see who they always were. They don't become anybody new; they just become themselves. On *Lost*, that usually takes the form of, say, Jack Shephard hurling himself against a wall, again and again, hoping he gets a slightly different result. But in the case of Sawyer, it goes somewhere sweeter and more unexpected. Here's a guy that even his own show wrote off, who still surprises you. Wouldn't you want to keep that guy around? Wouldn't you want to build a life—or a TV show—with him? —*ESJ*

"NAMASTE"
—
SEASON 5, EPISODE 9
ORIGINAL AIRDATE 3/18/09

In 1977: Jack, Hurley, and Kate join the Dharma Initiative with Sawyer's help, while a confused Sayid stumbles out of the jungle and gets treated as a Hostile.

In 2007: Flight 316 has a bumpy landing on the Hydra station runway that Kate and Sawyer helped build just off the Island's coast; and Sun and Frank leave Ben and the rest of their traveling party behind so they can row over to the crumbling Dharma barracks, where they learn that their friends are stuck in the past.

Lost launched with a cast of familiar faces and relative unknowns. Then, as the series rolled on, each of the guest stars and new regulars tended to be drawn from the ranks of veteran character actors and foreign TV stars, such that at times the original batch of Oceanic 815ers could seem a little overmatched, acting-wise. "Namaste," though, is one of the best acting showcases for *Lost*'s core cast, because it calls on their characters to adjust to a situation that's a mix of the familiar and the unfamiliar—leading to complex emotions, between reflectiveness and trepidation.

"Namaste" is effectively a pilot episode for the second half of Season Five—and, in a way, for the remainder of *Lost*. The season's first quarter offered a mix of mind-bending on-Island thrills and haltingly slow-paced off-Island woes. By the end of "This Place Is Death," the writers had introduced so many complications and so many hints and teases about how everything was going to fit together that it took three more or less stand-alone episodes to tell us everything we needed to know before "Namaste." When he left the Island, what did Locke do that ultimately led to his death? Watch "The Life and Death of Jeremy Bentham." How did (most of) the Oceanic Six get back to the Island? Watch "316." How did the 815ers who stayed on the Island end up joining the Dharma Initiative? Watch "LaFleur."

As for any lingering questions about how Kate and Sayid ended up taking Flight 316 and why Ben looked all bruised and battered on the plane . . . well, we're not done with the off-Island flashbacks, so stay tuned. But before *Lost* gets back to that, we get to enjoy watching the reunions of these characters with each other and with the Island, after three years apart. We get Hugo's genuine enthusiasm at seeing Sawyer alive, as well as his delight at discovering that Jin's English is now "awesome." We get Sawyer's twinge of guilt and sorrow at learning that—as far as everyone stuck in 1977 knows—Locke is dead. We get Kate's generally dazed reaction to everything, putting her friends at risk. (When Sawyer refers to the Hostiles and then reminds a confused Kate that they're the same as the Others, he sounds a little frustrated, as if saying, "Get back up to speed, Freckles.")

Plus, we get a lot of scenes where the writers shine at what they do very well: showing these characters making complicated plans. In the past, Sawyer scrambles to integrate his old friends into an organization, Dharma, that is exclusive, secretive, and somewhat distrustful by nature. In the present, the 316ers scatter to follow their own agendas, which leads to Sun and Frank encountering Christian Shephard's ghost and being shown a picture of their friends in Dharma jumpsuits. How is Sun going to find Jin now? It seems impossible. But then so is most of what they've been doing to get back to the Island.

It all ends back in 1977 with Sayid patiently (to a point) being treated once again as an enemy, as he arrives inconveniently in the Dharma camp and Jin makes the snap decision to pretend he's a Hostile. And then Sayid finds an unexpected ally in a Dharma teen who offers him a sandwich and says his name is Ben. Like the rest of his traveling companions, Sayid knows this place, and he knows some of these people. But nothing is quite the same. —*NM*

"HE'S OUR YOU"
—
SEASON 5, EPISODE 10
ORIGINAL AIRDATE 3/25/09

On the Island: Sayid feels abandoned by his Dharma-bound colleagues, so he decides to let the young Ben help him escape.

In the flashbacks: Sayid completes Ben's anti-Widmore kill list and then wrestles with who he really is and how he should live the rest of his life.

At one point in "He's Our You," Juliet stares out the window of the house she shares with Sawyer, and while looking at Jack and Kate, she sighs, "It's over, isn't it?" Juliet knows that from the moment the 316ers landed back in their lives, the clock started ticking. It's only a matter of time before she and her man will be traipsing through the jungle, dodging bullets and looking for time machines or spaceships or some other freaky game-changer.

This is ostensibly the reason that Sawyer gives to Sayid about why he can't just let his old buddy out of Dharma jail. He doesn't want this idyllic life he's built with Juliet to end before it has to. And if that means Sayid the Torturer has to get tortured himself—by a mild-mannered but ruthless Dharman named Oldham (William Sanderson)—then hey, it's not like Sayid is some noble innocent.

On some level, Sayid understands this, too, even if he doesn't like it. The flashbacks in "He's Our You" to Sayid's off-Island life (in multiple eras) are to some extent unnecessary, because it wasn't absolutely crucial to connect the dots between some of the missing pieces in Sayid's biography: like what happened to him after "The Economist," and how he ended up being taken onto 316 in handcuffs by Ilana. But in a character-development sense, this episode is pivotal—especially since Sayid wasn't given a lot to do in *Lost* between "The Economist" and "He's Our You." Here he gets the chance to think about how much of his life he's spent committing acts of violence against other people, under orders.

So, Sayid decides to go freelance. He's not waiting for Sawyer to figure out a way to free him. And he's not worrying about what the Island wants or the "rules" of time travel or any of that junk. He gets Ben to help him escape, with the aid of a diversionary flaming vehicle. And then he shoots Ben right in the chest. What can Sawyer do about that? The man who was doing so well as "LaFleur" quietly grumbles that he'd gone three years with no burning buses; and then within one day of Jack, Kate, Hurley, and Sayid returning . . . chaos. —*NM*

"WHATEVER HAPPENED, HAPPENED"

—

SEASON 5, EPISODE 11
ORIGINAL AIRDATE 4/1/09

On the Island: Our heroes debate whether they have any responsibility to save Ben's life, until a frustrated Kate takes matters into her own hands and hands Ben over to the Hostiles, who pledge to heal him but warn that he will never be the same.

In the flashbacks: Kate pays two visits, first to Sawyer's ex-girlfriend Cassidy and then to Claire's mom Carole, to whom she hands over Aaron before making her way onto Flight 316.

After Sayid completed his contract as Ben's hired gun, he lived a quiet and penitent life for a while, until Ben came calling again to tell him that someone had killed Locke (but not to confess to being that someone). He suggested that Sayid needed to come out of retirement and get back to doing what he does best. And in a roundabout way, when Sayid shoots Young Ben in 1977, he does what the adult Ben employed him to do in 2007. He exacts revenge for the murder of John Locke.

There's much in "Whatever Happened, Happened" exploring irony and fate, and the question of whether anyone has any personal responsibility on a mystical Island where magic occurs on the regular. That's certainly on Jack's mind, when he's presented with the opportunity to use his surgical skills to try to save Young Ben's life, just as he once operated on Older Ben. Jack has returned to the Island to try to become a different kind of person, and here he's being asked to repeat himself. The Island hasn't yet revealed to Jack who that person should be. What he does know is: The adult Ben ruined and/or ended many people's lives; Jack has already saved Ben's life once before, and the outcome to that wasn't great; and most importantly, since the adult Ben exists in 2007, Young Ben probably didn't die in 1977. So, Jack probably could do nothing and the kid'll make it anyway. Maybe.

The off-Island flashbacks are laced with strong emotions, and bolstered by an excellent performance from Evangeline Lilly, as Kate sorts through her feelings about Aaron and tries to separate them from her feelings about Sawyer and Jack. This is one of the best of the Kate episodes, because the flashbacks are so quiet, subtle, and human, as Kate talks woman-to-woman (and mother-to-mother) with first Cassidy and then Carole. This new maternal instinct is perhaps what pushes her to advocate so hard for saving Young Ben.

But it's the philosophical musings in this episode—underscored by the title—that provide most of its substance. When Jack talks to Kate about how familiar it is that he is asked to save Ben's life . . . well, it's true. It is familiar: Jack, Kate, Sawyer, Juliet, and Ben, doomed to repeat the same scenario. That's the way the Island works. It repeats things until it gets the sequence right, like a computer trying to crack a code—or find a bug.

The irony, of course, is that Jack not saving Ben forces him into the arms of the Hostiles, which turns Ben into the monster he'll inevitably become. Just like how Sayid, by shooting Ben, created Ben. Fate will always have its way. —NM

"DEAD IS DEAD"

—

SEASON 5, EPISODE 12
ORIGINAL AIRDATE 4/8/09

On the Island: As Locke takes Ben on a trip to the Temple to face the judgment of the Smoke Monster, Ben has the opportunity to reflect on some of the crucial and in some cases regrettable choices he has made.

At the time that Kate hands the mortally wounded young Ben Linus over to Richard Alpert, the Island faction known as "The Hostiles" are being co-led by Charles Widmore and Eloise Hawking. Or at least they think they're the leaders. At the end of "Whatever Happened, Happened," Richard waves off the warning that Widmore and Hawking won't approve of him healing Ben, because Richard answers to the older, deeper power on the Island. And he knows that at least part of that power—the darker part—will be all too happy to have Ben as a new puppet.

But what does it mean, to be healed by the Island's malevolence? Back in Season Three, "The Man Behind the Curtain" delivered what seemed to be Ben's origin story. Here's this lonely, motherless child, with a bitter dad who drags him to a dangerous scientific outpost, where the boy is treated like a nobody until he allies with the Island's unfriendly inhabitants and helps them purge the scientists, en masse. "Dead Is Dead" tells the rest of that story, in pieces drawn across decades. It focuses less on the "poor kid breaks bad" angle and more on the "bad guy does bad things."

In the rundown of important incidents from Ben's post-"healing" life—which includes agreeing to work for Widmore, deposing and exiling Widmore, and trying to murder Widmore's daughter Penny and her boyfriend Desmond—the one awful thing he does that almost seems forgivable is abducting Alex. At the time, he's under orders from Widmore to kill Rousseau and her baby. Instead, he saves Rousseau's life (while making her permanently paranoid by telling her to watch out for "the whispers") and keeps Alex. He says he did this because he didn't think

Jacob would want to harm an infant. But really, he has a soft spot for children, having been a broken little kid himself.

In fact, one of the main points of "Dead Is Dead"—even if it doesn't become entirely clear until the season finale—is that Ben has no real idea what Jacob wants. Like Widmore and Hawking before him, he's just a figurehead, a pawn.* The Island's darkness has turned him cold and merciless (except toward minors) and made him willing to do what others wouldn't, by using lies and manipulation to cruel ends. But either those ends don't matter to the Island at all or they're what the Island wants. This part of Ben's origin story isn't about how he rose to power. It's about how he never had much power in the first place. —*NM*

FORCE GHOSTS

"SOME LIKE IT HOTH"

—

SEASON 5, EPISODE 13
ORIGINAL AIRDATE 4/15/09

It's easy to go too far with finding secret messages and hidden codes in every line and moment in *Lost*, as though Lindelof, Cuse, and their writers intended each second of the show to connect to something—which, as is very obvious by the end of the series, isn't so. Sometimes the writers dropped in cultural references or introduced cool ideas because in the rush to fill out an episode, they tapped whatever might be on their mind at the time. This is just what happens, making weekly episodic television.

In other words, when it comes to "Some Like it Hoth," there's no reason to make too much of Hurley deciding to spend his time in 1977 writing, from memory, the screenplay to *The Empire Strikes Back*, in hopes

---

*   Before Ben killed him, Locke seemed like he might be on that same course, to be another Island dupe.

of helping out the movie's producer, George Lucas. Sure, Hurley himself draws parallels between the Luke Skywalker/Darth Vader son/father relationship and Miles Straume's relationship with his dad Pierre Chang. And sure, this whole show is filled with characters who have Darth Vader–level daddy issues. But for the most part, this whole *Star Wars* digression is just a way to inject a little levity into *Lost*'s fifth season before the story takes some very dark turns.*

Except . . . Maybe there *is* something more to Hurley's whole *Star Wars* deal? It's *probably* not intentional, but there is some thematic resonance in the idea that Hurley, trapped in the past, is tinkering with and trying to improve something that already exists in his present. Isn't this what our time-lost heroes are doing this season: not just living through the Island's history but in small ways trying to "fix" it?

"Some Like It Hoth" is *Lost*'s only true "Miles episode,"† giving everyone's favorite sass-talkin' corpse-whisperer the showcase fans had been waiting for since he was introduced in the strike-shortened Season Four. On the Island, Miles spends the bulk of his airtime teamed up with Hurley, the show's other consistent source of comic relief. The result is arguably the funniest *Lost* of the season. But "Some Like It Hoth" doesn't spare the tension, pathos, or plot developments either.

You can't go wrong with an episode that has Hurley and Miles delivering a corpse‡—along with some sandwiches dressed with Hurley's famous garlic mayo—to Pierre Chang at the Orchid, all while having a conversation about their unique experiences of talking to dead people. Throughout, Hurley is hilarious, starting with his insistence that he and Miles carpool to the Orchid to help prevent global warming ("which hasn't happened yet"), and continuing with his dismissing Miles's skepticism

---

* In the preceding episode's podcast, Damon Lindelof and Carlton Cuse outright stated that "Some Like It Hoth" was intended to lighten things up a bit before a heavier final stretch.

† In "Confirmed Dead," Miles shares space with his fellow non-commando Freighties.

‡ The music in this episode includes "It Never Rains in Southern California" by Albert Hammond (father of the Strokes' guitarist, by the way), and "Love Will Keep Us Together" by the Captain & Tennille. Which raises a question: Do the Dharma folks listen to the K-tel *Gold Rock* collections in their vans, or do they have a low-wattage radio station broadcasting somewhere on the Island?

about whether he can actually *see* the ghosts he chats with and suggesting that his own superpower is better.

When Hurley and Miles arrive at the Orchid—still under construction—Chang is initially irritated that Miles has brought along someone he wasn't supposed to; and he threatens Hurley with reassignment, mentioning that the polar bear feces probably needs shoveling. And when Hurley mutters to Miles that Chang is a douche, Miles drops the secret that all of *Lost* fandom guessed back in the opening scene of the Season Five premiere: "That douche is my dad."

What happens next pushes "Some Like It Hoth" to places unexpected. Once Hurley realizes that Miles has been living on an island with his mother and his father and an infant version of himself—born during his time there!—he takes it upon himself to bring father and son closer together. (He explains to Miles that if everything breaks right, maybe Chang will let him hold Baby Miles.) Miles is having none of it, since he bears a lifelong grudge against his dad for abandoning him and his mom for some never-explained reason back in 1977 (ahem). But Hurley brings him around using his extended Luke/Vader metaphor. How much galactic destruction could've been avoided if the Skywalker boys had just hugged it out?

So, Miles peeks in on his father's house and sees Pierre bouncing Baby Miles on his knee and reading him a book (about polar bears!), giving this half of the episode a well-earned emotional button.

Miles's off-Island flashbacks, meanwhile, function more like a supernatural thriller, with director Jack Bender using horror-movie-like handheld shots during a scene where the young ghost-whisperer finds a dead body in a cruddy LA apartment complex, and lingering on the wonderful incongruousness of Teen Punk Miles trying to extract information about his hazy past and weird powers from his mother before she dies.

The flashbacks extend from Miles's youth to the moment where he meets Naomi Dorrit for the first time and gets the offer to work for Charles Widmore (for $1.6 million . . . exactly half of what he asks Ben for in "Eggtown"). Naomi tests Miles by leading him to a corpse and asking what he can read in the dead man's mind, and Miles passes the test by saying that the stiff was delivering photos of empty graves and a purchase order for an old airplane to Widmore. Later, after grabbing some grub, Miles is kidnapped by some surprisingly friendly commandos, who urge him not to work for Widmore, and instead tell him that if he joins their cause he'll learn "what lies in the shadow of the statue"—as well as all he needs to know about his family and his "gift."

This B-story has its own nice button, relating to a bit of phony ghost-talking that Miles does for his client Howard Gray (played by Dean Norris, at the time becoming better known for his role as Hank on *Breaking Bad*). Miles tells Howard that his dead son knew he loved him; but after he gets the Widmore gig, he comes back and admits he was lying. He doesn't come clean to help Mr. Gray; he does it for the son, who Miles feels deserved to hear his dad say he loved him when he was alive. Another well-earned moment.

"Some Like It Hoth" has a final twist. Chang asks Miles to drive him to the dock to pick up some scientists from Ann Arbor. One of those scientists? Daniel Faraday. The time for goofy *Star Wars* references and warm family reunions is passing. Our whiz-bang '70s adventure is coming to an end. —*NM*

RUNNING OUT OF TIME

"THE VARIABLE"

—

SEASON 5, EPISODE 14 (EPISODE 100!)
ORIGINAL AIRDATE 4/29/09

For someone who didn't arrive on *Lost* until the show was in its home-stretch, Daniel Faraday ended up mattering a great deal—to the fans, to the story, and to the emotional heart of the show. A lot of that was due to Jeremy Davies, an inspired casting choice, blending soulfulness and weirdness into a character who always looked like he was one second away from breaking down completely. But it also had to do with how Lindelof and Cuse use Faraday.

Faraday is the guy who can ask the questions the writers need answered—and the guy who can explain what those answers mean, being a physicist. Equally at home with hard science and abstract philosophy, Faraday isn't just interested in how "the strange properties of the Island" work, but also why.

In "The Variable," for example—the Faraday showcase episode—Davies is able to bring multiple meanings to a simple line, as when he walks up to Jack in 1977 and asks how he made it back to the Island. From episode one, *Lost* is preoccupied with the notion of free will versus destiny, which means Daniel's question isn't a logistical one, but rather an existential one: What particular life path has brought Jack to this point? Is it as it's supposed to be? According to Daniel, the answer to the latter question is no.

"The Variable" is one of the most intense, action-packed episodes in *Lost*'s run, yet it's also one of the most philosophical and thought-provoking—and one that confirms some pieces of long-suspected *Lost* mythology while shaking up others. At the center of the whole hour is Daniel Faraday: a man in a hurry, trying to maximize the time he has left before life-changing events occur. With Daniel, everything's always about time.

Specifically, Daniel claims early in "The Variable" that in about six hours, the Dharma Initiative is going to tap into a pocket of electromagnetic energy that will unleash a "catastrophic" effect. This will go down in Dharma history as "the Incident," and will lead to the Swan station being repurposed as a kind of elaborate venting system for these destructive forces. One day Desmond will fail to push the Swan's buttons in time, and Oceanic 815 will crash, and Charles Widmore will send a freighter with Daniel Faraday on it, and so on and so on. So, here's what Daniel proposes: He wants Pierre Chang to order a general evacuation of the Island. And then he'd like to avert "the Incident" by detonating a hydrogen bomb.*

Apparently, the old Daniel Faraday of "Whatever Happened, Happened" had a change of heart during his years off the Island in Ann Arbor. Where before he was focused on "constants," now he's thinking about

---

* Jughead! The bomb first seen in the Season Five episode titled, well, "Jughead."

"variables." Maybe there are some random, destiny-bending elements out there. During his few remaining hours on the Island, Daniel acts like a total wild card. He tells Dr. Chang that Miles is his son from the future. He goes against what he swore three years ago and tells young Charlotte to escape. He's ready to throw off the shackles of fate and live the life he's never been allowed to live before.

Cue flashbacks.

The tales of Young Daniel in "The Variable" are far-reaching in scope and seasoned with little revelations and moments of poignancy.

We see Daniel as a boy, playing the piano for Eloise and hearing from his mother that he'll have to forget about frivolous pursuits like music because he has important scientific work to do. (When told that it's her job to keep him from wasting time, he tellingly replies, "I can make time.") Then we find Daniel graduating from Oxford and being forced by Eloise to leave his girlfriend/assistant Theresa behind so he can receive the leather-bound journal that will be so central to his life.

We move then to Crying Dan, from back in Season Four's "Confirmed Dead," and we learn that his brain has been fried from all his time-travel experiments, such that he weeps over the news of the crash of Oceanic 815 without really knowing why. Then he receives a visitor: Charles Widmore, who confesses that he staged the underwater 815 wreckage, and that he wants Daniel to travel to the Island so that his brain will be healed and he can continue his important work. (Here we see the influence of Marvel Comics on the *Lost* writers, as Faraday follows in the footsteps of psychologically damaged superhero scientists like Bruce Banner, Reed Richards, and Henry Pym.)

Finally, we see Daniel just before his trip to the Island, unable to play the easy piano piece he knew as a kid, and receiving his final, fateful instructions from Eloise that he must take Widmore's offer and go to the Island, for reasons she can't really divulge (because they're just too terrible).

While this isn't really part of the Daniel flashbacks per se, a lot of "The Variable" is also about Eloise Hawking, who we see at the hospital where Penny is fretting over Desmond's gunshot wound.* Long story short:

---

* The timeline gets really tangled in Season Five between all the flashbacks and time travel, but in "Some Like It Hoth" we learn via flashback that Ben shot Desmond before boarding Ajira 316.

Desmond's going to be OK. Short story that probably could've been longer: We also learn that, as suspected by many, Charles Widmore is Daniel's father.*

The flashbacks and off-Island business mostly establish that Daniel has been through a lot and has found himself more capable of change than he once might've expected, including now believing that maybe people who are unstuck in time can and should change the future—or fix the past. On the Island, he is thrust into the middle of multiple long-simmering conflicts, some of which have been instigated by his asking to be taken to the Hostiles so that he can get his hydrogen bomb plan rolling. He travels with Jack and Kate, while Miles and Hurley† and Jin join Sawyer and Juliet in packing their bags to head back to the beach.

None of this, of course, comes easy. Jack and Sawyer bicker over whether they should leave the compound at all, with Sawyer pleading with Kate not to help Daniel, and Juliet stepping in and giving Kate and Daniel the code for the Sonic Weapon Fence. That "paradise lost" feeling that's been nagging Sawyer and Juliet ever since Jack and Kate and the gang returned becomes a full-blown reality.

As we reach the end of Season Five, the show seems to be rushing headlong toward crisis—as is usually the case with *Lost* finales. The writers are experts at ratcheting up the intensity as they approach finish lines. Nevertheless, this episode still finds time for some tender moments, like Sawyer grabbing Juliet's hand, and him apologetically asking if she still has his back. (Her terse, I-love-you-but-I'm-still-mad-at-you reply: "You still got mine?") And it has time for some quirky moments, like Daniel asking if Kate had any guns "for a beginner," shortly before a thrillingly choreographed shoot-out with Radzinsky's crew.‡

This episode keeps the viewers thinking about time throughout—often in subtle ways, through the dialogue, whether it be Daniel noting that Pierre Chang arrives at the Swan "right on time" or the way he tells Jack and Kate he'll be "back in ten minutes" before he goes to talk to

---

* During the time-hopping episodes earlier in Season Five, we learned that Charles Widmore and Eloise Hawking used to live on the Island and serve Jacob. Sawyer would later ask Faraday if his mother was an Other.

† Hurley, getting caught up on what his friends have been up in the three years since he last saw them, refers to 1954 as "Fonzie-times."

‡ Radzinsky is especially irritated at getting shot by a physicist.

Charlotte. Everything surrounding Daniel just seems so orderly and on schedule, including his fateful arrival in the Hostiles' camp, where he's ultimately shot and killed by . . . Eloise Hawking.

Why did Ms. Hawking groom her son to be the victim of her younger self? If Daniel could go back in time and do it all over again, would he maybe take off his jumpsuit and come into the Hostiles' camp with his gun down? Or did all of this happen exactly as it was supposed to?

And then there's this: Just how amazing is Daniel Faraday? A tremendous lot. —NM

"FOLLOW THE LEADER"
—
SEASON 5, EPISODE 15
ORIGINAL AIRDATE 5/6/09

In 1977: The Dharmans and the Hostiles each figure out that our heroes are not who they have said they were, and they react either with anger and violence, or with a willingness to help them achieve their goals (which is either to leave the Island or to detonate a hydrogen bomb).

In 2007: Locke unnerves Ben and Richard with demonstrations of his uncanny connections to the Island's forces, before announcing his intention to visit—and kill—Jacob.

What was the Dharma Initiative's actual purpose? The Dharmans arrived on the Island to study and perhaps find some humanity-enriching use for its "unique properties," but soon found themselves sidetracked by their conflict with the Hostiles, who had been on the Island for . . . ?

Let's start again. What were the Hostiles (aka the Others) actually doing on the Island? Aside from the ageless Richard (whose origin story will come in Season Six), the folks we see camped out on the plains or usurping Dharma's built structures don't seem to have much of an agenda outside of protecting the Island. They have a temple, but we don't see much worship. They have a hierarchy, but no one seems very happy about it.

Like a lot of *Lost*'s pre-finale episodes, "Follow the Leader" serves as a kind of extended prologue, mostly setting up what's to come—which in this case is a season finale that will effectively end the story of the Dharma Initiative and, by extension, begin winding down the story of the Hostiles/Others, who throughout the show are largely defined by their opposition to interlopers. In Season Six, the Island's longtime residents will mostly be bystanders, as the interlopers fight among themselves and in some cases unwittingly serve as pawns of the Island's true protectors. In the past, our heroes argue about whether they should take drastic measures to try and reset the timeline, perhaps bringing back some of their dead in the process, or if they should stay the course and try to make a new life in the late '70s. In the present, Locke takes total command of the motley band of Island vets and newcomers, ordering Richard around★ and announcing his plan to drag Jacob out of the shadows so that he can answer for all that's happened here. In both eras, there are Gordian knots that these men and women of action are more than ready to cut straight through.

But before we say goodbye to the violent conflict of the Dharma years, we should take a moment to recognize how the Island can turn even hippie idealists into bitter, vengeful types, who gripe about their status and are willing to use deception and torture against the people they perceive to be their enemies. At a certain point, "communing with the Island" seems to matter less to the people who live there than clinging desperately to some small piece of the place.

It's no wonder that Jack—who has spent his entire time since returning to the Island looking for a sign from Jacob or whomever about what he should do with his life—hesitates for so long to take any action at all. And then finally, he hears an idea he likes, which speaks to his own simmering rage and frustration.

He wants to blow the whole place up. —*NM*

★ Closing the loop on the scene between Richard and Locke in "Because You Left," the Locke in this episode leads Richard to the spot where the Locke in that episode was shot, so that Richard can treat his wound and tell him to leave the Island (and die).

EVERYTHING'S
EXPLODING

"THE INCIDENT"
—
SEASON 5, EPISODES 16 & 17
ORIGINAL AIRDATE 5/13/09

Way back in *Lost*'s first season, the show introduced the motif of The Game. The castaways find two skeletons in a cave, with two stone game-pieces in a pouch: one black, one white. Locke spent a lot of time playing backgammon. The characters kept shuffling back and forth to different spots on the Island, like pieces on a board. It's the one hint to the larger point of the Island—and of *Lost*—that held on the longest and strongest from the earliest episodes. While viewers were asking questions like "Are the 815ers dead?" and "Is the Island the literal biblical Hell?," Lindelof and Cuse had really already given the audience the juiciest answer to what all of this is about. It's a game. Someone is playing a game.

But who? This is the question that the Season Five finale answers.

The two-part "The Incident" has the heft and sweep of a great movie—even though it's a movie that no one who hadn't watched the previous 100 episodes of *Lost* would understand. If Season Five was about shading in all the finer details of the Island's history (minus two more essential origin stories, saved for Season Six), the finale is about wiping the slate clean, to make way for the end. Forget about the Dharma Initiative. Forget about introducing important new characters with their own backstories and arcs. Starting with "The Incident," *Lost* starts paring the cast and the scope down to what matters most, to finish the story.

That narrowing down disappointed a lot of fans, who were hoping to learn more about some of the *Lost* characters' parents and their own connections to the Island.* But even in a game, the players eventually have to settle on a strategy. There might've been a different path through *Lost*'s labyrinthine narrative that Lindelof and Cuse and company could've chosen; and it might've even been effective in its own way. This endgame is the one that we get.

The bulk of the episode takes place in 1977, where the time-traveling 815ers (plus Juliet and Miles) are in their usual mode of arguing about their next move. Jack wants to follow Faraday's plan and detonate Jughead, in a maneuver he believes will send them back to 2007, just ahead of the infamous "Incident" that the Dharma artifacts they found in the present day warned them about.† Sawyer would rather escape the Incident by taking the Dharma submarine off the Island and living happily in the outside world in 1977 with Juliet. They all fight with each other. They all fight with the Dharma Initiative. But eventually—inevitably—they blow everything up, thanks to Juliet sacrificing her life to make the bomb go off.

Meanwhile, in 2007, different groups are moving across the Island toward Jacob's real home, in a chamber at the base of what once was a giant statue of the Egyptian goddess Taweret, but which is now just a big ol' foot. One faction is led by the entity claiming to be the resurrected Locke, who has the wary backing of Richard‡ (and thus the rest of the Others) but is treated with fear and distrust by Ben, in part because this Locke wants Ben to kill Jacob. The other faction is led by Ilana, the Ajira 316 passenger who actually works for Jacob in the outside world. The two groups arrive nearly simultaneously at the Statue, where Ilana reveals to Richard that the real Locke is still dead—right around the same time that the thing pretending to be Locke does in fact goad Ben into killing Jacob, by reminding him of the decades Ben has spent on the Island serving a master he'd never even met.

---

*   Like what was the deal with Sun's father, who apparently had business with both the Hansos and the Widmores?
†   Unless, of course, the detonation *is* "the Incident." When this theory is floated, Miles ruefully quips that they haven't really thought any of this through.
‡   Richard has seen a lot of weird and miraculous things on the Island, but a dead Locke coming back to life genuinely frightens him.

But it's the flashbacks in this episode where the action's really happening. Whenever "The Incident" isn't ratcheting up the tension by crosscutting between the increasingly intense situations in 1977 and 2007, there are some more-relaxed interludes featuring pivotal, previously unseen moments from various characters' lives—each, in its own way, an "incident." We see a young Kate almost get caught shoplifting; a young Sawyer mourning his father; the moment when Sayid's true love Nadia was killed in a traffic accident; Ilana recuperating in a hospital room; Locke lying on the ground in the seconds right after his father pushed him out a window; Sun and Jin's wedding day; Jack still in a discombobulated state after performing surgery; Juliet being told that her parents are getting divorced; and Hurley getting released from jail, not long before he boarded Ajira 316.

What connects all these vignettes? These are moments that changed who these people are; and with the exception of Juliet's flashback, each of them features a visit from Jacob. He paid for the lunchbox Kate was going to steal. He handed Sawyer a pen to write a letter to the man responsible for destroying his family. He distracted Sayid, keeping him from saving Nadia. He got the wounded Ilana to pledge to help him. He revived Locke with a touch, and apologized while doing so.* He handed Jack an Apollo Bar. He convinced Hurley to return to the Island by reassuring him that he is not crazy. All of this—again, aside from Juliet's story—is a final confirmation of something *Lost* fans had been hoping for since Season One. The people who crashed on this Island are there for a reason. They matter to Jacob—so much so that he's willing to sow destruction and discord in their lives to get them where he needs them to be. In fact, he may have *wanted* them to be marked by tragedy, frustration, and sorrow, because that makes them angrier and more argumentative . . . ready to compete in the larger game he has in mind.

There are two other significant scenes in "The Incident," though one of them at first seems just like a cute bit of fan service. When Kate, Sawyer, and Juliet leave the submarine, they paddle ashore in a dinghy and run into Vincent, Rose, and Bernard, who have been living peacefully on their own throughout the mid-'70s, away from all the Dharma-versus-Hostiles

---

* And what book was Jacob reading just before Locke fell? Why it's Flannery O'Connor's *Everything That Rises Must Converge.*

nonsense. Rose explains that they're "retired" and no longer want to take part in people trying to kill each other. They don't care if they die when or if the Island is destroyed. They also make an offer to Juliet to join them in sitting on the sidelines—which Juliet, tragically as it turns out, declines.

The most important scene in the episode, though, is the first one. We see a man in white—Jacob—weaving in front of a fire, then fishing, then cooking his fish while staring out at a ship. A man in black—never named—walks up and blames Jacob for bringing the ship to the Island. "We know how it'll end," he says, claiming that there will be violence. Jacob notes that even though they know how it'll end, what happens before the end is "just progress." The Man in Black says he'd like to kill Jacob, but knows he can't until he finds a "loophole." Jacob says he'll be waiting.

Obviously, by the end of "The Incident," The Man in Black—in the guise of Locke—will have found his loophole, using Ben as his assassin. The implications of all this will be what Season Six is partially about. But before Season Five ends, *Lost* introduces some provocative and, in some ways, disturbing ideas.

It's clear from that opening that Jacob and The Man in Black have been competing with each other for a long time: Jacob as the guy in charge of the Island, and his nemesis as the guy who loathes everything Jacob stands for. (What we don't know yet is exactly *what* he stands for, just as the goals of the Hostiles and the Dharmans remain vague; but in Jacob's case at least, we will learn what we need to know in Season Six.) In the process of bringing people to the Island—or judging them as unworthy of the Island's gifts—how much collateral damage have they done? What about Nadia? What about the people on Oceanic 815 who aren't on one of Jacob's lists? What about that pit full of Dharma Initiative corpses? Heck, what about John Locke, who loved the Island dearly but was used as a tool by both Jacob and The Man in Black? If this is all a big game, apparently the two main players don't mind losing a lot of material to win.

It's no wonder that Rose and Bernard want no part of it. But then again . . . Is that a responsible choice?★ The Man in Black argues that fate will keep causing the same conflicts to occur over and over to the

★ Jacob always insists that the people he taps for service have a choice, but he and The Man in Black sure do a lot to narrow those choices way down.

same ends, so what's the point of having any conflicts at all? And Jacob is arguing that even though the results may be the same, the details change, and that is what's important.

And so, as Juliet detonates a hydrogen bomb and Ben kills Jacob, the board gets reset, with different sets of pieces and new people moving them. Game on. —*NM*

FURTHER READING: TOWARD A UNIFIED THEORY OF *LOST* (OR: WHY ARE THERE SO MANY *DEADWOOD* ACTORS ON THIS SHOW?)

As early as *Lost*'s first season—heck, as soon as the first episode ended—the show's fans began combing over every major and minor detail of the show, looking for clues to the big mystery of the Island itself. What did it mean that Walt was reading a superhero comic book that featured a picture of a polar bear? Was Locke's love of backgammon relevant? Did Locke's *name* have a hidden meaning?

The cultural references in *Lost* are dense and wide-ranging, but a good place to start contemplating them is with the characters' names. The pilot episode introduces John Locke, whose name directly nods to an influential British philosopher who—among other things—advanced the theory that the human mind is a blank slate★ and that the self is formed through experiences. Later we meet characters whose names clearly refer to other philosophers and scientists: Rousseau, Hume, Faraday, Hawking . . . and also Jeremy Bentham, the pseudonym Locke adopts after leaving the Island. (Let us not forget either that Jack's father has the very loaded name of Christian Shephard.)

When *Lost* fans first started trying to decode the show, they headed straight to the library to try and learn more about the real-world people

★   Or "tabula rasa" . . . just like the title of a Season One *Lost* episode!

behind these names. Over time, some of them seemed *especially* relevant to *Lost*'s story, including French philosopher Jean-Jacques Rousseau, who argued that it's better for humans to follow their natural instincts than to follow the dictates of society; David Hume, a Scotsman who expressed skepticism toward the concept of free will; Michael Faraday, a pioneering researcher into the properties of electromagnetism; Richard Alpert, a psychologist who changed his name to Ram Dass and won followers with his book *Be Here Now*, exploring Hindu spiritualism. Some of the connections between these old academics and the *Lost* characters were clear—the time-and-space-obsessed Eloise Hawking is obviously named for *A Brief History of Time* author Stephen Hawking, for example—but even when the links were more tenuous, they got the show's more keen-eyed viewers thinking.

The *Lost* writers' slyest bit of name-foolery, though, was the introduction in Season Two of "Henry Gale" (later revealed to be Benjamin Linus, incognito). Henry Gale is both the name of an American astrophysicist known for studying the effects of the Earth's rotation on light waves and the name of Dorothy Gale's uncle in L. Frank Baum's Oz novels. The *Lost* version of Henry Gale claimed he'd been blown off course while hot-air ballooning and had accidentally landed on the Island. In the movie version of *The Wizard of Oz* and in the first book in Baum's series, the seemingly all-powerful "wizard" (who turns out to a charlatan) admits he ended up in the magical realm of Oz after flying off course in—yep—a hot-air balloon.

Clearly, Lindelof, Cuse, and company meant for viewers to chase those Oz connections, just as they wanted us to recall the hidden worlds in *Alice's Adventures in Wonderland* while watching the *Lost* episodes titled "White Rabbit" and "Through the Looking Glass"—and to think about the works of the fantasy author C. S. Lewis when we meet the scientist Charlotte Staples Lewis, who grew up on the Island, which is a kind of otherworld akin to C. S. Lewis's Narnia.

Is there a point to dropping all of these references? Almost certainly. Some of the names and titles are meant to spark connections in the audience's mind, getting us thinking outside the frame of any one particular moment or episode. If we see Ben has a copy of *Flowers for Algernon* on his shelf, maybe we think about science experiments gone awry and the people who get hurt by them. If Locke picks up a book containing

Ambrose Bierce's short story "An Occurrence at Owl Creek Bridge," maybe we remember that its protagonist is a hanged man, who in the seconds before his death imagines everything that happens in the story.

The same goes with all of the board games the characters play throughout the run of *Lost*. Backgammon, *Risk*, chess, *Connect Four*, Senet, *Mouse Trap* . . . We're meant to register the motif of competition, with one set of colored tokens against another. This is ultimately reflected in the revelation that our heroes are "candidates," jostling to win an incredibly important job.

But there are other reasons why *Lost* is so littered with cultural Easter eggs, beyond the merely thematic. These little winks and homage express the tastes and obsessions of its creators—and perhaps especially of Damon Lindelof, who has spoken openly about how he is influenced and inspired by *Star Trek*, *The Lord of the Rings*, *Watership Down*, the *Star Wars* movies, the comics of Alan Moore, the novels of Stephen King, and the *Lost*-like TV series *The Prisoner*, *The Twilight Zone*, and *The X-Files*. (Many of these are directly referenced in the show, through images, dialogue, and plot.)

That taste extends to *Lost*'s casting as well. The actors introduced in the first episode were, at the time, a mix of newer faces and a few familiar ones. The most recognizable stars were Matthew Fox (only a few years removed from completing six seasons of *Party of Five*), Terry O'Quinn (an accomplished character actor and a cult favorite thanks to his performance in the satirical B-movie *The Stepfather*), Harold Perrineau (who had been in the *Matrix* sequels and Baz Luhrmann's *Romeo + Juliet*), and Dominic Monaghan (fresh from a substantial role in the *Lord of the Rings* trilogy). Once the show became an established hit, though, the cast list—regulars and guest stars—became a who's who of indie film stalwarts, prestige cable TV stars, and old pros from the UK.

Michael Emerson, Néstor Carbonell, Fionnula Flanagan, Jeremy Davies, Jeff Fahey, M. C. Gainey, Clancy Brown, Alan Dale, Katey Sagal, Mark Pellegrino, Patrick Fischler, Fisher Stevens, Lance Reddick, Doug Hutchison, Jon Gries . . . These were all great gets for *Lost*. And that's not even taking into account all the actors from HBO's beloved western *Deadwood* that ABC roped into appearing, including John Hawkes, Robin Weigert, William Sanderson, Paula Malcomson, Kim Dickens, and Titus Welliver.

The point is that once *Lost* became a success—and once the writers realized they'd probably need to fill over 100 episodes—the writers could broaden the scope of their references, influences, and personal preferences, using the show as a channel for whatever might be on their mind.

But—and this is crucial—Lindelof, Cuse, and company did this without, for the most part, losing the thread of what *Lost* is about. If anything, over time the breadth of references became inextricably intertwined with the show's plot and, more importantly, its themes.

If you wanted to describe *Lost* in one pithy line—something many have tried—you could say it's "a story about stories." On a fundamental level, the plot of *Lost* sees an eclectic batch of characters from around the world being drafted against their will into an audition to see who will become the new protector of a mystical piece of real estate—bound to keep the world safe from ancient destructive forces. All these broken people, each of whom seems to have stepped out of their own separate pulp melodrama (the medical thriller, the con-man thriller, the fugitive thriller, and so on), are auditioning to be the ultimate hero of an epic saga.

On a straightforward narrative level, we see the effect of this in what becomes a gradual winnowing-out process. Some characters die. Some abandon a game they didn't even know they were playing. The Smoke Monster looks into the souls of some of these folks and tests their mettle, before flinging them against the trees. The Others test them. The Temple tests them. Jacob tests them.

On a meta level, this describes what we were doing as *Lost* viewers. We took a long look at everything the characters and their creators did, and we judged accordingly. This also describes what the show's writer and producers did. As much as they publicly professed that the whole series was planned out, the truth was they tried a bunch of stuff that didn't always work as intended. Some actors lacked the right energy; others impressed more than expected. Some subplots ran into dead ends; others proved surprisingly fruitful. Some writers left; others stepped in. Changes were made.

Put all this together—the evolving scope of the story, the assemblage of references, and the churn of *Lost* employees—and you have a backstory to the creation of *Lost* that resembles the messiness, serendipity, and inspiration-by-necessity that has defined so many epic tales and foundational myths.

At heart, *Lost* is about how legends and belief systems get distorted by broken human beings—which is to say all human beings. Our heroes go through several cycles of trial and error, working their way through personal narratives that touch on just about every significant bit of philosophy and fiction known to humankind. In the end, they learn that waiting on absentee parents and ancient lore to tell them what to do gets them nowhere, and that they should rely more on the people already by their side.

How much of this message was consciously intended by *Lost*'s creators, as opposed to being the result of them throwing all their influences into a blender? Hard to say. As with Mark Twain, Charles Dickens, and Marvel Comics, the tricky thing about popular serialized entertainment is that in seeking to divert and provoke on the installment plan, the goals can shift from beginning to end.

But that's also part of the thrill of a big story told in tiny pieces. Myths are made of moments that connect broadly and linger in the memory, across generations. Twenty years after *Lost*'s debut, new viewers are still discovering the show; and the original viewers are still thinking about Hurley, hatches, the Smoke Monster, and Sawyer. The arguments about *Lost* rage on, because that's what myths are for. They're made for us to find meaning—or to misinterpret. —*NM*

SEASON SIX

CHECKLISTS

Let's talk about endings.

When it comes to dramas and comedies—especially those that are more of the slice-of-life variety—often the ending is everything, and where the author chooses to punctuate the story is the ultimate indicator of what the story is about (i.e., its ideas). But fantasies, adventures . . . these genres frequently get their ideas out of the way early, to clear a space at the end for action. Whether it's superhero movies ending with a bunch of costumed characters frantically blasting rays at each other or crime stories that end with car chases and shoot-outs, often these endings feel a little pro forma—like moving the last few cards onto the base piles in a game of solitaire, or filling in the final squares in a crossword puzzle.

So, let's say this about how *Lost* ends: It does not feel by-the-numbers. For years, fans had speculated about where this show was headed and what Lindelof and Cuse were hinting at with all their oblique references in interviews and podcasts about the Island being a "cork." No one had predicted anything exactly like Season Six.

Season Five is so complicated that it takes notecards, corkboard, and string to follow properly. But Season Six? Half of it proceeds in a straight(ish) line from start to finish. The other half is off the charts entirely.

The on-Island story is relatively simple. After Juliet explodes the H-bomb in the Season Five finale, all the time travelers are wrenched back to the present day, where they are immediately thrust into the crisis that had developed in their absence. Ben has killed Jacob. The Others are in disarray. Richard is disillusioned. Ilana and Jacob's other agents from Flight 316 are galvanized to take revenge. The Man in Black has taken the form of John Locke—when he's not in raging Smoke Monster mode, that is—and is looking for a way to leave the Island and to wreak havoc in the outside world. The 815ers find themselves caught between these various factions, trying to reconvene as best as possible in order to hop on the still-intact Ajira jet and fly home.

But there's still the matter of what Jacob actually wanted from all of them in the first place.

Lindelof and Cuse could've spent the whole season just on the Island, answering all the lingering questions fans had accumulated over the previous five years. Instead, they really only addressed the mystery of the Island itself, explaining that it is a kind of guard station, protecting the powerful "light" at the heart of reality itself from any forces of darkness that might exploit it and destroy everything. Jacob had drawn people to the Island over the years, looking for "candidates" to take his job as the primary protector; and The Man in Black had worked his own mojo on those candidates, to prove his own theory that people are inherently terrible.

But while telling this last story about the 815 castaways running and hiding and shooting and fighting on the Island—with Jack and Locke (or "Locke") again at the center of the struggle—Lindelof and Cuse also decided to keep *Lost*'s "flashing" structure, by trying something entirely new. Rather than flashing backward or flashing forward, throughout Season Six—in nearly every episode—the story flashes "sideways," to a universe where Oceanic Flight 815 lands safely in Los Angeles and our main characters go on about their lives. Except that "their lives" aren't exactly like the ones we had seen before.★

Is this some kind of parallel universe? An alternate timeline? *Lost* would string viewers along for nearly the whole season, not explaining the sideways flashes until close to the very end. When viewers found out what was really going on? Well, not everyone was thrilled.

★ One of the sly themes of this season is that even with the deck reshuffled, the game plays much the same. Season Six turns characters we thought we knew into different people—and not just in the sideways universe. On the Island, Claire's not quite Claire, Sayid's not quite Sayid, and Jack, Hurley, Kate, and Sawyer have all been profoundly changed in the three years since they last sat around a campfire with a guy who looks like Locke.

There are a lot of ways to take the divisive reactions to *Lost*'s big finish—and to Season Six in general. One thing to consider is that fans had cooked up a lot of theories by the final season, and many of those *Lost* die-hards had become smitten with their own ideas, vastly preferring them to what Lindelof and Cuse eventually settled on. Early in the show's run, the big surprises were a delight. Toward the end, they jerked the plot away from what a lot of fans wanted.

But the more important thing to consider is the nature of what *Lost* sprung on audiences in Season Six: the notion that its sideways universe is a kind of way station on the way to the afterlife, where all the people who meant something to each other on the Island meet again as a slightly altered version of themselves, to address any unfinished business. Just as the Island has Jacob—a protector who helps people understand their responsibility to the universe—the outside world's main father figure is Jack's actual father, the late Dr. Christian Shephard, who appears to our heroes to guide them toward being better people in general.

This was many viewers' main problem with Season Six: the touchy-feely "step into the light, my child" stuff. But you see, *Lost* always cared about both halves of its storytelling structure: the Island woo-woo and the deep dive into who these people are. By the finale, the most memorable moments from the pilot episode—that plane crash on a beach, that monster in the trees, and that mysterious transmission in French—were settled business. What *Lost* wanted to give viewers at the end was some closure on the characters themselves, rather than one last round of Island "answers." Lindelof and Cuse took an abnormal show and brought it home with a normal(ish) kind of TV finale, full of hugging, goodbyes, and warmth.

Did that sell out all the harder ideas *Lost* had been grappling with for six seasons? Well, that debate still rages. But what should be obvious is that Season Six and its finale episode did not retroactively ruin *Lost*. All the good stuff that fans loved is still there, waiting to be enjoyed by newcomers and old-timers for as long as the show can be streamed or telecast or purchased—in whatever universe that exists. —*NM*

MIGHT HAVE BEEN

"LA X"

—

SEASON 6, EPISODES 1 & 2
ORIGINAL AIRDATE 2/2/10

From its very first frames, *Lost*'s final season premiere unveils a massive shift in its storytelling. The flashbacks and flash-forwards that reigned in the first five seasons have given way to something new: the flash-sideways. The whole conceit is bold, brilliant, and incredibly foolhardy. Even here, in the very first episode of the season, it's tempting to wonder how the show can *possibly* land this entirely new plane alongside all the other ones it has aloft. Wouldn't it be fitting for this series to end with a metaphorical fiery crash? Tune in next week, folks!

The flash-sideways depict a world in which the Island rests at the bottom of the Pacific and Oceanic 815 made its way through some bad turbulence before landing safely in Los Angeles. With the characters' lives thus diverted, viewers get to see what the story might have been like had, say, Locke and Jack bumped into each other at baggage claim, where spinal surgeon Jack offered wheelchair user Locke a free consult.

It's the sort of idea that could *only* work in a final season, where the sense of an approaching end creates a willingness in the audience to look back over what's transpired. Several TV shows★ have tried to build their entire runs around the idea of examining what happens to characters in two or more separate versions of reality, but they inevitably run aground when the audience wants to know which reality is "real."

In its final season, however, *Lost* can use the flash-sideways to comment on characters we already know exceedingly well. The alternate reality exists less as a storytelling device and more to reflect on how far

★ The 2012 series *Awake* and the 2021 series *Ordinary Joe*, to name two you've probably forgotten about.

276

the characters have come from where they started out—and how far the show has come, too.

In addition, the show bounces between the flash-sideways stories and the on-Island action, where Juliet's explosion of the hydrogen bomb at the end of Season Five has sent everybody back to the same time period, and . . . that's about it, so far as we can tell. Her ghost tells Sawyer (via Miles) that "It worked," but it's hard to say what she means. From what we can tell, the characters are simply right back where they started. The Swan station was built, then destroyed. The course of Island history proceeded as it always had, and whatever happened, happened. Whatever the flash-sideways are, our characters are not aware of them.

In addition, "LA X" sets up one major difference between Seasons Five and Six. Season Five was a "man of science" sort of season, showcasing its philosophy of a time travel that can't actually change anything and a web of time that holds us in place, predestining us to do certain things. Season Six, on the other hand, is a "man of faith" season through and through. If we didn't realize it from Hurley getting led around by Jacob's ghost, we surely get there once the characters are brought to yet another new Island location: the Temple.★

In general, *Lost* works best in one of two modes: going all in on inexplicable mystical hooey, or going all in on rigorously defined scientific principles. It's at its strongest, however, when the two play off each other, when the show never quite lands on either side of its science/faith dialectic. For better or worse, however, "LA X" all but announces, "We're going all in on the mystical hooey, folks. Get off this train while you still have the chance! Next stop is a weird lighthouse that feels left over from *Myst*."

The Temple is exactly the kind of mystical nonsense that runs directly counter to the series' stronger sci-fi qualities. The castaways bring a gravely wounded Sayid to said Temple after Jacob's ghost tells Hurley to do so. At the Temple, the Others shove Sayid in an oddly off-color pool, holding him down until he drowns. They proclaim him dead, but by episode's end, he's rising from the floor, good as new. Why? Mystical nonsense!

★   Technically speaking, we've seen the outskirts of the Temple before, most notably when Jin traveled there with Rousseau's group in Season Five. This, however, is the first time we've seen the inner sanctum or the people who live there.

These might sound like complaints, but they're really not. Few shows in TV history have ever been as good as *Lost* at coming up with moments that beggar belief, then asking you to simply believe in them. Too many other shows would have one of the Others immediately explain why Sayid was healed, but the Others seem as mystified as Jack and company. With Jacob dead, none of this should be happening. The pool should be glowing, and it's not. The normal rules have been suspended, and our characters never figured out those normal rules to begin with.

If "LA X" introduces a bunch of new stuff for viewers to puzzle over, then it also painstakingly confirms certain things we most likely already know or at least suspect. The ghost of Locke reveals himself to be a manifestation of the Smoke Monster, spitting out, "I'm sorry you had to see me like that," to Ben after turning into his wispy alter ego and killing some of Jacob's men. Similarly, flight attendant Cindy and the kids Zack and Emma, last seen in Others' custody many seasons ago, pop up at the Temple, if only to reassure us that they're still alive.

The revelations in this episode work on two levels. On one hand, we need to know the stakes of this final set of episodes. We need to know that Locke and the Smoke Monster are one and the same, so the series can finally tell us who the real villain is. On the other, the show wants us to think about where we've been, where we are, and where we're going. Seeing Locke as evil incarnate makes his death even sadder—he wanted to serve the Island, only to be used by a being that wants to destroy it.

Thus, the flash-sideways. Maybe the Locke that we see in this timeline isn't Locke at all, but in the alternate reality, Locke landed in Los Angeles, still feeling underestimated and misunderstood but very much still alive and his cantankerous self. You'd be forgiven for worrying that all these new mysteries dumped atop the old ones create a situation where nothing can possibly be resolved satisfactorily. And, yes, when TV shows start adding whole new batches of questions to answer this late in their run, that's often a concerning sign.

In this case, however, the flash-sideways and set pieces like the Temple dig into the essential thematic mysteries of the show: Why are we alive? What mark do we make on the planet? Do we have a destiny, or free will? If Season Five offered some possible answers to those questions from a more rational point of view, then it's only fair to let Season Six take a stab at the same from a traditionally less logical one. Sometimes, you can't answer every question. Sometimes, you just have to step back and let the mysteries be. —*ESJ*

"WHAT KATE DOES"

—

SEASON 6, EPISODE 3
ORIGINAL AIRDATE 2/9/10

On the Island: The Temple-dwellers are unnerved when Sayid comes back to life, while Sawyer storms off to the Barracks intending to mourn Juliet alone (but is followed by Kate).

Off the Island: Kate befriends Claire and helps get her to the hospital to give birth to Aaron.

It's fascinating to look back at the reviews and reactions for the early Season Six episodes, before it was entirely clear what was going on in the "flash-sideways" scenes. In interviews and on their podcast, Damon Lindelof and Carlton Cuse would insist that the sideways universe wasn't an alternate reality, but until we had a context for what they meant by that, *Lost* fans had to proceed on the assumption that when Juliet detonated Jughead, two things happened. Our heroes on the Island in 1977 rematerializing in 2007 was one outcome. Their original Oceanic 815 flight landing safely in Los Angeles in 2004 was the other. And the connection between the two . . . ?

Well, that's what made Season Six such a challenge to watch at times. In the previous seasons, the flashbacks and flash-forwards fed viewers necessary, character- and plot-developing information, while—at their best, anyway—infusing the present-day action with an extra note of poignancy. But when an episode like "What Kate Does" first aired, it was hard to see how one piece informed the other. The drama on the Island has to do with Jack defending the resurrected Sayid and defying the Temple-dwellers, Jin crossing paths with the feral Claire while looking for Sun, and Kate listening to Sawyer's laments about missing Juliet. What did any of this have to do with Kate and Claire becoming friends in a parallel world?

As for that parallel world, if in fact it was meant to be Los Angeles in 2004 if Oceanic 815 had never crashed, then why did everything feel a little . . . off? In the sideways scenes, "What Kate Does" answers one of the questions fans had been kicking around since Season One: Who was the "nice couple in Los Angeles" who were going to adopt Claire's baby? It turns out they were a couple of nobodies, unrelated to the larger Island narrative—and that the husband had changed his mind and left his wife. But when Claire goes into labor and Kate drives her to the hospital, they are greeted by Dr. Ethan Goodspeed,★ who on the Island was an Other. What is he doing in LA? So many new questions, even as we answer the old ones.

The eventual explanation for what is going on—that Lindelof and Cuse were being honest and that this is not a parallel reality but rather a kind of "settling unfinished business" pre-afterlife reality—doesn't retroactively make "What Kate Does" a more coherent episode. It still feels like just a lot of scattered business, on and off the Island. But some poignancy creeps in, in retrospect. On the Island, Kate's friends are enduring unimaginable pain and splintering once again into subgroups. The Others want to kill the resurrected Sayid before he turns irredeemably evil. Jin wanders off to find Sun and gets caught in a trap set by Claire. Sawyer returns to the place where he and Juliet were happiest, where he shrugs off Kate's attempts at sympathy.

Off the Island, meanwhile, Kate and Claire (and Aaron) form a bond. It's a simple story, but one that points to where these sideways tales are bound to go. On the Island, our heroes are hurting. Off it, the healing has begun. —*NM*

★   Another way that this reality feels strange: Ethan is using his father Horace's last name, rather than Rom.

"THE SUBSTITUTE"
–
SEASON 6, EPISODE 4
ORIGINAL AIRDATE 2/16/10

On the Island: The Man in Black tries to recruit Sawyer to his cause by taking him to a seaside cave and showing him how Jacob has been tracking and manipulating their lives for years.

Off the Island: Locke returns from Australia and finds out he has lost his job, but with the help of some familiar faces and the support of his fiancée Helen, he finds a new job as a substitute teacher.

There are three John Lockes in "The Substitute." One is Jacob's brother, The Man in Black, who wears Locke's form but is more confident and icier than the real Locke ever was. One is flash-sideways John, who is back in his wheelchair and still plagued with bad luck—but who also has Helen by his side and generally seems more mellow and content than the guy we saw in the previous seasons' flashbacks.

And then there's the corpse of John Locke, which gets buried and paid tribute in this episode's strangest, sweetest scene. Before traveling to the Temple with Ilana, Sun insists on holding an impromptu funeral for Locke, up at the beach's picturesque Oceanic 815 Memorial Cemetery & Stick-Cross Emporium. There, Ben says a few words about Locke being "a believer" and "a better man," before saying, "I'm sorry I murdered him."

With that bit of business out of the way, we're free to deal with the other two Lockes, and to wonder whether they have anything in common. The Man in Black often relies on others to accomplish his goals, which the now-dead Locke was also known to do. (Getting Sawyer to kill Anthony Cooper, letting Ben turn the Donkey Wheel, etc.) Here, in a thrilling and dramatic sequence, The Man in Black comes to the embittered Sawyer and leads him to a remote seaside cave, where the walls are covered with the names of many of the 815 survivors.* He explains that Jacob was choosing a candidate to protect the Island, but he insists that there's nothing special about this place, and urges Sawyer to help them both just leave. He wants Sawyer to defy Jacob and exercise his free will—but won't Sawyer just be following someone else's?

Both The Man in Black and Locke have also been, in some way, trapped: the former bound to the Island, and the latter in a wheelchair. Stretching the analogy even further, both of them are in their respective predicaments because they've been conned. As we will see later in the season, Jacob's been able to keep The Man in Black in check for so long because of tricks and semantics. (He's reminded of this in "The Substitute" when a little blond boy appears as an apparition before him, and reminds him that "the rules" state that he can't kill Jacob, prompting the Locke-ian reply: "Don't tell me what I can't do!")

In the flash-sideways, meanwhile, we meet a Locke who seems to have a sense of humor about his condition: chuckling when his van hydraulics get stuck, or when he falls out of his chair onto his lawn just as the sprinklers come on. But the more time we spend with him, the more we see some of the familiar dissatisfaction. He wants to be independent, and is frustrated by how much he needs people: Helen, his new employment counselor Rose, his new acquaintance Hurley. The story of this Locke—and maybe the actual Locke, and maybe even The Man in Black—seems to be about coming to accept his circumstances. Sometimes there are things he can't do. But sometimes there are people who can be persuaded to help. —*NM*

---

* When they enter the cave, The Man in Black sees a scale with a white rock on one side and a black one on the other. He tosses the white rock away, telling Sawyer it's a "private joke."

"LIGHTHOUSE"
—
SEASON 6, EPISODE 5
ORIGINAL AIRDATE 2/23/10

On the Island: Jacob's ghost tells Hurley to show Jack the lighthouse Jacob used to observe his "candidates," while Jin sees how Claire has gone mad since being abandoned by the other 815 survivors for three years.

Off the Island: Jack finds out that his teenage son David is an accomplished pianist and he apologizes for being such a stern father in the past.

One of the under-recognized strengths of *Lost* is how the storytelling structure reflects the ideas the show explores. Long before the characters started traveling through time, viewers were traveling through time, via flashbacks and flash-forwards. Season Six is split between two realities, but also devoted to alternate realities within those realities. For our heroes, choosing a side between Jacob's earnest followers and The Man in Black's nihilist army isn't just a matter of allying with friends against enemies. It's also about subscribing to a worldview. It's about picking a reality to live in.★

"Lighthouse" is a Jack episode, and as such both halves of it are devoted to catching up with where his head is at now. The sideways version of Jack seems less anguished than the one we've known—as is the case with most of *Lost*'s main characters in this new universe. But he still has daddy issues, which he's at risk of passing on to his son David (Dylan Minette), who seems to resent his father in part for the usual vague teenage reasons and in part because this version of Jack appears to be in a bit of a fog, uncertain about the details of his own life. When he learns about

---

★ Claire, we find out in this episode, has chosen The Man in Black's reality. While looking after Jin in her jungle hideout, she talks about how she's survived the past three years with the help of her "friend," who turns out to be, you guessed it, *Lost*'s Big Bad.

David's musical talents—and that has son has been afraid to share them, because Jack is so demanding, he pledges on the spot to chill out, even though he doesn't fully remember anything about his past relationship with David. He just knows he wants to be a new Jack.

On the Island, meanwhile, Jack rebels once again against Jacob's call for him to be a hero, though in this case it's a rejection Jacob expects—a necessary step on the way to embracing his fate. Hurley takes Jack to Jacob's lighthouse, where they discover—as Sawyer did in the cave in the previous episode—a list of names with numbers beside them, corresponding to the degrees at which the lighthouse mirrors can be turned. Jack orders Hugo to turn the dial to 23—the number for "Shephard"—and he sees the house he grew up in. So, he smashes the mirrors. Jacob shrugs this off, telling Hurley it was more important for Jack to know that he's special than for the lighthouse to remain functional. Acceptance is a process.

Perhaps more importantly, though, "Lighthouse" takes the rough form of what it's ultimately about. As Jack is reflecting (in two realities) on how far he's come as a person and who he wants to be, Hurley is talking about how it's "very old school, you and me, trekking through the jungle, on our way to do something that we don't understand." In a meta way, it's as though these characters are realizing what they're best at: being on *Lost*. —NM

"SUNDOWN"
—
SEASON 6, EPISODE 6
ORIGINAL AIRDATE 3/2/10

On the Island: Sayid is given one last chance by the Temple-dwellers to prove he hasn't been infected with evil, but instead he kills two of the Others' leaders and lets The Man in Black in to wreak havoc.

Off the Island: Sayid tries to help his brother out of a jam with some mobsters without resorting to violence, but he ends up killing several men.

Although most of the mainstream TV critics who were writing about *Lost* every week ultimately had positive things to say about Season Six and the way the series ended, early in the season those same critics filed a lot of understandably mixed and at times outright skeptical reviews. Their complaints ranged from a lack of emotional engagement with the flash-sideways scenes to grumbling that the on-Island story followed the same "nobody asks questions" / "walking from here to there to here again pattern" that *Lost* usually employed when it was stalling for time. And in its finale season, a show shouldn't have any reason to stall.

James Poniewozik (at the time the *Time* magazine TV critic, later hired by the *New York Times*) made one of the most cogent criticisms of Season Six's early episodes on Twitter, writing, "What, now, is the objective? What, exactly, are we rooting for Jack et al to do?" On the Island, everyone is separating into factions even though they (and by extension we) haven't been told exactly why. Off the Island, characters who look like our heroes (but who have subtle behavioral and biographical differences) are just living their lives, with no goal line in sight.

"Sundown" is definitely one of those patience-testing episodes, even though on its own merits it's impressively grim and often terrifying. Ultimately, it's the story of two Sayids, neither of whom is exactly our Sayid. Both have been pigeonholed as torturers, killers . . . evil to the bone. And both ultimately prove their doubters right. Both, when pushed, take lives. In the sideways universe, Sayid reconnects with Nadia (now married to his shady brother Omer); and to protect the people he loves, Sayid kills the crooks who've been squeezing money from Omer . . . one of whom is Martin Keamy!* On the Island, he realizes that the Temple leadership† are sending him to his death by pitting him against The Man in Black, who awaits them outside; and in retaliation, he initiates a rampage that leaves many of the Others dead.

---

*   Sayid also discovers that Keamy and his men have captured the sideways Jin. We'll learn more about that side of the story in a few episodes.

†   They don't get to do a lot this season, but the two main Temple leaders are Dogen (Hiroyuki Sanada) and Lennon (John Hawkes). Both characters are introduced in the season premiere and initially seem like they're going to be major new additions, given the pedigree of the actors playing them. A few episodes later, they're dead.

So, what's the point? Well, on a macro level this is a show about old battles, being fought over and over; and Season Six is about finding a way to break those patterns. And on a micro level, this season is about taking different angles on the characters we know and asking if they can change. In "Sundown," the answer for Sayid is no—and it's devastating.

But the season isn't over. —*NM*

THOSE WHO CAN'T DO

"DR. LINUS"

—

SEASON 6, EPISODE 7
ORIGINAL AIRDATE 3/9/10

I've asked this before, but it bears repeating: Did the Others—or the Hostiles, if you prefer—ever have a real function on the Island? And if so, was Ben Linus meant to be their leader? Jacob looked all over the world for candidates to replace him and never seemed to consider Ben; and for the longest time Ben was treated by the de facto Island bosses Charles Widmore and Eloise Hawking as kind of an unworthy usurper. He was not born to this life. He's "new money," so to speak.

But Jacob didn't seem to want to pick an Other, either—not even Richard Alpert. It's almost as though the Others/Hostiles were The Man in Black's recruits, with Richard embedded by Jacob to keep those weirdos in check.

What does all this have to do with "Dr. Linus"? Well, as *Lost*'s last full-on "Ben episode," it's also the last chance to ask these kinds of questions about a man whose great ambition masks a deep need. Throughout his life, Ben tried to overcome his feelings of abandonment by maneuvering his way into paternal and/or man-in-charge positions— even if they turn out to be phony. Ben doesn't really know much about

Jacob or the Candidates, and may not even know much about what the Temple was really for. He's just always been very good at pretending.★

So it goes with the flash-sideways scenes in "Dr. Linus," which are like an alternate origin story for Ben Linus, Evil Mastermind—but with a different outcome than the one we're used to. In this world, Ben is a high school history teacher,† unhappy with the indifference of his fellow faculty members and of his boss, Principal Reynolds (William Atherton). At home, Ben takes care of his infirm father, Roger, who wonders what might've happened if they'd stayed on the Island with the Dharma Initiative. Ben's only source of pride seems to be the school's History Club, and his prize student: Alexandra Rousseau, who's trying to get into Yale.

Then, during one AP test-prep session, Alex lets slip that Principal Reynolds is having an affair with the school nurse. Immediately, the latent Evil Ben rises to the surface, as he makes deals with the computer-savvy Doc Arzt‡ to help him tap into the school's emails so that he can gather enough evidence to push out Reynolds and take his job. (Arzt calls him a "killer" . . . again, pointedly.) But when Ben presents his blackmail offer to Reynolds, the principal offers Ben a choice of his own: He can go through with the coup, but if he does, Reynolds won't write a recommendation letter to Yale for Alex.

Meanwhile, on the Island, Ben has reconnected with Ilana's crew, only to find he's not welcome. Unlike Ben, Ilana actually takes Jacob and the Island seriously. One of the most moving moments in the episode sees Ilana, cradling a sack full of the ashes of Jacob—the dearest father-figure in her life—and weeping. She has been trying to do the job that Jacob

---

★ As a case in point, when Ben talks in this episode about what Sayid did at the Temple, he says our zombified hero killed Dogen and "the interpreter." He doesn't mention Lennon by name. Does he even know the Temple crew?

† One of the lessons we see him teach involves Napoleon's final days as a mere figurehead. Every scene and line in this episode seemed designed to make sure that we got the point about the cruelty of fate, the burden of power, and so on and so on.

‡ Is it a coincidence that the subject of the Black Rock dynamite comes up on the Island in the same episode that Arzt returns in the sideways universe? Probably not.

asked her to do, protecting the Candidates.* It's irrelevant to that task whether Ben Linus lives or dies.

So Ilana hands her sack of Jacob-ash to Miles and asks him to listen to what the dead man has to say about how he died. What Miles sees is Ben standing over Jacob's body with a bloody knife. (Making matters worse, Miles later tells Ben that among Jacob's last thoughts was that he hoped he was wrong about Ben.) Ben tries to cozy up to Ilana and use his usual tricks to sow seeds of doubt about Miles; but instead, she chains him to a tree and gets him started digging his own grave.

On both sides of the "Dr. Linus" story, a version of John Locke gets involved. On the Island, The Man in Black frees Ben and invites him to Hydra island, to begin the transfer of Island power into Ben's greedy hands. Off the Island, Locke encourages Ben to do whatever he must to become the principal. The outcomes in the two worlds diverge, though. In the alternate Los Angeles, Ben sacrifices his ambitions to save Alex. But on the Island, he sticks with The Man in Black, believing it to be his only option.

When talking about their decision to introduce the "sideways" story-telling technique to *Lost*, Lindelof and Cuse said they were intrigued by the question of what would happen if the exploding Jughead really worked as Faraday said it would. To paraphrase their interview with *Entertainment Weekly* at the time: "For at least a couple of years, we knew that the ending of the time-travel season was going to be an attempt to reboot. And as a result, the audience was going to come out of the 'do-over moment' thinking we were either going to start over or just say it didn't work and continue on. Wouldn't it be great if we did both? That was the origin of the story."

"Dr. Linus" shows the fruits of this approach. In a way, it's a heartening answer to "Sundown." That episode was chillingly bleak, with its depiction of unchanging characters guided strictly by fate. "Dr. Linus," on the other hand, by showing the sideways Ben behaving more altruistically than the Island Ben ever has, pulls back a bit to suggest that free

---

*   Once again, the women on *Lost* get a raw deal, story-wise. "Will Sun find Jin?" "Who will Kate end up with?" Ana Lucia, Libby, Juliet, Shannon . . . all dead. And now here's Ilana, assigned as protector of Candidates but not a Candidate herself?

will actually does exist (at least for those who choose to embrace it). The difference between Jacob and The Man in Black is getting clearer here. The former allows people to join if they choose. The latter says "join or die." —*NM*

THE WORLD'S FORGOTTEN BOY

"RECON"

—

SEASON 6, EPISODE 8
ORIGINAL AIRDATE 3/16/10

Walt Whitman once said that we all contain multitudes, embracing different tastes, emotions, and points of view depending on the time of day and the company we keep. That kind of fragmentation multiplies in the *Lost* world, where time and reality itself often splinter—and where people don't so much change as they respawn.

Take Sawyer. Although the character grows and progresses during his time on the Island, it's fair to say that Pre-Crash Sawyer is almost an entirely different person from Post-Crash Sawyer—who himself is almost entirely different from Dharma Sawyer, aka Jim LaFleur.

And what of James Ford, Supercop?

"Recon" is maybe the most "fun" Season Six episode,★ because it's the one with the most wildly entertaining sideways-universe story: all about a Sawyer who is living a surprising new life but is still the same old lovable rogue.

★   There was no "previously on *Lost*" when this episode originally aired. It's like the producers were saying, "You don't need to prep. Just sit back and enjoy."

In some ways, his life is unaltered in this otherworld. The man named James Ford was still orphaned as a boy; and he's still been on a worldwide hunt (including in Australia!) for Anthony Cooper, the man he blames for the loss of his family. This Jim is still a liar, too, hiding his true intentions behind a devil-may-care attitude and a killer smile. But where the Sawyer of old was a con man, James Ford is a con-man-*catcher*: a proud member of the LAPD Bunco Squad, working alongside his partner, Miles Straume.

Speaking strictly in terms of plot, not much actually happens in the sideways scenes in "Recon." We do get to see a little of James Ford's police work in the opening,★ when he gets the drop on a fugitive woman, calls her "dimples," and then signals his backup with his special code word: "LaFleur." (Magnificent.) But this episode is more about our hero's personal life. Miles sets Jim up on a date with his friend Charlotte, who works at a museum with Miles's dad, Pierre. Jim and Charlotte hit it off (and get it on!†) but when she stumbles across the file on Cooper in his bedroom drawer, he flips out and kicks her out. Then Miles finds out Jim lied about his trip to Australia, creating a rift between them. Jim tries to patch things up with Charlotte and fails. He has better luck later with Miles.

Aside from dropping a few more old friends into the mix—like Charlie's brother Liam, who we see asking questions about Charlie at the police station, and Kate, who crashes into Jim and Miles and then gets nabbed by them when she flees—there's not a whole lot of incident here. But that's OK. James Ford and his buddy Miles, fighting crime? That would be good TV in any era.

The Island material in "Recon" is more action-packed, and anchored to a question Miles asks Jim in the car toward the end of their storyline

---

★   Notably, this police work involves Sawyer undercover, pretending to run a con but actually working a sting operation. A con within a con (in a sideways universe)!

†   Our Jim is clearly not meant to be with Charlotte, who has a different soulmate in the sideways world. Besides, he seems much happier enjoying a night alone, with a frozen dinner, a beer, and *Little House on the Prairie*. (It's a relevant *Little House* too, in which Pa reminds Laura that life is about "laughing and loving each other" and that "people aren't really gone when they die.")

in the sideways universe. Looking at the name scrawled on top of the Cooper file, Miles asks, "Who's Sawyer?" Throughout the Island business, as Sawyer travels from place to place, making deals and plans, that question resonates. Who *is* Sawyer, really? A good guy? A bad guy? Or something else entirely?

He certainly spends a lot of his Island time in this episode with the villains, all freshly returned from the Temple: The Man in Black, the possibly soulless Sayid, and Crazy Claire. The Man in Black even takes the increasingly disillusioned and disaffected Sawyer into his confidence, admitting at last that he actually is "the black smoke" who has tormented the 815ers ever since they crashed. He also asks a favor from Sawyer, wanting him to take a boat over to the Hydra station, to see if there are any lingering Ajira survivors and if the coast is clear to get the airplane back up and running. He says he knows Sawyer's the man for the job, because he's a con man, and can make up any story he needs to stay alive.

It says something about Sawyer's innate confidence—or perhaps his deep-rooted nihilism—that he's brazen enough to speak his mind to a rampaging Smoke Monster. (The Man in Black seems a little annoyed at times at Sawyer's impertinence during their conversation; but then he absently mutters, "I forgive you," as though those were magic words that allow him to keep dealing with this irreverent whelp.) "Recon" then kicks into several higher gears once Sawyer arrives on Hydra, and first wanders around his old polar bear cage—where Kate's dress still hangs, forlornly—before spotting a pile of dead Ajira passengers and meeting a woman named Zoe who claims to be the sole remaining survivor.

Zoe is not who she says she is—because this is a Sawyer story, after all. She's an agent of Charles Widmore. Zoe's boss invites Sawyer onto his sub to make a deal. Sawyer, adopting the same flippant tone that he takes with The Man in Black, tells Widmore he'll gladly bring the Monster over to be killed or contained by Widmore's sonic pylons, so long as his own people remain safe and Widmore gets them off the Island. Widmore agrees; but then Sawyer rows back to The Man in Black and spills everything he knows, including the deal he made. And then he tells Kate his real plan: to let these two yahoos fight it out while he and Kate swipe the sub and leave.

Ironic, isn't it, how Sawyer is working his greatest con by telling everybody the truth?

As the episode ends, we still don't know whether Sawyer's good or bad in the grand scheme of things. He's just Sawyer, looking out for himself. Widmore even chides Sawyer about how little he really knows about the Island and its history, when they talk about who's responsible for all the dead Ajira folks. But what makes "Recon" such a great episode is that—like Sawyer—we also don't have to know what's really going on to be excited or delighted. There's a person we know. Call him James Ford or Sawyer or LaFleur . . . whatever the moniker, he's an easy man to root for. —*NM*

IN JACOB WE TRUST

"AB AETERNO"

–

SEASON 6, EPISODE 9
ORIGINAL AIRDATE 3/23/10

Is it better to rule in Hell or serve in Heaven? What about if you serve in Hell, but you're, like . . . really high up?

A useful poker term is "pot-committed," which refers to that point in a hand where you've got so many chips at stake that you pretty much have to call any raise by your opponent, no matter how big. Like a lot of poker-speak, "pot-committed" has applications even when you step away from the card table. Consider Richard Alpert. For 140 years, he has worked as Jacob's intermediary in the world, guiding people to the Island (and guiding them once they're on the Island) to an end that Jacob has only vaguely explained. Richard has trusted that Jacob knows what he's doing, and that the other guy—The Man in Black, the first one to touch Richard and offer him help on the Island—is an evil force that Jacob's keeping in check. Not much more seems to have been clarified for Mr. Alpert, ever.★ He's primarily been acting on faith; and with Jacob dead at the end of Season Five, that faith is as shattered as the giant statue that used to guard this Island. What was it all for, ultimately? Is it time for Richard to fold, or does he need to stand behind his bet, now more than ever?

"Ab Aeterno"† is an episode that a lot of *Lost* fans had been anxiously awaiting: the big Richard Alpert origin story, with promises of major reveals about the Island mythology. It largely takes place in 1867, with an extended explanation of how Richard found himself in Jacob's service in the first place. There's a different kind of mood about it. Michael Giacchino's score sounds different, particularly at the start of Richard's story, which introduces a new musical theme.‡ The framing of shots catches parts of the Island—an overgrown tree, the beach with the Statue—not seen much during the run of the series. The overall thrust of all these creative choices is that this is a tale from Richard's perspective, and that the way he experiences this world has been affected by the 160-plus years he's been alive.

One of the best aspects of *Lost* is how any given episode can whisk viewers to other places and tell stories in any genre. "Recon," the prior episode, is basically a buddy cop show. This one is a tragic Victorian romance, with biblical overtones.

We start on the Canary Islands, where poor Richard needs a doctor to save his feverish, consumptive wife Isabella. She gives him her heavily symbolic gold cross to pay for medicine, but the doctor refuses it—calling it worthless, layering meaning upon meaning—and an agitated Richard accidentally kills him. Isabella dies and Richard is imprisoned, where he's given a choice between death-by-hanging or joining a man named

---

★ At one point in this episode, Ben bitterly notes that he's known Richard for a long time, and that Richard doesn't know anything about the Island, really. And if anyone's an expert on Island ignorance, it's Ben.

† Named for a Latin term loosely translated as "from eternity" or "from the distant past."

‡ In the DVD commentary for this episode, writer Melinda Hsu Taylor told Néstor Carbonell about the theme, saying that it's cued to Richard's wife's cross. She said, "When Michael Giacchino scores these episodes, he watches them start to finish. He doesn't want to know the ending first, he doesn't want to know the plot points or twists and turns. He likes to experience it. The music comes to him from that."

Mr. Whitfield on an expedition to the New World on *The Black Rock*. Only after Richard makes the choice to live does he learn that Whitfield means him to be a slave, "property of Magnus Hanso."

The Black Rock soon gets caught up in a storm and heads toward the Island, where it catches a big wave, crashes into the Statue, and demolishes it, before washing up way inland.* Mr. Whitfield begins slaughtering all the slaves so that they won't be a drain on Hanso's resources, but Richard is spared when the Smoke Monster comes whooshing in, killing everybody. A few days later, Richard sees the ghost of his wife and hears her scream when the Monster returns. Then the Monster comes back yet again, in human form this time, and tells Richard that "the devil" has Isabella down on the beach by the shattered Statue, and that Richard can get her back if he slays the devil with a special dagger. He's not to listen to a word the devil—Jacob—says, because if he does, it'll be too late.

But alas, Richard does listen. Jacob repels Richard's attack easily, then quickly convinces Richard that The Man in Black is the bad guy, and that Richard, no matter what he believes, is not dead and not in Hell.† He proves this by dunking Richard in the ocean three times—ritual baptism, in other words—after which Richard is born again, and ready to do as Jacob asks. Jacob explains that The Man in Black is a dark stain that will spread throughout the world unless he's contained in his bottle by "the cork" that is the Island. He explains that his adversary has a gift for manipulating people and bringing out their worst tendencies. Richard asks why Jacob doesn't use his own powers of persuasion on the opposite side, and Jacob explains that it's not right for people to be led to the proper path rather than finding it themselves. But then he seems to take Richard's idea under consideration and asks if Richard would mind going out into the world as his representative.

So, how does all this fit into *Lost* as we know it?

Note that Jacob says he can't bring Richard's wife back and can't absolve Richard of his sins, though he can grant eternal life. Those sound like the promises of a supernatural being, yes, but not necessarily a Christ figure (baptism and gold crosses aside). Note also that when Jacob makes

---

*   Hey, it's a magic island. Sometimes stuff just . . . happens.

†   This reassurance was perhaps also aimed at all the fans still convinced that the Island was some kind of afterlife.

his offer to Richard, he's essentially repeating the offer made by Whitfield. Richard is as good as dead, then Jacob offers him life—but only in service. That parallel isn't coincidental.

As for what makes "Ab Aeterno" a *Lost* story, note that it has a narrative structure which puts the protagonist in shackles and in the dark for a good chunk of the episode. That's *Lost* in a nutshell, yes? There's so much we want to see, and so much we want to know, yet again and again, the writers lock us into one place, and leave us there in ignorance until our spirits are broken. Then just when we're about to give up they take us someplace new and unexpected, and we're so grateful that we'll believe anything they tell us. It's quite canny how often *Lost* becomes a metaphor for itself.

Richard's story plays out against the backdrop of the old rivalry between Jacob and The Man in Black. When Jacob explains that there'll always be a cork to contain the malevolence, The Man in Black responds by smashing a bottle (thus illustrating that there may be more than one way to escape). In 2007, Richard is in such despair that he swings to The Man in Black's side, digging up Isabella's old cross, buried on the Island 140 years ago, and calling for The Man in Black to take him onto the dark team as he promised to way back when. Richard's ready to quit.

Then Hugo shows up, carrying a message from Isabella's ghost to stay in the game. It's a beautifully conceived, staged, and acted scene—rivaling the more emotional Desmond/Penny scenes—with Richard and Isabella standing right next to each other and communicating through Hurley. *Lost* is not Jacob's story or The Man in Black's story. It's the story of how these characters we've lived with for six years deal with the choices and opportunities being offered by those two entities. Following Jacob may not always be the right thing to do; but it does give Richard a sense of purpose and hope that he doesn't have at the start of the episode. In the end, he's an existential hero. He can't go on; he'll go on. —*NM*

"THE PACKAGE"

—

SEASON 6, EPISODE 10

ORIGINAL AIRDATE 3/30/10

On the Island: The conflict between Widmore and The Man in Black intensifies, with Widmore abducting Jin and trying to sway him to his cause.

Off the Island: Jin loses the money he was supposed to deliver to his future father-in-law's criminal associates (who look a lot like the Island villains Keamy and Mikhail) and needs help from a stranger named Sayid to avoid being killed.

How many scenes did Daniel Dae Kim and Yunjin Kim shoot together after the first season of *Lost*? In the early going, Jin and Sun's story was about a controlling husband and a secretive wife, who were insepara-ble even if one of them would have preferred to have more freedom. Then they fought, and split up, and reunited, and learned to appreciate each other again, then split up again. By the time Season Four rolled around, the story of Jin and Sun was about a couple who'd finally real-ized what they meant to each other, but who kept getting separated by circumstance.

"The Package" doesn't vary much from the Jin/Sun episode struc-ture that had been in play for years—and in fact in some ways the Jin/Sun storylines feel a bit tacked-on, in an episode that is just as much about The Man in Black and Charles Widmore coming face-to-face at last and effectively declaring war. Even the title "The Package" refers to the sur-prise arrival at the end of the episode: Desmond, who has been brought to the Island against his will by Widmore (or perhaps, in a roundabout way, summoned a few episodes ago by Jacob's lighthouse).

A lot of the Jin/Sun parallels here feel a bit forced. In the sideways universe, Jin bumps his head. On the Island, Sun bumps her head—and loses her ability to speak English. In both universes, they're making deci-sions they hope will reunite them, but which instead draw them further apart. On the Island, Sun resists Jack and company's plan to go to the Hydra station and disable the airplane (to keep The Man in Black from escaping); but she has no idea that Jin is already at Hydra, with Widmore's army. Off the Island, Jin tries to make things right with the people to whom he was supposed to deliver a parcel of money, unaware that those people were being paid to kill him.

"The Package" lacks the kind of poignant resolution that Jin/Sun episodes usually have (although in the sideways universe she does reveal to him that she's pregnant) and in a way the sideways scenes mainly close the loop on "Sundown," which ends with Sayid finding Jin being held captive by the same crooks he's after. But there is a touching moment early in the episode, when Mikhail escorts Sun away from Jin. There's something in their eyes: a sense that if they let someone pull them apart, they might never be together again . . . as though they know what kind of *Lost* episode they're in. —NM

"HAPPILY EVER AFTER"

—

SEASON 6, EPISODE 11
ORIGINAL AIRDATE 4/6/10

On the Island: Widmore tortures Desmond with electricity and tries to convince him that he's the key to saving the Island.

Off the Island: While trying to arrange a special Drive Shaft concert for his boss Charles Widmore—and Widmore's wife Eloise and son Daniel— Desmond begins to experience flashes of the "other" reality.

Prior to "Happily Ever After," Damon Lindelof and Carlton Cuse described the episode as the start of a "new chapter" in Season Six, which would "change the conversation" about what was happening with the flash-sideways scenes. So naturally they built the story around Desmond, the one *Lost* character who has consistently delivered some of the series' most eye-opening and emotional moments. Desmond begins to bridge the gaps between the two Season Six universes, establishing—finally—where the sideways stories are headed.

To that end, most of "Happily Ever After" takes place in Los Angeles, with the sparse on-Island scenes devoted to showing Widmore trying to break Desmond down (unlike in the sideways world, where Desmond enjoys a good relationship with Widmore . . . perhaps because in the sideways world Desmond has never even heard of Penny). The main takeaway from the Island scenes is how Desmond gradually moves from despair—having been returned once again to this place he spent so long trying to escape—to a kind of stubborn resolution. If he's the only one who can save the Island, then by Jacob, he'll get it done.

Off the Island, Desmond goes through a change, which also involves a sacrifice. Superficially, everything in LA is going OK for him. He has a steady job; and he has a friendly relationship with Charles Widmore, a man who hated him in the other reality. But he doesn't have Penny, and as he crosses paths with people the other Desmond knew on the Island—Charlie and Daniel, mainly—he realizes that they also sometimes have a sense that they've lost a woman they once loved. As Desmond's déjà vu with these new acquaintances intensifies, he makes the decision to find more people in the sideways reality that he vaguely remembers, and to help them understand that something's not quite right.

"Happily Ever After" doesn't explain the sideways universe exactly, but it does make it clear that this place is not a happy ending for our heroes—not really. Here they are experiencing some things that were missing from their old lives, but at the expense of some other things that were essential to who they were. From this point on in Season Six, the sideways scenes will start putting all the pieces back together, just as the story on the Island is careening toward tragedy. —NM

"EVERYBODY LOVES HUGO"

—

SEASON 6, EPISODE 12
ORIGINAL AIRDATE 4/13/10

On the Island: Hurley hears from Michael's ghost, who urges him to stop his faction from blowing up the plane at the Hydra station.

Off the Island: A wealthy and successful Hurley meets Libby, who begins to remind him of his other life.

In one of Season One's most memorable moments, the doomed Dr. Arzt was in the middle of delivering a pedantic lecture about the dangerous instability of old dynamite when he accidentally proved his point by blowing himself up. In "Everybody Loves Hugo," Hurley is trying to convince his friends that their plan to use that same old dynamite to destroy an airplane will get a lot of people killed. And sure enough, Ilana quickly proves him right by mishandling the explosives and splattering herself.

These are shocking moments—and, yes, darkly funny. And "Everybody Loves Hugo" has another one at the end of the episode, when Sayid brings Desmond to The Man in Black, who gives a little history lesson about Islanders digging wells where the magnetic energy is wonky—before pushing Desmond into one of those wells.

But hey, in a show where sometimes the revelations come in dribs and the action is often unnaturally drawn out, there's something to be said for a sharp, sudden jolt. And "Everybody Loves Hugo" is about that, too. Just as "Happily Ever After" represented the beginning of the end for the sideways universe—by having the sideways Desmond "wake up," and embark on a mission to be a kind of cosmic alarm clock to his former Island acquaintances—"Everybody Loves Hugo" shows just how everyone's going to snap out of their sideways fog. For Hurley, it happens

299

when he kisses Libby, who in this world is institutionalized because she sees the truth about the fake reality around her. Later, Desmond intentionally runs over the sideways Locke with his car, in an attempt to set Locke's awakening in motion.

The point is: Revelations can hurt. They're abrupt and destructive, and even if you survive them, there's no guarantee that the people you share them with will believe you—especially if they have reason to cling to the status quo. This is the situation—and the dilemma—that will define the remaining *Lost* episodes. —*NM*

"THE LAST RECRUIT"
—
SEASON 6, EPISODE 13
ORIGINAL AIRDATE 4/20/10

On the Island: Finally, all in one place again, the castaways try to sneak away on a boat, but both Widmore and The Man in Black aren't so eager to let them go.

Off the Island: The sideways versions of the 815ers continue to cross paths, steered by Desmond.

As "The Last Recruit" begins, nearly all the surviving 815ers are back together, under the watchful eye of a monster who looks like Locke. Meanwhile, Ben's on his way back to the Others' camp with Richard— exactly where they both were when this whole adventure started in Season One. And Desmond? He's stuck in a hole in the ground. Sound familiar?

And yet, as Jack astutely notes in this episode, they're "all different now." Throughout its first five seasons, *Lost* cycled through various kinds of storytelling modes, examining how the characters did and didn't take charge of their respective stories. Season Six makes that theme more explicit by literally turning the characters we thought we knew into different people. On the Island, Claire's not quite Claire, and Sayid's not quite Sayid. Jack, Hurley, Kate, and Sawyer have also been profoundly changed in the years since they first sat around a campfire with a guy who looks like Terry O'Quinn. And in the sideways universe? Everyone's profoundly different . . . although in "The Last Recruit," when Jin and Sun arrive at Jack's hospital at the same time that Locke rolls in with Ben, a panicked Sun has a flash of recognition upon seeing Locke's face.

As proof of how much things have changed, consider Jack, who throughout Season Six is determined not to be a leader anymore, unless the Island makes it clear that he's supposed to take charge. He defers at times in this episode either to The Man in Black or to Sawyer, though each has weaknesses.

The Man in Black's method of leadership involves pulling people aside, spilling secrets, and making subtle suggestions and insinuations. According to Claire, as soon as you let him talk to you, you're on his team. But the problem with the-devil-on-the-shoulder method of leadership is that as soon as Locke steps down off the shoulder, he loses his prey's attention. Witness Sayid, who dutifully walks off into the jungle to kill Desmond, only to hesitate when Desmond asks whether The Man in Black's rewards are worth it. Even if Locke can bring Nadia back, as he has promised, what will he tell her when she asks what he did to revive her? Away from The Man in Black's smoke, his followers start to see more clearly.

As for Sawyer, his leadership style is driven to a significant degree by a lifetime of defensiveness, and a need to prove that he's no hayseed. He's a shrewd son-of-a-bitch with no patience for doubters or debaters. So, when Jack wonders aloud whether deceiving The Man in Black and allying with Widmore is the best idea, Sawyer demands an immediate up-or-down vote. When Jack chooses down, Sawyer orders him out of their boat, telling him to take "a leap of faith" (echoing something Eloise Hawking said to Jack in "316").

How much have things changed? Well, in this show where the phrase "We have to go back!" is practically a motto, Sawyer preempts even the suggestion of that after he orders Jack to go overboard. As Jack swims to shore, Sawyer hisses that they're done going back. —NM

"THE CANDIDATE"

—

SEASON 6, EPISODE 14
ORIGINAL AIRDATE 5/4/10

On the Island: Jack and Sayid help The Man in Black free Sawyer's party from Widmore's goons, but then The Man in Black gets a bomb onto the submarine our heroes were using to escape, killing Sayid, Sun, and Jin.

Off the Island: Jack tries to convince Locke to have an operation that could help him walk again.

One of the hallmarks of *Lost*'s storytelling was wheel-spinning. Characters make big pronouncements one week and then back off of them the next. New people are introduced and then killed for no apparent reason. Our heroes spend a whole episode walking across the Island and then have to return from whence they came. It's all busywork.

This is the case in "The Candidate" as well. In "The Last Recruit," Jack dramatically leaves Sawyer's group, and in "The Candidate" he's back with them. Later, when the bomb is ticking away on the submarine, the gang wastes time arguing about whether or not the bomb even *can* blow up, given what the people inside it mean both to the Island and to The Man in Black. Meanwhile, in the sideways universe, Jack spends the whole episode violating his patient John Locke's privacy in order to build the case that Locke should get surgery—and Locke still refuses. More busywork. More wheel-spinning. Except . . .

Canonically, "The Candidate" is the episode where Sayid, Sun, and Jin all die, so what happens in the episode is consequential. Perhaps it doesn't mean as much given that characters died on *Lost* throughout its run and then came back, and given that Sayid, Sun, and Jin are all alive in the sideways universe at the end of "The Candidate" (as is Locke, who died two seasons ago). But everything in this episode—one of *Lost*'s most intense and nerve-wracking overall—certainly feels meaningful. There's a sense that all the cycling is coming to an end. We're passing a point of no return.★

Even in the sideways universe, the versions of Jack and Locke seem to be realizing their connection, as they both toss around a lot of familiar phrases, like "Push the button," "I wish you had believed me," and, inevitably, "What happened, happened."

Add in boats blowing up, characters drowning, people trying to leave and then washing up on shore . . . well, to quote Sawyer, "Feels like we're running in circles." But this time the recurrences feel more thematically rich, and not a case of the writers running out of ideas. This is what Season Six is about, in part. What happened before happens again, over and over . . . until someone gets it right. —NM

THE SECRET OF GLOWY CAVE

"ACROSS THE SEA"
—

SEASON 6, EPISODE 15
ORIGINAL AIRDATE 5/11/10

When J. J. Abrams and Damon Lindelof were writing the *Lost* pilot, there was no Jacob and no Man in Black; and while Abrams and Lindelof may have had some vague idea of what cosmic purpose the Island served, they almost certainly hadn't talked about a cave bathed in golden light, leading to the heart of all good and evil in the world.

★ Once again, even Michael Giacchino's score emphasizes how significant the moment is when an explosion causes the escape submarine to flood. He cycles through multiple standard *Lost* motifs; and then as Jin and Sun drown, he settles on the plaintive melody that often plays as characters either die or are reunited. (Both are true in this couple's case.)

Across the six years of fans theorizing about the origins of this epic, centuries-spanning saga—with its dozens of characters and mind-bending time-jumps—nobody on the online forums probably ever said, "I'm picturing a cave." So, is this the genius of *Lost*? To deliver what few would have expected? Or is the Glowy Cave in "Across the Sea" a case of the *Lost* writers sabotaging all their super-cool ideas with something woo-woo and drippy?

For example, who would've guessed back in 2004 that we'd get from the events of the pilot to what happens in "Across the Sea," an episode set thousands of years in the past, and dealing with The Source of All Life, and how it both inspires and corrupts. And who would've guessed the episode would answer so much, and yet still leave so many questions—most of which were never resolved.*

To be fair to the naysayers, whenever *Lost* deals directly with the transcendental—rather than just glancing at it—the show can get awfully gooey, and painfully blunt. Given that the first half of this episode features Young Jacob and The Future Man in Black asking Big Questions and getting simple answers, "Across the Sea" really tests the audience's willingness to sit through talk of good and evil and truth and lies and mystical lights under the water.

But those conversations sound better on reflection, and spark some deeper thoughts. What's legitimately great about "Across the Sea" is that when all is said and done, the answers it offers really aren't so simple. Sure, the implications may be. *Lost* in Season Six clarifies just who the villain of the piece is and what the responsibilities of the heroes are vis-à-vis said villain. Yet the roots of that hero/villain dynamic remain awfully tangled, and indicate that when it comes to faith versus reason, and choice versus no-choice, there's a continuum. Even in a story about white stones versus black stones, there's still quite a bit of gray. "Across the Sea" has a real biblical feel, as just as with the Holy Bible, there's a lot here that's open to interpretation.

Here's one interpretation:

---

* Not to get too far ahead of myself, but among those questions: Who were the other people on the Island and how did they get there? Why didn't the Woman destroy them earlier? How does she destroy them? *What is the history of this place?*

Once upon a time, two brothers—twins—were born on a mysterious island, and raised by a woman who taught them right from wrong, and taught them also that they were destined to protect the Island from ill-intentioned interlopers who would exploit the Island's unique energies and spread wickedness throughout the world entire. But the younger twin—the Bad Twin—didn't trust the Woman, and went to live with some of those interlopers, helping them to tap into what the Island has to offer. So, the Woman punished the Bad Twin for straying, and in return he killed her. The Good Twin banished his brother, consigning him to roam the Island as a monster, and effectively drafting the Bad Twin in the ongoing campaign to keep outsiders at bay.

And here's another interpretation:

Once upon a time, a woman stumbled across a pregnant castaway on the beach of a mysterious island, and after helping her deliver her babies—twins—the Woman killed the Mother and claimed the offspring as her own.* The Woman lied to the brothers about what lay beyond the confines of the Island. She lied to them about why they were there, and what they were meant to do. She pitted one brother against the other, by indicating she had different expectations for each. She stifled their interests and crushed their ambitions. Then the younger twin—the Good Twin—rose up against her and killed her. In repayment, he was chained to the land he despised.

There are further wrinkles to explore. For example, while living with the Island's interlopers, the black-clad brother comes to hate them, because he sees that the Woman was right, and that men are by nature egotistical, avaricious liars.† Meanwhile, the white-clad brother—Jacob—watches these men from afar and sees a lot of good in them, even as he dutifully stays by the Woman's side. And there's more: The Woman demands that Jacob cement his status as the Island's protector by speaking a Latin oath and drinking from her special bottle of wine—although Jacob is reluctant to do so. (After he drinks she says that the two of them are "the same," which is pretty ominous given how awful

---

* Echoes, part one: Claire was told not to let Aaron be "raised by another." Jacob and The Man in Black definitely were not raised by their proper mom.

† Echoes, part two: The Woman is a crazy person in the wilderness, distrusting the Others, just like Rousseau.

the Woman can be.) Then later, after The Man in Black stabs her, she tells him that she's always loved him, and that she meant him to be the protector all along. As she dies, she whispers, "Thank you," indicating that she's glad to be free of the burden of fighting, lying, and killing to keep people away from whatever lies at the bottom of Glowy Cave.

"Across the Sea" is a whopper of an origin story (and *Lost* was always good at those). It explains why Jacob and The Man in Black are obsessed with games; how The Man in Black is responsible for the construction of the Frozen Donkey Wheel; and how Jacob pushed his brother into Glowy Cave and turned him into the Smoke Monster. But the episode also shows how origin stories can change over time, and take on meanings far different than their, well, origins. Yes, the Smoke Monster came into this world because The Man in Black broke his Mother's rules. But Jacob is just as much to blame, for forcing his brother into the water. Jacob created a lot of the problems that he's spent centuries trying to solve.★

And yes, there are still questions. ("Every question I answer will simply lead to another question," the Woman promises, in one of the episode's many meta-moments.) Like, how did the Woman get there? When she meets the boys' pregnant mother, the Woman says she's the only one on the Island—but we know the Woman lies. And how did she make the kids immortal? How long has the Island been in existence? How did the villagers learn about the Island's power and how to exploit it?

For anyone who tuned in to "Across the Sea" hoping for those kinds of answers? No dice.† And given that it came close to the end of *Lost*'s run, the episode disappointed some fans, because it seemed to (and more or less did) close off all further possibility that the show would explain the Island. But then *Lost* was never about the Island per se, or even a

---

★   Is it also possible that in order to be the Island's protector, you have to be willing to be a little evil sometimes? Is that why he let people like Charles Widmore and Ben Linus lead the Others?

†   In the DVD commentary track for this episode, Carlton Cuse said, "Who built Taweret? Who were all the ancient people that were here that built some of these inner workings of the Island that we've seen? That sort of fell out of the spectrum of the story that we were telling in our series. But what did, in our opinion, fall into that spectrum was: 'Who is Jacob?' 'Where did he come from?' And, 'What is the origin of the relationship between Jacob and the Man in Black?'" Cuse also admitted that he and Lindelof were genuinely surprised that so many fans were so angry about the episode.

story of Jacob and The Man in Black. Those were all only ever part of the backdrop for a story about the people who come to the Island, and what being there reveals about them.

As "Across the Sea" ends, we see Jacob take the dead bodies of his brother and the Woman and put them side by side, with a pouch containing two stones from the game that he and his brother liked to play.* And then we flash back to *Lost's* sixth episode, "House of the Rising Sun," and relive the moment when Jack, Kate, and—most ironically—Locke discovered the bones of The Man in Black and the Woman, and dubbed them "Adam and Eve."† It's a haunting moment, made all the more so by the reminder of how easily Locke reduced the corpses to the echo of a simple story—the ultimate origin story, really—while we know it's far more complicated than that. —NM

"WHAT THEY DIED FOR"

—

SEASON 6, EPISODE 16
ORIGINAL AIRDATE 5/18/10

On the Island: The Man in Black wins the war against Widmore and announces his plan to use Desmond's special powers to destroy the Island, while Jacob appears one more time to Hurley (and Jack, Kate, and Sawyer) and anoints Jack as the Island's new protector.

Off the Island: Locke changes his mind about letting Jack operate on him, while Desmond and Hurley arrange for Kate and Sayid to get out of jail, in time for them all to make it to the Drive Shaft concert.

---

*   The game is Senet, one of the oldest in the historical records—and one that no one today really knows the rules of, aside from speculation. Another subtle metaphor?

†   Lindelof in the "Across the Sea" DVD commentary insisted that as far back as the episode "House of the Rising Sun," he knew that the skeletons in the cave would be, in some way, responsible for Oceanic 815 crashing and setting this whole epic saga in motion.

"What They Died For" was difficult for *Lost* fans to evaluate when it originally aired, since it came one week after the divisive "Across the Sea"—which had disappointed many with its prosaic approach to a story about myths and magic—and just five days before a finale that the diehards hoped wouldn't just explain everything but would retroactively redeem everything about Season Six that they had found off-putting.★ And while "What They Died For" does steer the show toward its ultimate conclusion, it doesn't do so in a way that would alleviate any anxieties for the "Across the Sea" haters.

If anything, the episode doubles down on its predecessor's bluntness. By the end of the hour, the only real remaining "mystery" per se for the show to solve is the explanation of what the sideways universe is. Granted, that wasn't the only mystery the fans wanted Lindelof and Cuse to resolve. In the weeks leading up to the finale, the entertainment media was filled with essays and listicles summing up every remaining unanswered *Lost* question . . . and there were quite a lot.† But as far as the creators of the show were concerned, "Across the Sea" and "What They Died For" covered most everything they felt needed to be addressed before "The End." In fact, part of what makes the finale so entertaining is that most of the "answers" that mattered had already been given, freeing the show up to deliver a rush of action and emotion.

Jacob is responsible for the last big answer-dump, stating plainly some things that a lot of *Lost*'s audience had already sort of assumed. The crux of it: Jacob brought the Oceanic 815 "candidates" to the Island because the monster that used to be his brother was inevitably going to kill him one day, and it was essential for someone trustworthy to step up and keep doing the job of preserving and protecting the Island's powerful forces.

★   To be clear, Season Six has a lot of supporters, including the authors of this book, but for many the general emphasis on the sideways universe over Island mythology rubbed them the wrong way.

†   On the day that this episode aired, Gizmodo rounded up fifty questions that "*Lost* really does need to answer," including: Why the Dharma Initiative had Egyptian symbols inside the Swan's countdown mechanism; why Libby's backstory shadowed Hurley's so closely; why the Smoke Monster killed some Island visitors but let others live; why the Smoke Monster wanted the Island moved; what caused the fertility problems on the Island; why Jacob didn't consider some of the castaways proper Candidates; *what's the deal with the numbers?!?!*; and more.

But Jacob says a few other things too, worth contemplating before "The End." He says he selected the candidates because they were broken and unhappy in their regular lives and would thus be open to starting over on a magical uncharted isle; and he adds that he's not selecting his replacement, but rather his replacement must step forward and claim the job. In other words: "Fate" has less to do with this process than the people caught up in it may think. (Nevertheless, Jack drinks the sacred water and accepts the responsibility, which makes sense in dramatic television terms, because he's been the de facto lead character of *Lost*, which makes him the inevitable choice to be the ultimate hero.★)

Lost in its final season veered close at times toward the side of "Yes, fate exists and evil exists and the whole reason our heroes are here is to slay a dragon." But even then, it never lost the angles of "Yes, The Man in Black is a bad dude, but he has reasons," and "Yes, the castaways are here for a reason, but only because someone meddled in their lives." To the end, *Lost* held to the idea that people do the wrong thing for the right reason—and vice versa. The process is never clean. —*NM*

MOVING ON

"THE END"

—

SEASON 6, EPISODES 17 & 18
ORIGINAL AIRDATE 5/23/10

EMILY: Before we begin talking about "The End" in earnest, I need to tell you, Noel, that my thinking on this episode has been shaped immeasurably by something you said, offhand, in a bar, to a person who wasn't even me. I just happened to be present. Just what was it you said? Well,

---

★   Perhaps! There is still one episode to go.

in true *Lost* fashion, I want to circle back to that. Before we get there, some bona fides.

I loved "The End" when it aired, writing thousands upon thousands of words about the episode in the week after its debut. I had quibbles, to be sure. But *Lost* was always a show made better by its imperfections, so I would hate if the finale were some sparkling TV diamond. My overall impression was overwhelmingly positive, even as fan opinion on the episode turned rancid. The finale bet hard on concluding the characters' journeys rather than having someone sit down and offer a long series of "answers." That call was the right one for me, but for many fans, it very much was not.

I then set "The End" aside for a decade. In May 2020, in the early depths of the Covid-19 lockdown, the finale's tenth anniversary arrived and brought with it a wave of reappreciations. As you and I had just started working on this book, my wife and I thought we would rewatch it on one of those long, lonely nights when our apartment started to feel both like a prison and like our entire world all at once. Seen in that environment, I lost all critical objectivity. I cried buckets. In that environment, "The End" was exactly what I needed to see.

I've rewatched it a couple of times since then, just to see if the experience of that rewatch holds up, and it very much does. After a decade of series finales that could feel like locking puzzle pieces into place without much emotion behind them, *Lost* going for broke on Jack dying quietly in the very place he woke up on the Island, with Vincent falling asleep beside him, plays better and better. I don't want TV to tell me things I already know. I want it to make me feel things I can't find anywhere else.

When I think of the main wound time has healed for me, however, it has to be the flash-sideways timeline, the one where we see what all of the characters' lives would have been like without the Island. In 2010, in the midst of fervent theorizing about what it all meant, even I—a finale super-fan—was mildly disappointed that the answer was "Eh, it's a celestial waiting room★ for the afterlife." I remember thinking, *"That's it?!"*

★   A few discussions of the finale were the first place I saw the word "bardo" to refer to the Buddhist concept of a state between life and death, which came to greater prominence in American pop culture in the 2010s after the publication of the George Saunders novel *Lincoln in the Bardo*. The idea had, of course, been discussed and then mostly coming around on it. The various scenes of characters "waking up" to the reality of their lives on the Island worked well for me then and even better for me now, but the overarching superstructure of the idea . . . is a huge reach.

To be clear, with every year I get older, I love the idea a little more, but every time I watch it, I do think of something Noel said at a bar in San Diego for Comic-Con 2010: "I don't need answers. I care about what happens to these characters. I'm just not sure I care about what happens to them after they die."

NOEL: And I stand by that! Well . . . sort of. Look, I have two main criticisms of "The End" (which, I hasten to add, is a TV episode that I wrote a hugely positive review of on the night that it originally aired, and an episode which I still mostly like). My first criticism is exactly as you remembered: If you're the sort of person who likes to think of *Lost* as one long, cohesive narrative, then the ending doesn't exactly fit with the beginning. It has almost nothing to do with the mysteries introduced in "Pilot."

Now, it's not unusual for an epic saga to conclude with a lengthy epilogue; and I think if the flash-sideways in Season Six had shown us the lives of our heroes after they got off the Island, then even the most disappointed fans would've been more forgiving. Instead, "The End" asks us to be moved by the final day for characters who are not *quite* the ones we'd been following for six years. We have no idea what Sawyer actually did between flying away from the Island and ending up in this strange way station to the afterlife; and as fun as it is to watch the adventures of James Ford, Supercool Cop (and it *is* fun!), it feels like a cheat to be denied the real details of his post-Island story.

My second criticism is that "The End" presumes a kind of ride-or-die camaraderie between these people that is rarely seen in the previous hundred-odd episodes. The idea that Sayid would be eager to attend some kind of cosmic high school reunion with, say, Kate or Claire? I don't know . . . Was he even really friends with either of them? A lot about the sideways universe feels forced in that way.

And yet! Do I tear up when Sawyer's hand touches Juliet's and they simultaneously experience a rapid-fire montage of their time together

often in other countries, but in the American culture that tended to influence *Lost*, the idea felt pretty new.

on the Island? Oh, you better believe I do. All of those "waking up" moments in "The End" really land, because the truth is that some of these characters really did form a bond—with each other, and with us. The finale boldly offers the simple, satisfying pleasures of episodic TV that the creators of *Seinfeld* once mocked as passé. The *Seinfeld* crew promised "no hugging, no learning." *Lost* ended with a lot of both.

But let's flash sideways now in the other direction, because while a lot of the attention paid to "The End" today is focused on the pocket universe and the final gathering at the church, I think the way the episode wraps up the Island story is pretty sublime. So much of *Lost*'s plot is about moving pieces around the big board that is the Island; and the finale offers that one last time, as some characters trudge off to Glowy Cave for a final standoff while others make their way to the Ajira plane to escape. So much of *Lost* is *also* about the complicated, kludgy mechanisms that make the Island magic work, and we get *that* again too, as first Desmond and then Jack wrestle with the heavy stone plug that apparently keeps humanity safe. The action throughout is both exciting and weird . . . my favorite kind of *Lost*.

EMILY: The final season of *Lost* has a strong whiff of religious hokum to it, and it could become overpowering in, say, the episodes focused on the mysterious Temple hidden on the Island. Similarly, the resolution of the flash-sideways arc confused many when it took place in a church and seemed to be endorsing some sort of vaguely Christian afterlife. If you weren't spiritually inclined, then this religiosity could turn you off really quickly.

Yet if there's something Damon Lindelof excels at time and again as both a TV and film writer, it's portraying the ways in which a bit of storytelling becomes a bit of myth becomes a bit of religious doctrine. And for me, when Jack makes Hurley the Island's protector, handing him an Oceanic Airlines water bottle with a muted "Now, you're like me," it's the best of both sides. It's a hugely important character moment for both Jack and Hurley, but it also suggests a kind of proto-religion, a wellspring from which all other belief follows. You hear something that seems true to you, that speaks deeply to your soul, and it's as though the person who told you that is saying, "Now, you're like me." You've been changed, even if you can't explain how. It's a little like Mother's rules for her boys, come to think of it.

Earlier in this book, I alluded to the fact that the writers never quite explain what the Island is, which is both true and not true. On the one hand, the final handful of episodes provide about as good of an explanation as you could possibly get, given the extreme metaphysical weight of everything we know about the Island. It's a kind of divine protection mechanism, to keep forces of pure evil at bay, and everything about it that seems strange scientifically is exacerbated by this extra layer of mysticism. It places *Lost* firmly within the literary subgenre of "mythic fiction," which is a subgenre of fantasy that draws from mythological and religious tropes, then transplants them to a world much like our own. The subgenre includes work by writers such as Angela Carter, Susanna Clarke, and John Crowley, all of whom are among my favorites of all time, so of course I find this resolution to *Lost*'s biggest mystery a good one.

I also said, however, that it's *true* the writers never explain what the Island is, and that's because you never get a real sense of how any of this works. Jack needs to put a rock back in a hole, and that starts everything humming again. Sure. Why does it work that way? How does it work that way? Who designed the system to work that way? *Lost* doesn't have answers for these questions, nor does it care to. Nor, ultimately, are those answers that important. The world is the way it is; what's important is how we choose to live in it.

The interesting thing about *Lost* is that you can go incredibly deep into the series' lore if you really want to. I've spent hours reading Lostpedia and reminding myself of the ephemera that built up around this series. Yet the lore also has its limits. The history of the Island is detailed but flimsy, and the periods not depicted directly in the show have a tendency to feel like they would fly away if you blew on them.

When people say that *Lost* didn't explain what the Island was, I think that's what they mean: The explanation we got was insufficient because it didn't offer a complete, deep, satisfying explanation for everything that happened on the show. A lot of the show's fans expected the Island to have some central *core* that was tangible and approachable and possibly even rational. In the days leading up to the finale, the theories posted online had become so all-consuming that it was inevitable something as simple as what the show offered would disappoint a lot of people.

Yet it doesn't fall into the easy trap of fundamentalism either. Within the world of *Lost*, there are good and evil, and each force has its avatar, but good and evil exist independently of any of these characters or even the Island. To "explain" the Island is to attempt to explain ancient mysteries not just within the show but within human existence. In its on-Island action, "The End" goes big before at least some of the characters go home.

NOEL: The water bottle baptism is a favorite of mine too, because unlike the later scenes deep within the Heart of the Island, nothing overtly magical happens. It reminds me of an exchange at the start of the episode, when Sawyer says to Jack, "So you're the new Jacob, huh?" and asks whether Jack feels any different. Jack answers, "Not really." But for those of us who've been watching Jack since "Pilot," we can see that he *is* different, in subtle ways. He may not be bathed in radiant light—and his changes may or may not have anything to do with Jacob—but as the series ends Jack is clearly a much humbler man and more open to what other people need.

Y'know, in *Lost*'s middle seasons, before Lindelof and Cuse started explaining more about the Island's history, the 815ers didn't really have a vocabulary yet to talk about what was happening all around them; and I used to cringe a bit when they would use the kind of words that *fans* were using, like "the monster." That kind of woo-woo just sounded strange in the context of the show's more super-serious conflict and action. But here at "The End," it suddenly feels much more natural for everyone to be discussing "candidates" and mentioning Jacob—perhaps because now they actually know what they're talking about. It even feels OK when Sawyer calls The Man in Black "Smoky," directly to his Locke-face.

But you're right that some mystery persists—like when Sawyer speculates that The Man in Black intends to use Desmond to destroy the Island and Jack isn't so sure, because Jacob didn't tell him anything about that.[*] And then later, when the good guys cross paths with The Man in Black and Ben, Jacob's old nemesis raises an eyebrow at the idea that Jack was picked to be the new Protector, given the oblique strategies Jacob usually uses. ("You're sort of the obvious choice, don't you think?")

---

[*] This cues Hurley to give *Lost* one last chance to reference *Star Wars*, as he calls Jacob "worse than Yoda" and adds, "I've got a bad feeling about this."

Except that Jacob didn't pick him—not really. Jack volunteered. And in the end, he's not even the right guy; Hurley is. There's more of that Island kludginess I keep mentioning. Everything is much harder and much more inexact than one would think it would be for a mystical piece of real estate that keeps the world safe.

Yet as Jack also notes to Desmond as he prepares to sacrifice his life for the Island, it is the nature of this place that "there are no shortcuts, no do-overs." The instruction manual is incomplete, even though it is very important to follow the rules. Isn't that how life itself feels, sometimes? To quote some very *Lost*-appropriate lyrics from one of my favorite bands,★ "This pattern's torn, and we're weaving."

EMILY: I think that overall feeling of life's random, terrible beauty peeking through everywhere is a big part of the reason the show's ultimate reveal about the flash-sideways sequences has worn so well with me over the years. Intellectually, I agree with your argument that they wrap up a version of the story that is completely different from the one we've been following. Emotionally, though, they create a bridge between the characters on the show and all of us watching at home. We're going to die, too, and *Lost*'s vision of the afterlife is one I find tremendously moving, even as I agree that, like, Sayid would probably want to be reunited with Nadia after death, not Shannon. Quibbles!

I suspect that one reason I'm not as bothered by the "they're not the same versions of the characters as I followed" criticism, which I've heard from many people other than you, is that my life as a trans woman means I'm used to the idea of identity being flexible and entirely arbitrary. The me who watched the *Lost* pilot amid that sticky Milwaukee summer of 2004 is extraordinarily different from the me writing these words, in ways that are immediately, visually obvious to anybody who looks at me. Yet I'm also the same person. It makes intuitive sense to me that a Sawyer who's a con is the same person as a Sawyer who's a cop, even if their circumstances are different. There is some core self that cannot be touched by the events that befall us, and I like to believe that core self—call it a soul—persists after we move on.

There's another reason I think the afterlife ending is perhaps necessary. *Lost* has always taken death seriously. Its pilot asks quite literally

★ Pavement, "Frontwards."

315

how these characters will survive a life-and-death situation, and by the time we've reached the finale, the show has killed off a tremendous amount of its cast. The characters who escape the Island are Kate, Claire, Sawyer, Richard, Miles, and Lapidus, which is such a random assortment of characters from across the run of the show that it feels exactly right. Hurley and Ben stick around to protect the Island. Desmond lives, though whether he returns to Penny and their son is left for outside the show. Rose and Bernard stay on the Island. "New Man in Charge," the short epilogue produced for the complete series DVD, catches up with Walt. But everybody else dies.

That's a high body count for almost any TV show,* but what's notable to me across the run of the show is how seriously *Lost* takes those deaths. When a late episode includes the deaths of Sayid, Sun, and Jin, the show takes time a couple of episodes later for those deaths to *matter*—indeed, that episode is called "What They Died For," and it takes seriously the idea that none of these lives is easily expendable for either the audience or for the other characters.† This series was born amid America's collective grief over 9/11, and it never entirely lost that quality. It almost *needs* to end with a story that allows for a sense of powerful release, and I think it's interesting that when I rewatched the finale, during the Covid lockdown, it played even better for me than it had in 2010. I needed somewhere to put the messy, scary despair that was threatening to overwhelm me, and there was *Lost*, an antidote to a lot of the grim TV of the 2010s.

I want to conclude with thoughts on "answers." In a 2023 episode of the podcast *Blank Check with Griffin and David*,‡ comedian and filmmaker Scott Aukerman posits that his disappointment in the show's finale stems from how often the series seemed to be leaning into visual symbolism that suggested an ultimately scientific explanation for the

---

* Arguably, it's only rivaled by *The Walking Dead* and *Game of Thrones*, two shows that learned many lessons from *Lost*.
† I want to note, in line with our earlier writing about the show's take on race, that the characters who escape the Island are almost all white. So few characters survive at all that it's perhaps less notable than it would be on some other shows— looking at you, *Walking Dead*. But it's still worth pointing out.
‡ "T2: Trainspotting with Scott Aukerman & Shaun Diston," released April 23, 2023.

Island's many oddities. People would tap on keyboards or vent electromagnetic energy or dig down into the earth. It all felt like it was heading somewhere plausible or at least somewhere steeped in *X-Files* science—which is to say fantastical but seemingly non-supernatural.

The more mythic, religious place where the series ends is, for me, a powerful one, but I won't deny that some part of me wishes that the show had just been, like, "The Island is a crashed alien spaceship, got it?" I think that would have been a much weaker ending than the one we got, but some part of me really would appreciate its cleanness.

NOEL: Before I pivot to my final thought, I'll stand up one more time for the people who were disappointed with the finale because they felt its focus was . . . well, let's just say *off*. You and I have both written about a lot of serialized television over the past twenty-plus years, so we're both familiar with the all-too-common phenomenon where the people making a show get so committed to one story idea or one character that they can't see how they're sabotaging their own creation.

The Walking Dead is a prime example. That show went in so many infuriating directions, which the showrunners insisted were necessary because they believed the most important story they were telling was the one about Sheriff Rick Grimes. The deaths of fan-favorite characters were often handled disrespectfully or too casually, because to the writers those deaths only mattered for how they affected Rick. See also *How I Met Your Mother*, where the writers built an entire series around the premise *in the title of their show* and then opted in the final minutes of the finale to redirect the story so that it was about the main character's lingering feelings for someone else.

I'm not saying that fans always know better than creators how a story should go; I'm only saying that TV showrunners can be so far inside their own heads sometimes that they don't even understand why their viewers are so mad about the choices they make. So, I'm sympathetic to angry *Lost* fans. I get where they're coming from.

But I don't share their outrage. There's just too much I love about *Lost*'s final season and final episode. We've covered most of this already, but I do have one more winning element I want to bring up from Season Six: the way that the flash-sideways gives us the real John Locke back (or at least *a* real John Locke), after multiple seasons where the entity possessing Locke's body was bitterly opposed to everything Locke stood for.★ This is what Season Six does so well: give us back the characters we found so fascinating back in Season One, without all the years of damage the Island did to their personalities and their relationships. This clearly mattered to Lindelof and Cuse, and in "The End" it mattered to me, too.

TV critics and TV fans have every right to criticize creative choices that they genuinely feel don't work. But before jumping to that conclusion, I do think it's best to let the creators tell the story they want to tell and see how it plays out. And once it's all put together, *Lost* mostly works for me. It makes sense. It has a point of view. It's expressing something consistent and coherent.

My wife is a professor in an interdisciplinary university honors program that requires their freshmen to take a class that's essentially a "history of thought," guiding them through all the major belief systems—religious, philosophical, political, and economic. At the core of that class is an idea that students should play "The Believing Game," approaching each new concept—even contradictory ones—as believers. They need to make an honest effort to understand these beliefs and explain them from the perspective of someone who shares them. They don't have to give up what they *actually* believe; they just have to try on someone else's worldview for a while.

If I had to define the way I approach criticism, I'd say I play The Believing Game. This doesn't mean I end up liking everything. (I have written plenty of pans in my life.) But I do always try to ask myself, "What if I were a person who liked this? Why might that be?" And sometimes, when I'm imagining myself as that person, I talk myself into becoming it. With *Lost*, I guess that would make me a Jack, becoming the person the Island always wanted him to be.

But if I'm being honest? When it comes to *Lost*, I was always a Locke. It was never that hard for me to believe.

★   One of the most satisfying moments in the finale is when Jack says, out loud, that he now believes Locke was "right about just about everything."

AFTERWORD

ON THE NEXT EPISODE OF . . .

Since it left the air in May 2010, *Lost* has remained a fervent topic of conversation. Even if you didn't like the show or never watched it, *Lost* has seeped so deeply into our pop cultural groundwater that you've almost certainly seen something influenced by it.

The most obvious influence the show has had stems from its cast and crew, many of whom have gone on to have massively successful careers in film and television. Co-creator J. J. Abrams's career was already on the upswing when he worked on *Lost*, but he's gone on to direct massively successful blockbusters in the *Star Wars* and *Star Trek* franchises. He has also produced a gamut of acclaimed TV shows, including HBO's sci-fi series *Westworld*, which has more than a few things in common with *Lost*.

Damon Lindelof and Carlton Cuse, co-showrunners for most of the series' run, have seen similar success. Lindelof's post-*Lost* TV work has included cult favorites (HBO's three-season series *The Leftovers*) and massive, Emmy-winning successes (HBO's miniseries *Watchmen*), while his work contributing to screenplays has mostly resulted in films people complain about online.★ Cuse has served as an executive producer for a wildly diverse slate of TV projects, from docudramas (the Hurricane Katrina–set *Five Days at Memorial*) to horror prequels (the *Psycho* spinoff *Bates Motel*) to comics adaptations (*Locke & Key*). He also

★ Like *Star Trek Into Darkness* and *Prometheus*, though this author would submit people are wrong about *Prometheus*, which is good, actually.

wrote the screenplays for two Dwayne Johnson vehicles, *Rampage* and *San Andreas*.

To run down every single TV series that someone who wrote on *Lost* has worked for—and often improved—would require another book. Suffice to say that those who passed through the series' writers room have gone on to create both massively successful series like *Once Upon a Time* (created by *Lost* alums Adam Horowitz and Edward Kitsis) and beloved cult favorites like *The Middleman* (created by Javier Grillo-Marxuach).★

The series' lead director, Jack Bender, has also charted an eclectic path post-*Lost*, including directing stints on shows as varied as *Game of Thrones* and the short-lived, deeply trippy "dream crimes" show *Falling Water*. Of late, he's entered the Stephen King universe, helping to bring the author's books *Mr. Mercedes* and *The Outsider* to the small screen. His most recent project, the *very Lost*-ian *From*, about a small town surrounded by monsters that let no one escape, reunited him with *Lost*'s own Harold Perrineau, who is *From*'s star.†

Speaking of Perrineau, the show's cast has spread far and wide across the film and TV landscape, often bringing a distinctly *Lost* flavor to even the most mundane of projects. Michael Emerson, for instance, headlined *Person of Interest*, a seemingly prosaic CBS crime procedural that leaned into his creepy affect to become a series about the rise of artificial intelligence and what freedoms humanity might sign away for security. Evangeline Lilly has become a fixture of the Marvel universe, while Josh Holloway has lent his charismatic machismo to a wide swath of popular TV shows including the alien-invasion drama *Colony* and the massively successful prime-time soap *Yellowstone*. Daniel Dae Kim hopped right from *Lost* to *Hawaii Five-o*, another wildly successful show filmed in Hawaii, then went on to produce the similarly enormous medical drama

★ If you take one recommendation from this book, it might be to watch *The Middleman*, a wonderfully delightful piece of TV entertainment that will make you sigh and say, "They just don't make 'em like that anymore!" It's available on an out-of-print DVD that, nevertheless, remains pretty easy to find.

† *From* is one of my go-to shows when people ask for something they've never heard of that they'll enjoy watching. If you like this sort of show—and considering you've almost finished a book on *Lost*, you almost certainly do—definitely check it out.

The Good Doctor. And that's just scraping the surface. *Lost* actors have been everywhere since the show ended.★

The show's influence has perhaps been most profound on all the shows *Lost* alumni *don't* work on, however. Even as *Lost* was airing, lots of other shows were trying to distill its essence and offer their own spin on it. Many of those shows failed,† as most TV copycats do. But series like the superhero drama *Heroes* and the sitcom *How I Met Your Mother*, both of which cribbed from *Lost* in several ways, had long, healthy runs that overlapped with *Lost*.

After *Lost*'s run was over, however, the floodgates really opened. *Lost*'s influence could be felt everywhere, not just in genre series like *The Walking Dead*‡ and *Game of Thrones*, which took up its mantle of "the show everybody's talking about." *This Is Us* blended *Lost* with the family drama. *The Good Place* blended it with the high-concept sitcom. *Orange Is the New Black* blended it with the ensemble drama. *The Handmaid's Tale* blended it with dystopian fiction. *Yellowjackets* blended it with stark horror. And those are just five obvious examples. Dig around in the skeletal structures of most of your favorite shows post-*Lost* and you'll surely find a little *Lost* in there.

Yet all these shows iterated on the *Lost* model as well. *This Is Us*, for example, shared a love of mystery-driven storytelling and flashbacks with *Lost*, but it also centered on a single family, which meant it could use its flashbacks to uncover the tragic moments the family didn't want to talk about. Instead of the flashbacks being secrets the characters kept from each other, as on *Lost*, they became the secrets the characters kept from themselves, a painful reflection of the way foundational traumas can reverberate through a family structure. Similarly, on *The Good Place*, the many twists and turns within that series' version of the afterlife reflected not just an exciting story packed with big reveals but

---

★ I haven't even brought up that Elizabeth Mitchell continues to play Mrs. Claus in the *Santa Clause* franchise, a role she technically originated pre-*Lost* but one she continues to perform to this day.

† Though I recommend checking out the one-season series *Invasion*, which took a *Lost*-ish approach to an alien invasion storyline, wedded to a surprisingly intimate family drama.

‡ Which began mere months after *Lost*'s run ended.

also a thematic reflection of the idea that living "a good life" is almost impossible. Just when you think you've figured out how to live ethically, the rules can change on you.*

Finally, you cannot have made it this far in this book without noticing just how much *Lost* impacted our TV and movie viewing culture. Sure, most *Lost* viewers were casual ones, tuning in every week to see what happened next on the Island. Yet the deeply passionate fans who debated twists and turns and tried to solve the show's mysteries became synonymous with "*Lost* fans" to the degree it was easy to forget all those casual viewers. The longer the series ran and the more impenetrable its mythology became, the more it seemed to cater to those hardcore viewers, who invested ever more deeply with each passing week.

We now live in a world where the hardcore fans are catered to almost as a matter of course. Whether it's the Marvel Cinematic Universe or *Star Wars*, viewers' ability to maintain an encyclopedic knowledge of deep lore is increasingly considered a prerequisite to enjoyment. The recent struggles of, say, superhero films suggest that we're exiting this particular period of storytelling, but it will take a long while to extract the claws of telling stories mostly for "true fans" from our culture. *Lost* wasn't the first example of a series catering to those fans,† but it was one of the earliest examples of how you could still be hugely successful by slowly eschewing everybody who didn't want to learn everything about your series.

Yet the series made audiences more adventurous, too. It was one of the first US TV series to heavily utilize subtitles, for instance, and it made many casual viewers more comfortable with nonlinear storytelling that forced you to pay attention. It normalized the idea of appointment TV, of shows you *had* to watch every episode to keep up with. The American viewing public has gotten more open to lots of different kinds of shows in the last twenty years, and it's not hard to see *Lost*'s influence in that regard.

---

*   I could also point to how skillfully the teen cannibal drama *Yellowjackets* uses its own blending of past and present timelines to replicate the ways that trauma survivors can sometimes struggle to distinguish between the present moment and the horrible events that happened in the past, but I now work on that show and feel weird saying anything more about it outside of a footnote.

†   That's *probably The X-Files*.

Few pop cultural objects of the twenty-first century have had as massive an impact as *Lost*. Wherever you look, you can spot its tendrils reaching out to affect the culture you love. That's how art works, of course. Something resonates with people, and its influence spreads far and wide. All creativity is one part sudden, imaginative spark and nine parts iteration on what's come before. *Lost*, which blended so many cultural influences into its stew, provided lots to iterate upon.

With all of that said, then, perhaps the title of this book is a bit of a misnomer. We never had to go back to the Island. In so many ways, we never left. —*ESJ*

WORKS CITED

Note: Due to the ephemerality of the internet, there are some citations in this book that are difficult to source with absolute accuracy. The authors both reviewed Lost *while it was airing, and some of those reviews quoted blog posts and Twitter posts that have since disappeared from the web, for various reasons. But we have endeavored to be as thorough as possible in compiling the sources we've quoted that are still accessible.*

DVD SPECIAL FEATURES

"The Genesis of *Lost*." *Lost: The Complete First* Season *DVD, Disc Seven*. Buena Vista Home Entertainment, 2005.

"*Lost*: On Location." *Lost: The Complete Second Season DVD, Disc Seven*. Buena Vista Home Entertainment, 2006.

"Secrets from the Hatch." *Lost: The Complete Second Season DVD, Disc Seven*. Buena Vista Home Entertainment, 2006.

"'The Man from Tallahassee' Commentary Track." *Lost: The Complete Third Season DVD, Disc Four*. Buena Vista Home Entertainment, 2007.

"The World of the Others." *Lost: The Complete Third Season DVD, Disc Seven*. Buena Vista Home Entertainment, 2007.

"'Ab Aeterno' Commentary Track." *Lost: The Complete Sixth Season DVD, Disc Three*. Buena Vista Home Entertainment, 2010.

"'Across the Sea' Commentary Track." *Lost: The Complete Sixth Season DVD, Disc Four*. Buena Vista Home Entertainment, 2010.

PODCASTS AND YOUTUBE

Cuse, Carlton, and Damon Lindelof, hosts. Official Lost Podcast, February 12, 2007.

Cuse, Carlton, and Damon Lindelof, hosts. Official Lost Podcast, April 9, 2009.

Lin, Alice. "Damon Lindelof of *Lost*: Relevant Storytellers Talk at Disney 10/19/11." YouTube, uploaded October 23, 2011, https://www.youtube.com/watch?v=XYC8Apc62gw.

Newman, Griffin, and David Sims, hosts. *Blank Check*, April 23, 2023.

Shepherd, Jack, and Jacob Stolworthy, hosts. *The LOST Boys*, July 31, 2018.

BOOKS, JOURNALS, MAGAZINES, AND WEB ARTICLES

Anders, Charlie Jane. *50 Questions "Lost" Really Does Need to Answer. Gizmodo.* May 18, 2010, https://gizmodo.com/50-questions-lost-really-does-need-to-answer-5540279.

Contributors to *Lostpedia* (conducted by TheAma1). *The Lostpedia Interview: Carlton Cuse & Damon Lindelof. Lostpedia.* April 17, 2009, https://lostpedia.fandom.com/wiki/The_Lostpedia_Interview:Carlton_Cuse_%26_Damon_Lindelof.

Gray, Jonathan, and Jason Mittell. "Speculation on Spoilers: *Lost* Fandom, Narrative Consumption and Rethinking Textuality," *Particip@tions* 4, no. 1 (2007).

Jenkins, Henry. *Transmedia Storytelling 101. Pop Junctions.* March 22, 2007, http://henryjenkins.org/blog/2007/03/transmedia_storytelling_101.html.

Jensen, Jeff. *"Lost" (S4): Mind-Blowing Scoop.* EW.com, *Entertainment Weekly.* February 22, 2008, https://ew.com/article/2008/02/22/lost-s4-mind-blowing-scoop/.

Jensen, Jeff. *"Lost" (S4): A Desmond Fact-Check.* EW.com, *Entertainment Weekly.* March 6, 2008, ew.com/article/2008/03/06/lost-s4-desmond-fact-check/.

Jensen, Jeff. *Confused by the "Lost" Premiere? Never Fear! Damon and Carlton Explain a Few Things About the Start of Season 6.* EW.com, *Entertainment Weekly.* February 2, 2010, https://ew.com/article/2010/02/02/lost-premiere-damon-carlton/.

Jensen, Jeff. *"Lost": How a Volcano Would Have Changed the Ending.* EW.com, *Entertainment Weekly.* April 10, 2017, https://ew.com/tv/2017/04/10/lost-volcano-alternative-ending/.

Jones, Steven E. *The Meaning of Video Games: Gaming and Textual Studies.* Routledge, 2008.

Litman, Juliet. *The Best TV Episode of the Century Is . . . The Ringer.* July 31, 2018, https://www.theringer.com/tv/2018/7/30/17627614/best-tv-episodes-of-the-21st-century-explained.

Mittell, Jason. "Playing for Plot in the *Lost* and *Portal* Franchises," *Eludamos: Journal for Computer Game Culture* 6, no. 1 (2012): 5–13, doi: 10.7557/23.6134.

Murray, Noel. *Interview: Damon Lindelof and Carlton Cuse.* The A.V. Club. April 23, 2008, https://www.avclub.com/losts-damon-lindelof-and-carlton-cuse-1798213783.

Schneider, Michael. *"Lost" Found on Many Platforms. Variety.* April 10, 2008, https://variety.com/2008/digital/features/lost-found-on-many-platforms-1117983862/.

Sepinwall, Alan. *How "Station Eleven" Told a Pandemic Story That Didn't Depress the Shit out of Us. Rolling Stone,* January 13, 2022, www.rollingstone.com/tv-movies/tv-movie-features/station-eleven-finale-interview-1279145/.

ACKNOWLEDGMENTS

Lost: Back to the Island would not have happened without a team pulling together to make sure it did. We sold the book literally one month before the Covid-19 lockdowns, and the process of writing and editing it ended up being more stressful than expected. What kept it from becoming overwhelmingly stressful was the hard work of great editors like Eric Klopfer, Asha Simon, Ruby Pucillo, and Zack Knoll. Zack, especially, carried this project over the finish line.

Thank you to Bonnie Nadell for believing in this book and pushing to get it sold, even at a time when *Lost*'s reputation might have been better. Thank you, also, to our wonderful cover designer Charlie Davis.

Finally, the two of us met working at The A.V. Club, thrust together by the then-editor-in-chief Keith Phipps. Without him realizing the two of us were kindred spirits, this book would not exist. He remains a wonderful cultural critic and friend.

EMILY: My thanks to the many, many, many TV critics I've bounced thoughts about this show off of over the years, especially Joanna Robinson, Maureen Ryan, Alan Sepinwall, and Kathryn VanArendonk, all of whom have changed how I think about this series. Over the years, I've also interviewed Damon Lindelof many times, and those conversations have informed this book. I would not have been a TV critic for so long without Matt Zoller Seitz taking a chance on me for his blog *The House Next Door*. My colleagues at *Yellowjackets* have helped me think about this series from a perspective of actual TV production, instead of just from the outside looking in. (*Lost* comes up perhaps more than any other show in our room.)

Maggie Furlong provided an enormous screen on which to watch the series finale back in the day, an experience that still colors my memories of that episode. The editors at the *Los Angeles Times* gave me a space to cover the final season of the show for their sadly defunct TV blog (RIP).

My daughter has no idea what *Lost* even is yet, but I am so glad to wake up every morning and get to see her doing her thing. She made the experience of writing this book at least three times more pleasant.

Finally, my wife, Libby, has been a constant companion to my *Lost* viewing, going so far as to turn every finale viewing into an event. I spent most of the run of the show in a dysphoric haze, penetrated only by great TV. *Lost* was one of those shows, and I'm thankful both for it and for the woman who watched every second of it with me. Twice.

NOEL: I had the good fortune to be in The A.V. Club stable when the site first added television reviews; and I had the even better fortune to be assigned to cover *Lost*, a show with such a fervent fanbase that I could've scribbled 1,000 words of absolute nonsense into my weekly write-ups and we still would've gotten hundreds of thoughtful comments. So I have to give thanks first to the A.V. Club commenters, who were an appreciative audience and—even better—sometimes a really tough one, pushing me to think more deeply and write more precisely. Those *Lost* years were fun times.

I've already mentioned a lot of the colleagues who helped make writing about *Lost* less of a lonely proposition, but I want to express my appreciation especially to Myles McNutt and Jason Mittell, who introduced me to the academic side of TV criticism and welcomed me into their company even though (as my college professors would attest, if they remembered me at all) I am certainly no scholar.

I am grateful to the high school teachers who encouraged my writing habit and pushed me to do better; and I am extra-grateful to Bob Stackhouse, Lois Dunn, and Kent Cathcart in that regard. I miss my late friend and editor Jim Ridley, whom I worked alongside at the alt-weekly *The Nashville Scene* right after I graduated from college and who taught me how to be a more disciplined journalist and a more gracious person.

Lastly, my wife, Donna Bowman (an excellent TV critic as well as being the best college professor in central Arkansas), and our kids, Archer and Ash, put up with long stretches of me being cranky and distracted while worrying about and working on this book; and I know they're as happy as I am to have made it to the other side. *Lost*, like any big endeavor, is a journey, filled with setbacks and changes and, finally, resolution.

See you in another life.

ABOUT THE AUTHORS

EMILY ST. JAMES is a writer and cultural critic, currently writing on the TV series *Yellowjackets*. During her journalism career, she served as the critic-at-large for *Vox* and the first TV editor of The A.V. Club. Her work has also appeared in the *New York Times, Vanity Fair*, and *Vulture*. She is the co-author of *Monsters of the Week: The Complete Critical Companion to The X-Files*. Her debut novel, *Woodworking*, arrives in early 2025. She lives in Los Angeles.

NOEL MURRAY has been a freelance pop culture critic and reporter for over thirty years, and was a key contributor to the influential websites The A.V. Club and The Dissolve. His writing about TV, movies, music, comics, and more has appeared in the *New York Times*, the *Los Angeles Times, Vulture, Entertainment Weekly*, and *Rolling Stone*. He lives in central Arkansas.